INDIANA UNIVERSITY PRESS

Earth eats

Real Food Green Living

ANNIE CORRIGAN

with Daniel Orr

THIS BOOK IS A PUBLICATION OF

Indiana University Press
Office of Scholarly Publishing
Herman B Wells Library 350
1320 East 10th Street
Bloomington, Indiana 47405 USA
iupress.indiana.edu

Manufactured in China

Library of Congress
Cataloging-in-Publication Data

Names: Corrigan, Annie, author. |
   Orr, Daniel, author.
Title: Earth eats : real food green living /
   Annie Corrigan with Daniel Orr.
Description: Bloomington : Indiana
   University Press, [2017] | Includes index.
Identifiers: LCCN 2016044788 (print) |
   LCCN 2016054907 (ebook) |
   ISBN 9780253026293 (pbk.) |
   ISBN 9780253026934 (e-book)
Subjects: LCSH: Natural foods. | Local foods. |
   Sustainable living. | LCGFT: Cookbooks.
Classification: LCC TX369 .C667
   2017 (print) | LCC TX369 (ebook) |
   DDC 641.3/02—dc23
LC record available at
   https://lccn.loc.gov/2016044788

1 2 3 4 5   22 21 20 19 18 17

Contents

Preface

What is local food?

We've been exploring this question since *Earth Eats* aired its first episode and posted its first recipe in January 2009. Chef Daniel Orr shaped our local food platform in those early days by preparing recipes that featured seasonal ingredients grown by Indiana farmers. For some of my favorite episodes, he brought the "local" all the way home to his mother's front-yard garden in Columbus, Indiana. We collected knotty apples from an apple tree—the uglier the better, he said—and watched him slowly transform fruit that would never be featured at grocery stores into the most delicious apple butter.

As *Earth Eats* grew, we brought the "local" to more people. We learned that home cooks had been champions of local food since long before we'd launched the program, so we welcomed food bloggers to our website. We were eager to provide a platform for home cooks and chefs to share space and discuss the food local to their areas. Now, we could hear about the Stephanie Weaver's version of local in San Diego. Natalie Rae Good offered seasonal ideas from Brooklyn. And we could compare Dianne Venetta's food life in Florida to Heather Tallman's in southern Indiana. These bloggers are the heart of *Earth Eats*, and I'm proud to include their voices alongside those of professional chefs and farmers in this book.

We will never be completely local. Let's face it: a southern Indiana source of olive oil is probably not on the horizon. With each new episode, and in editing this book, we've tested the limits of the idea of local eating. I think all the contributors would agree that we try to stay true to our current definition of "local food": food grown close by, picked fresh, and prepared in your kitchen.

Earth Eats has grown from a weekly five-minute recipe-focused piece to a thirty-minute radio show and podcast that includes news and interest stories. On our website, we also feature content from more than a dozen contributors. This book is an exciting addition to our work. Thanks to everyone who was with me in the beginning, especially Adam Schweigert, Eoban Binder, Yael Ksander, and David Wood. And thank you to WFIU-Bloomington for supporting this program and encouraging its growth over eight years.

Let's see where local food takes us in the next eight.

Annie Corrigan

Earth eats

spring

❧ Ready, Set . . . Grow! Beginner's Guide to Gardening

DIANNE VENETTA

Planting time is one of the best times in the garden, second only to harvest.

Sowing seeds is a wonderful step in the process because it's filled with the thrill of anticipation, a dash into uncharted territory, and the belief that all things are possible.

You are the master of your garden. You control what grows where and when. You are ultimately responsible for the success or failure of the plants in your garden. Mother Nature does this all the time, but now it's your turn to play a more proactive role.

THE PERFECT LOCATION

First things first, you must determine a spot for this wonderful new adventure of yours. You'll need a sunny location for your garden. That is, unless you live in an especially sun-drenched part of the world. I've learned from experience that a little shade break during the afternoon in a hot, sunny climate can do your plants some good. Too much sun can quickly deplete your soil of moisture, burn your plant's leaves, and generally stress the entire system. Sure, you watered it for an hour this morning, but in places like Florida and Texas where the sun shines hot, by 3:00 PM your plants are acting as if they'd forgotten that they received their daily dose of water.

And speaking of watering your plants, be sure to select a spot close to your water source.

WHICH BED IS BEST

You'll want to determine whether your beds will be inground or aboveground. Raised garden beds can ease the pain in your back, but you'll have to build them. Inground gardens require more weeding, which can also be backbreaking work. Be sure to kill the grass before you begin. The roots will lose their grip after they've died.

Veggies like soft, yet dense soil, with good moisture retention and a rich organic lining. They also prefer a nice deep cushion of 8–12 inches, ensuring that their roots have plenty of space to spread out and spread deep.

Whatever you do, don't skimp on the mulch. Once you have sprouts, you'll need it to keep the weeds to a manageable level no matter which method of gardening you choose. Organic mulch serves a dual benefit. It prevents weeds, and it eventually becomes a source of nutrients for your plants as it breaks down into the soil.

PLANT WHAT YOU'LL EAT

Focus on what you like to eat, not what you think you can grow. While a variety of colorful vegetables may add to your garden's appearance, they'll ruin the effect when left withering on the vine because no one cared enough to harvest them. Imagine you're in the garden, short on time—What are you going to harvest? Your favorites, that's what. Choose your seeds with that in mind.

When planting your seeds in the ground, a good rule of thumb is to consider the size of your seed. Tiny seeds like carrots, lettuce, and broccoli are planted very shallow—about a quarter inch deep. If you plant them too deep,

CARROTS THRIVE IN RAISED GARDEN BEDS

If farmer Joseph Swain knows one thing about farmers' market customers, it's that they love carrots.

"If you only have one or two farmers at your market who are selling carrots, you can pull a pretty good penny," he says. One-quarter of Swainway Urban Farm is dedicated to growing carrots.

He constructed 12 raised garden beds in his backyard, giving him 3,000 feet of growing space. For the carrot beds, he mixed together peat, perlite, green sand kelp, and fertilizer. He has a long list of reasons why building raised beds is beneficial. You have control over the quality of the soil by adding amendments, compost, and organic material to a specific growing area.

Raised beds also provide a lush 6–8 inches of growing depth, which is key for a successful carrot crop. Plants can shoot their roots deep into the ground, which means Swain can plant his crops closer.

He hopes to be selling his first batch of carrots by the middle of June. He'll then plant two new rows of carrots every two weeks, so he should be well stocked for the rest of the summer market season.

they might not break through all that dirt to reach the surface. Stepping up in size are eggplant, squash, pepper, and beet seeds. These require a bit more coverage, about one-half inch depth. Then there are seeds like beans and corn, which prefer to be buried in about one inch of soil.

What about potatoes? They love to be underground and prefer a depth of about two inches. The same goes for garlic. This depth helps them burrow in for the long cold winter.

Companion planting is the idea of strategically planting certain fruits and vegetables close to one another in order to optimize natural growing conditions.

For example, if you know dill attracts the hornworm, and you know hornworms can devour a tomato plant down to the bare stem, you'll know to not plant these two next to one another. How about rosemary and cabbage? Rosemary acts as a natural repellent for the cabbage moth, which just so happens to love to eat cabbage plants. Corn and beans are great friends, as corn provides the trellis for beans to climb. Garlic repels aphids, while tarragon seems to disgust most insects. Take a look at your selection of seeds and do the research. It will save you a basket full of heartache later on.

TIME AND PATIENCE

While some climates allow for an extended growing season, most plants still need certain growing conditions to thrive. Play it safe your first time. Read the seed packet labels and sow accordingly.

You can plant vegetables several times throughout the season. That's called stagger

CANDY OF THE GARDEN: GROWING CHERRY TOMATOES

Whether you've gardened since childhood or are just now thinking about taking to the greens, here are some solid tips for getting the best out of your tomato plants:

- Don't overcrowd seeds. When starting the tomatoes from seed, give the seedlings plenty of room to expand. Crowded conditions keep them from reaching their full potential.

- Place in direct sunlight. Seedlings need to be in the sunniest part of your garden.

- Provide a breeze for your plants. Tomatoes need plenty of wind in order to develop stronger stems. You can even put a fan on them for 5 to 10 minutes a day.

- "Preheat" the garden. Before planting, cover your plot with a black tarp to heat up the soil.

- Bury deep. Tomatoes can grow roots all the way up their stems. If you're planting starters, be sure to bury your plants deep.

- Don't forget to mulch. Mulching helps conserve water. Make sure you mulch after the soil has warmed up.

- Remove leaves. When the plants are three inches tall, take away the leaves from the bottom inch of the stem.

- Pinch and prune. Remove the suckers that pop up in the elbows of the branches.

- And of course . . . be sure to water regularly!

planting. Let's take tomatoes. Many toma- toes mature at between 55 and 80 days. If your first planting date is May 1 and your growing season effectively ends in October, then you might consider planting in the first week of May, the third week of May, early- to mid-June, and the beginning of July. By staggering your planting dates, you'll stagger your harvest, giving you an endless stream of tomatoes fresh from the vine. You'll also ensure that your last batch is mature prior to fall's first frosty nip.

WHAT SHALL I FEED THEM?

Plants need nutrients to thrive and survive. Many nutrients like carbon, hydrogen, and oxygen can be obtained from the air and rainwater without your help. Other import- ant nutrients like nitrogen, phosphorous, potassium, calcium, magnesium, and sulfur are harder to come by.

These elements are present in healthy soil but usually not in sufficient amounts to pro- mote strong growth. That means the plants will rely on you to supply them.

Your powerhouse nutrients are N-P-K— nitrogen, phosphorous, and potassium.

Nitrogen helps keep the leaves green. When they begin to fade or turn yellow, con- sider adding nitrogen. When you need nitro- gen, composted manure (e.g., from chickens, rabbits, and cows) works well. Blood meal

and fish emulsion, both considered organ- ic fertilizers, are also great for a nitrogen boost. Plant cover crops for a "green ma- nure." Phosphorous helps your plants devel- op strong roots and produce fruit. Minimal flower growth and fruit production, as well as a purplish tint to the leaves, can be signs of phosphorous deficiency. To add phosphorous, consider bone meal and rock phosphate.

Potassium promotes the overall health and well-being of your plants. It helps reg- ulate their internal functions. Generally speaking, when your plants become suscep- tible to disease and seem a bit "thin-skinned," think potassium. Potassium can be found in sulfate of potash, wood ashes, and seaweed fertilizers. Infuse your garden with calcium, magnesium, and sulfur by adding limestone, eggshells, Epsom salts, and sulfur.

And don't forget the compost! Adding compost improves soil structure and provides organic material for your plants.

Saag: Indian Style Mustard Greens

DANIEL ORR

One of our mantras at *Earth Eats* is "Local ingredients with global flavor," and we're going there with a recipe for saag. This dish of pureed greens is usually served with paneer, a fresh cheese popular in the cuisine of South Asia.

Most American restaurants use spinach as the base, but we're using a Japanese mustard green called mizuna. Adding a bit of arugula and spinach will give the dish a nice balance, since mizuna can have a strong flavor. My general rule for cooking with aggressively flavored greens is to add a touch of sweet, a touch of heat, and a touch of fat.

This recipe calls for two pounds of greens, which may seem like a lot, but it will cook down to one quarter of that volume. Be sure you cook the greens completely to a velvety texture. This is not one of those dishes where you want crispy, crunchy greens!

You can serve this finished dish in two ways: right out of the pan, complete with big pieces of greens, or blended to a smooth sauce.

Ingredients:

- 2 pounds mustard greens, stemmed, or broccoli rabe, trimmed and chopped
- ½ pound cleaned spinach and arugula
- 2 tablespoons cornmeal
- 1 cup heavy cream
- 1 tablespoon toasted cumin
- 6 garlic cloves, chopped
- 4 jalapeños, seeded and finely chopped
- 1 2-inch piece fresh ginger, peeled and chopped
- 2 red onions, finely chopped
- ¼ cup vegetable oil
- salt (to taste)

Directions:

Bring a large pot of salted water to a boil. Add the mustard greens and cook for 2 minutes. Add the spinach and cook for 30 seconds. Drain the greens.

In a medium-heat pan with oil, combine the garlic, jalapeños, toasted cumin seeds, and ginger. Add the onions and cook until lightly browned.

Add the greens and cook for 4 minutes, stirring occasionally. Sprinkle the cornmeal over the greens. Add the heavy cream and combine. Serve when greens have completely wilted.

Or add cooked greens mixture to a food processor. Add another handful of spinach and a dash of water. Blend until smooth. Serve over paneer.

Green Goddess Breakfast Juice

Ingredients:

- 1 cup kale
- 1 cup baby spinach
- ½ cup parsley
- 1 carrot
- ½ cup pineapple
- small piece of ginger
- 1 cucumber
- ¼ cup citrus trio (start with equal parts lemon, lime, and orange juice, but feel free to adjust to your taste)

Directions:

Start by juicing the dry green ingredients. Juice the ginger, carrot, and pineapple. Finish with the cucumber. Finally, add the citrus trio. Serve over ice and enjoy!

Stir-Fried Baby Bok Choy vegan

NATALIE RAE GOOD

Ingredients:

- 1 pound baby bok choy
- 3 tablespoons sesame oil
- 4 cloves garlic, halved
- 3 tablespoons sesame seeds, toasted
- ½–1 teaspoon red pepper
- sea salt, to taste

Directions:

To toast the sesame seeds, place a dry frying pan over medium heat until hot (about 3 minutes). Add the seeds, stirring constantly. When they become golden, transfer to a bowl. Heat sesame oil over medium heat until hot. Then add garlic and red pepper, stirring often for about 3 minutes.

Arrange one layer of bok choy face down in the pan. When one side has browned, transfer to a covered dish while you repeat the process with the rest of your bok choy. Toss bok choy with sea salt and toasted seeds and serve immediately.

Sesame Roasted Kale

DANIEL ORR

Before we get cooking on this kale creation, cleaning the greens is step one. I find that washing veggies in lukewarm water gets the dirt and grit out better than cold water. You can also add a splash of vinegar to the water if you find little bugs hanging on to your greens.

We are only using the leaves for this dish, but don't throw the stems into the compost heap. Cut them into small rounds and toss them into soups and pasta sauces.

We want to keep the natural color and crunchiness of the kale, so we're simply wilting it in the pan. Be careful not to overcook it!

Ingredients:

- 1 bunch kale (cleaned with stems removed and sliced thinly)
- 2 cloves garlic, chopped
- 2 tablespoons olive oil
- 2 dashes sesame oil
- tamari (to taste)
- salt and pepper (to taste)
- toasted sesame seeds (garnish)

Directions:

Heat olive oil in sauté pan. Add garlic, sauté for 10 seconds. Add kale.

Cook kale with cover for 3–5 minutes. Add tamari, salt, and pepper.

Turn off heat. Add dash of sesame oil. Sprinkle with sesame seeds. Serve hot.

Massaged Kale Salad

Ingredients:

- 2 cups kale
- 2 tablespoons olive oil
- ¼ cup mint
- pinch black pepper
- pinch kosher salt (only a pinch!)
- juice of half a lemon
- juice of half an orange
- sliver of lemon peel, very finely diced into zest

Directions:

Slice kale into thin ribbons, or chiffonade. Rough-cut mint into large pieces.

Combine kale, mint, seasonings, olive oil, and juices. Massage kale forcefully with your hands for several minutes. This tenderizes the greens. Serve with an orange wedge.

Curried Kale Chips

This recipe can be the beginning of your love affair with kale. It has the satisfying crunch of potato chips. The bitterness of the greens cooks out in the oven.

You won't use the stems in this recipe, but that doesn't mean you should throw them in the compost. You can chop them up and put them in a soup, braise them with lentils, use them as skewers, and even pickle them.

Ingredients:

- 3–4 cups kale leaves
- 1 tablespoon olive oil
- pinch of kosher salt (only a pinch!)
- pinch of fresh ground black pepper
- healthy pinch of curry powder
- healthy pinch of garlic powder

Directions:

Preheat oven to 250°F.

Remove the kale leaves by running your fingers along the heavy stems. Leave the kale in large pieces, as they will shrink in the oven.

Massage oil and seasonings into kale. Spread kale onto cookie sheet.

Cook for 25–30 minutes or until crispy.

❧ Cooking Up a Healthy Compost Heap

"It's kind of like cooking," says Michael Simmons. "Some people use a very careful adherence to a recipe and others do it more by intuition." He teaches the Master Composter Class through the Bloomington, Indiana, Parks and Recreation Department.

He says the recipe for a building an active compost heap consists of four parts:

- The correct carbon and nitrogen ratio should be 25–30 parts carbon to 1 part nitrogen.

- The proper moisture content should be 60–65 percent, or that of a squeezed-out sponge.

- Airflow is important to a compost pile. It needs to be turned, or aerated in some other way.

- The pile should contain a source of microorganisms. That can be achieved by adding a few spades of garden soil or some finished compost.

BROWNS VERSUS GREENS

The browns are the carbon sources (e.g., straw, sawdust, and dried leaves). The greens are the nitrogen sources (e.g., food scraps, coffee grounds, and human hair).

If the pile has too much carbon, nothing will decompose. If the pile has too much nitrogen, it will give off an ammonia smell. Perhaps the best way to judge what's in your compost is with your eyes. Building a layered pile will allow you to keep track of your ingredients.

COMPOST NO-NOS

Knowing what *not* to compost is just as important, says Simmons.

Don't compost dairy products, meat, and bones. Those kinds of things will attract pests.

Domestic pet waste should not go into the compost. Theoretically, the high temperatures over a given period of time would be enough to kill any pathogens, but you don't want to chance it.

Avoid a lot of citrus, especially with a vermicomposting bin. (That's a compost bin full of worms!)

Avoid large quantities of garlic, because garlic is a natural antibiotic. It would kill the microorganisms you need working for you in the heap.

TURN IT UP

The temperature of the compost pile dictates when it needs to be turned.

The optimal operating temperature is 135–160°F. Measure that with a compost thermometer, which is a dial thermometer with a long shank that can be thrust into the center of the pile. When the temperature begins to fall, turn the heap. The reintroduction of oxygen will cause it to reheat.

Simmons often fields questions about the smell of a compost pile. Generally speaking, bad odors occur when the pile is starved for oxygen and parts of it have become anaerobic. A good turn should do the trick. You can also cut odor by covering the food waste with a layer of brown, carbon-rich materials.

The same goes for vermicomposting: there should be no odor. Often a smell comes when the worms are overfed and uneaten food begins to mold or decompose. When a worm box is started, it will take a while for the red wigglers to acclimate to their new living arrangements and to begin to digest the food. As they reproduce, they will be able to handle larger and larger quantities.

If the compost does start to smell, stop feeding the worms for a week or two to allow them to catch up.

BREAK IT DOWN

If you're patient, almost anything organic will break down eventually, but some items take much longer than others. Corncobs and avocado pits are especially hardy.

Eggshells also take quite a while to decompose. Crush your shells before throwing them in the heap and they'll break down more quickly. If there are eggshell fragments in the compost when you apply it to your garden, don't worry. They will continue to slowly release calcium as they break down.

You can add a little spice to your heap in the form of hot peppers. Some composters believe this discourages flies.

How do you know when the compost is ready to be applied to a garden?

Simmons suggests planting bean seeds in it. If the seeds sprout and grow, that usually means the compost is ready to use.

Build Your Own Compost Bin

DAVID WOOD

If you're like me, you get really excited about those first warm days in the Midwest. Visions of seedlings freshly planted and trips to the nursery dance in my head.

But Mother Nature has a way of reminding us here in Zone 5 that planting time's not quite here. The frost date is still in front of us, and we'll have to make do with what we've got for now: some lovely bulbs up and blooming, trees sending out their first leaves, and sub-freezing temperatures overnight.

So what can you do when you've got the garden itch and you're locked out of the soil by the threat of frost?

It's time to build a compost bin.

The idea is that with minimum supplies, tools, and skill (all necessary in this amateur's case), you can build a solid compost bin.

The design consists of a series of square frames that can be stacked as the pile gets larger. You can quickly disassemble it when you need to turn the compost heap. You can also easily move it to a new location in your yard if you need.

Start with these wooden pieces:

- 20 1-by-6 untreated wood boards, 36 inches long
- 20 2-by-2 untreated wood boards, 6 inches long
- I opted to have the local lumberyard cut the wood to length for me for a small fee.

Then, collect these tools:

- 80 2-inch woodscrews
- 1 quart of wood sealer (I used linseed oil for a nontoxic option)
- screwdriver (preferably electric)
- tape measure
- pencil
- wood saw
- wide paintbrush
- rubber gloves
- eye protection
- one small aluminum loaf pan (wait for it . . .)

Attach each 2-by-2 board to each of the 1-by-6 boards. They should be flush with an end but offset from the top edge by 1 inch. Drive two screws into each 2-by-2 through the 1-by-6. (When you stack the finished squares, the offset 2-by-2 boards will create gaps in the bin. This will allow air to flow through the pile. You'll also be able to insert a soil or compost thermometer through these gaps.)

Attach the non-2-by-2 end of each board to the 2-by-2 end of another board, forming a 90-degree angle. The long boards will be flush at the top, bottom, and outside edge. Attach with two woodscrews. Repeat this process with two more boards to make a square. After screwing all twenty 1-by-6 boards into squares, you will have five individual square sections.

Apply two coats of wood sealer, letting each coat dry in between. This should be done in a ventilated space or outside. Here is where the loaf pan comes into play. You can pour a portion of the sealant into the pan, which is more easily maneuvered than the can of sealant. You can reuse it for future applications of linseed in other fix-it projects. Once the sealant has dried, the frames can be moved outside to your compost spot.

I like to start a new compost pile with two frames. You can add more frames as the pile grows.

❧ The Birds and the Bees of Growing Food

SWARM OF BEES FREE TO A GOOD HOME (IF YOU CAN CATCH THEM)

This is swarm season, the time of year when bees reproduce and find new places to build hives. While it can be stressful for homeowners who discover a cluster of bees on their property, beekeepers see it as an opportunity.

When a swarm is announced on Bloomington's Bee Town Bee Club Facebook page, beekeepers race to call dibs.

Kara Krothe posted pictures of the swarm in her tree on a Thursday evening. "I thought it was pollen flying off the trees. I looked closer and realized they were honeybees," she says. "I texted the neighbor and told her to take her kids inside because I didn't know what was going on."

On Friday morning, beekeeper Jill Stowers was in Krothe's backyard looking up at the cluster of bees. After seeing the note on social media, Stowers left work in the hopes of capturing the wild bees. That means she's not wearing any protective gear, and the cardboard filing box in her left hand is what she's hoping to capture the bees in. But she's not concerned about her safety, because swarming bees are calm. "They're not defending a hive. They don't have a huge honey store they're defending. They don't have babies and pollen. So, we'll see how that goes." She's waiting on a neighbor to bring her a ladder. Her plan is to climb the ladder and shake the bees into the box.

Jill maintains several colonies on her hobby farm. Buying a package of bees through the mail costs her $150, so snagging these bees would be a money saver—if she can catch them.

And suddenly, the buzzing crescendos as the tight cluster from the tree evaporates into a haze around the backyard. "It's raining bees right now," as we notice drops of yellow goo falling from the sky.

"That's bee poop," says honeybee specialist and Purdue University professor Greg Hunt.

To understand why bees swarm, Hunt says, you have to understand how bees reproduce. There is only one queen per hive. She gives off a special pheromone so the drones know to not make new queen cells. In the spring, when a hive grows its numbers,

Bees cluster in a tree, while the scouts fly off in search of a new location to build their hive

sometimes the pheromone doesn't get evenly distributed to all the worker bees and they make a new queen.

It's time to swarm. The old queen leaves in search of a new home, taking most of the workers with her.

Hunt traces this season's intense swarming activity to abnormally warm weather in March. "This makes the bees build up their colony strength faster. Then we had that cold weather (in April), and the bees were cooped up in their hives. As soon as the weather gets good, off they go."

The clock starts ticking once they leave the old hive. They've tanked up on honey, so they need to find a new home where they can build comb and grow new bees before they run out of food. As most of the bees cluster in a tree or on a fence post, the scouts fly off to find good spots for the colony to set up shop. "These scouts come back and they do the waggle dance, the famous dance that bees do that tell each other where flowers are. Well, they also dance to tell where the new hive should be," he says. "Once they're all dancing for the same place, then it's kind of a democratic decision and they all get excited and fly off."

Hunt says swarming is a good thing for bees. It indicates they came from a healthy colony, and if all goes well, that swarm will become a new colony. They just have to make it through the winter.

Stowers and Krothe follow the swarm to the front yard.

"They're going high up in that tree across the street it looks like," says Stowers. "There's no ladder tall enough."

And just like that, the bees fade off into the distance. Stowers left empty-handed, but she has high hopes that as bees continue to swarm through June, she'll get another chance to re-home some pollinators.

NURTURING A DYING BEEHIVE THROUGH ITS FINAL SEASON

Ellie Symes hands me a beekeeper hat and mask. I struggle to fit it over my headphones. Then I wrap the string around my recording equipment and around my waist to secure the net. It's uncomfortable.

"Yeah, I'm so used to it by now," says Ellie, who also happens to be wearing shorts. She shrugs off the possibility of a bee sting. "You're technically not supposed to wear red either, but my Chiefs won last night."

We're preparing to crack open the hives she helps manage at Indiana University's Hilltop Garden and Nature Center. She is the president of Indiana University's beekeeping club, but she doesn't consider herself an expert. She's only been working with bees for three years.

"I don't get intimidated by the bees anymore," she says. "Once you understand their behaviors, it's just like, 'Oh, she's doing that now, so I'll do a little more smoke.'"

Yes, she has been stung before. She says each time was her fault, like when she nearly crushed a bee reinserting the frame. Or when she didn't use smoke when opening the hive. "It just shot out right away and got me in the leg," she remembers. That was her first sting as a beekeeper. "I was actually really excited, probably the only person who gets excited by a sting. Like, I'm a real beekeeper now!"

Ellie is a graduate student at Indiana University, but her beekeeping began in Columbus, Ohio.

It was the summer after her freshman year. "I was getting bored with lifeguarding and wanted to jazz it up, so I googled environmental volunteering and founded 'Beekeepers Assistant Needed,' and I thought that looks weird, I'll try that." She fell in love with it.

When she came back to school, she secured a research grant from the Hutton Honors College to establish the first hive at Hilltop in 2014. Since she was still a beginner, she connected with local beekeeping guru George Hegemen to learn the ropes.

More and more students expressed interest in bees, so Ellie helped form the IU Beekeeping Club. Forty students attended the group's second annual call-out meeting, and another two hundred signed their contact list.

"We don't need to raise a generation of beekeepers that start beekeeping after college," she says. "We just want to raise a more knowledgeable generation that understands this issue."

She grabs a handful of brown pine needles and shoves them into the smoker. It's a windy day, so it takes several strikes of her lighter before the smoker ignites. Ellie says the proximity to the pine trees was one of the reasons they chose this spot. The bees use the sap to seal the hive, and keepers have a ready supply of burnable material.

A few good puffs from the smoker and the bees are stunned. She can now open the hive. She shrugs, "This hive's kind of struggling. They're not going to make it through winter." She points to the edge of the frame where there's only a small portion of honey; in a healthy hive, the entire frame would be covered. There aren't many eggs or bees inside this hive either.

But she's still dedicated to her weekly task of providing additional food for the bees. She holds a mason jar filled with sugar water. The lid has several small holes in it. She inverts the jar and places it over a slit in the hive. They need this during the cold months when there isn't much nectar to collect. But Ellie's efforts can sometimes cause more harm than good. A couple weeks ago, she discovered a dozen bees had drowned in the water.

"Beekeeping is a soap opera, I've learned," she says. "Honestly, I used to get really upset and get really emotional about it, but now it's just like, 'Okay, well . . .'"

She adjusts the mason jar so it's positioned just right. And then she crushes a bee. Ellie recoils.

Other bees hover around their wounded comrade. "See her wiggling the tail, the other bee," she points out. That's a sign it might sting, so she puffs the smoker. Ellie lets out a deep sigh. "Okay, that was sad, I'm sorry," and she gently inserts the frame back into the hive.

THIS ORCHARD IS LOOKING FOR A FEW GOOD BEES

"Diversity is inherently built into an orchard," says Amy Countryman, a member of the board of directors for the Bloomington Community Orchard.

That's where bees come in.

At a volunteer workday, community members of all ages are wielding drills, saws, hammers, and paintbrushes to assemble honeybee hives and mason bee homes as a way of enticing these beneficial bugs into making their homes at the orchard.

The orchard purchased a starter colony of honeybees, called a nuc, from Hunter's Honey Farm.

Mason bees are a little different. Countryman hopes they'll just come. "We're trying to create an ecosystem that is complete and that has everything birds and bees and people would want," like a food source, water,

and shelter. "That's what makes me want to go places," she says.

Unlike honeybees, mason bees are solitary creatures. Each female makes her own nest. There are no worker bees. They don't produce any honey and they only sting if they feel especially threatened. While they are considered better pollinators then honeybees, their lifespan is much shorter—between 4 and 8 weeks.

Volunteers make 12 mason bee homes that will hopefully house some 30 bees each. They take 4-by-4 blocks of wood and drill holes in them, one-fourth by three-eighths of an inch in diameter. The eggs laid closest to the front of the hole are unfertilized and develop into male bees, so volunteers are careful to drill holes deep enough to encourage the production of females—4 to 8 inches deep.

When it comes to birds, some are welcome guests and others are pests.

Volunteers convert dried gourds into birdhouses, and the size of the hole determines what kind of bird can live in it. They saw a one-and-a-half-inch hole in a gourd, which should be ideal for bug-eating bluebirds.

⚘ Chickens: The Snack Food of the Wild Kingdom

JANA WILSON

After having chickens for several years, I have come to the conclusion that they are the snack food of the wild-animal kingdom. By taking some key precautions, you can minimize raids by the would-be killers, or even them ward off completely.

If you have your chickens in an urban or suburban setting, don't be fooled into thinking you are safe from the worst of these varmints. Many predators of city chicks seem to be the same ones that their country cousins need to be aware of, too. Of course, in certain rural areas, there are bears, minks, and even weasels to contend with, but we'll deal right now with the most common chicken attackers.

Here are some critters you need to be aware of when keeping chickens in the city or the country:

- Dogs—Either yours or your neighbor's. Any dog can get excited and go after a quick-moving bird and do it some real harm. A chicken can literally be frightened to death after being chased around by an enthusiastic dog.

- Raccoons—They've got those opposable thumbs and can open just about anything. Ever seen how they can get into the trashcan? They are pretty clever coop openers, so you may need to lock the doors and windows.

- Opossums—These nocturnal critters can be incredibly vicious, so don't try

Jana Wilson holds one of her young Sicilian Buttercup chicks

to corner one if you catch it going after your birds.

- Hawks—There are all kinds of hawks to guard against, depending on your part of the world. I have red-tailed hawks and Cooper's hawks to contend with. I mostly worry about my young chicks and bantams with them.

- Owls—Like hawks, they will hang around for a while to scope out their prey, so keep an eye out for one hanging up above in the trees.

- Coyotes and foxes—Yes, they've moved even into the city and suburbs, and they are looking for an easy meal!

The best defense, as they say, is a good offense. Start with your chicken coop and make sure it is predator proof.

The best thing you can do for your birds is to provide them with a sturdy coop that has a door that latches or even locks at night. Make sure all openings are covered with sturdy wire, such as a heavy-gauge wire mesh or screening. I recommend that the opening be one-half inch or less, as I have heard of rats and even a mink slipping through a one-inch opening.

Also, make sure there are no openings in the floors or walls, which are an open invitation to a night marauder. If your coop has a dirt floor, dig a trench around the coop and run the chicken-wire walls about 12 inches down into the ground, then splay it out away from the coop another 6–12 inches.

Your chicken pen should be nearly as secure as your coop in terms of keeping daytime creatures like the neighbor's dog out. If your chickens are in a pen for all or part of the time, it's best to have a sturdy fence that also has chicken wire extending about 12 inches under the ground. This generally deters all but the most persistent of predators.

Some people put bird netting over the top of their run, which will keep hawks and owls out. I recommend if you do have netting that you tie some bright, shiny ribbons or old CDs to the edges to deter the predatory birds. I once came home to find a young hawk caught in my netting, his desire for a snack trumping his observance of the net. (I cut his talons out carefully with scissors while wearing leather gloves, and he flew to freedom, hopefully never to return!)

If you let your birds free range all or even part of the day, there may be nothing you can do about a swooping hawk attack. As a result, you may want to keep an eye on the hens if they are out. I have never lost a full-size bird to a hawk, but I did lose a month-old chick in the yard running around with its mother. That was enough to convince me to let only my adult birds out in the yard and woods.

SIX TIPS FOR KEEPING YOUR BACKYARD CHICKS HEALTHY

1. Always have clean, dry food and clean, fresh water for the birds. Disinfect your water and feed bowls from time to time, especially after the summer heat brings out unwanted growth in the watering containers.

2. Keep coops clean and dry. This reduces harmful ammonia fumes, which can cause respiratory illness.

3. Keep an eye on lice and mites, and treat birds and coops on a regular basis. Little chewing bloodsucking critters can drain the health right out of your birds, making them more susceptible to diseases they might not pick up otherwise.

4. Wash your hands before you go into your chicken pen or coop to avoid transmitting disease. Wash your hands after you're done with the chickens as well.

5. Don't let strangers come into your chicken pens, especially strangers who have their own chickens at home. You never know what germs are clinging to the bottom of somebody's shoes.

6. If you have taken your birds to a county fair or other poultry show, isolate them for two weeks after you return. Gathering hundreds or even thousands of birds into one building can pass illness around in a New York minute.

Eat Your Flower Garden

SARAH GORDON

Denise Schreiber got an early start eating flowers. "When I was little, we lived with my grandmother who had a large flower garden, and I used to eat four o'clocks," she says.

Four o'clocks? But they're poisonous!

"I know! I don't remember getting sick, but I could have and just not connected the two of them together," she says. "But I loved the flavor."

Years later, traveling around England, she had her first adult experience eating flowers. It was rose petal ice cream served as part of an afternoon tea. "That's what started me on the journey."

Scheiber's love for floral culinary delights led her to publish *Eat Your Roses*, a recipe book for cooking with flowers. "This is just to add a little flavor to your diet," she says. "It's not meant to be anything more than fun."

Thanks to the locavore movement and growing popular interest in edible landscaping, more and more people are learning about the diversity of edible plants.

"It's not just edible flowers," Schreiber says, "It's also fruit trees and bushes that you normally don't think of. Blueberries are a wonderful shrub in the landscape. They get great fall color."

Blueberries, sure. It makes sense to eat blueberries, and even roses. But daylilies? Nasturtiums?

"Nasturtiums have quite a peppery flavor to them. And the leaves are edible, the stems are edible, the flowers are edible, and the seedpods are edible. A lot of people pickle the seed pods and substitute them for capers."

If you want to grow your own edible flowers, Schreiber has important advice. For one thing, don't pick from the side of the road. On top of emissions from cars, you don't know whose dog has been there.

Don't buy from a nursery, unless it's an organic nursery. Most nurseries will have sprayed their flowers with chemicals you probably don't want to eat. Like any food, it's important to know where your edible flowers come from.

If you're not a gardener but want to try cooking with flowers, commonly used varieties like roses and lavender are often sold dried in herb stores and grocery co-ops.

Time for Tea with Flower Sandwiches

DANIEL ORR

This is a perfect snack for a Midwestern high tea. It features flowers you might already be growing in your garden. (Be sure to use blooms that have not been treated with herbicides!)

Ingredients:

- several marigold and nasturtium leaves and petals
- ¼ teaspoon minced garlic, smashed into paste
- ½ teaspoon lemon zest
- ½ teaspoon fresh lemon juice
- 3 tablespoons butter
- pinches of salt and pepper
- basil leaves (garnish)
- rye bread

Directions:

Combine garlic, lemon zest, and juice with butter. Season with small pinches of salt and pepper.

Toast slices of rye bread. Spread with the prepared butter.

Place nasturtium leaves and marigold petals on buttered toast. Garnish with a couple basil leaves.

Chicken Fried Zucchini Blossoms

Ingredients:

- 16 large squash blossoms
- 1 (½ pound) lightly salted fresh mozzarella ball, at room temperature
- 1 clove garlic
- 1 teaspoon olive oil
- ½ teaspoon cracked black pepper
- ¼ teaspoon nutmeg
- pinch of salt
- 16 large basil leaves
- 4 eggs beaten with 1 tablespoon water
- 2 cups panko (Japanese breadcrumbs)
- flour as needed for dredging
- oil for frying
- tomato sauce as needed
- herbs or greens as garnish

Directions:

Open the flowers by ripping them down one side. Remove stamen. Lay the flowers flat on a cookie tray or large plate.

Cut the cheese into 16 small cubes and toss in a bowl with the garlic, olive oil, spices, and salt.

Wrap each cube of seasoned cheese in a large basil leaf, and place one in each flower. Wrap the petal around the cheese and fold the end over to form a package. Give the flower a light squeeze to tighten the package.

Beat eggs and water together and season with salt and pepper. Dredge in flour, then egg mixture, then breadcrumbs, and sauté or deep fry.

Serve with fresh tomato sauce and garnish with basil or other herbs or greens.

❧ Up Your Local Food Game with Community-Supported Agriculture

It's the early-spring waiting game for local food lovers. We still have a couple of months before spring crops will be harvested and farmers' markets start bustling.

But this is a busy and expensive time of year for growers. They have to buy seeds and soil amendments. They hire workers and improve their farms' infrastructure. To get an influx of money when they need it most, some farmers develop CSAs—community-supported agriculture programs.

When subscribers sign up for a CSA, they pay a sum of money to a farm early in the planting season, usually around March. Then during harvest season, subscribers receive boxes of food from the farm according to a predetermined schedule (usually weekly) for a fixed number of weeks (usually 20–25, depending on the region).

Under a CSA model, subscribers agree to adopt some of the risk that goes along with farming as an enterprise.

Farmers appreciate the fact that the model decreases, and sometimes eliminates, the need to take out early-season loans to pay start-up costs. Those loans would be taken out against the anticipated revenue that comes from selling the harvest, but if the harvest fails due to bad weather or other natural disasters, they still need to be repaid.

The origins of the CSA model are disputed. The most common narrative is that in 1965, a group of Japanese women were concerned by the possible effects of pesticides on arable Japanese land, and the associated increase in imports. These women started the first CSA projects, called *Teikei*, out of a desire to make

Olde Lane Orchard advertises its community-supported agriculture program at the Bloomington Winter Farmers' Market

local, pesticide-free food available in their communities.

Steve McFadden of the Rodale Institute traces the American CSA movement to Europe's biodynamic agricultural tradition. Considered the first modern take on organic farming, biodynamic agriculture is a holistic approach to land management, in which building healthy soil is as important as growing food and raising livestock. The two pioneering ventures were Indian Line Farm in western Massachusetts and Temple-Wilton Community Farm in New Hampshire.

The Temple-Wilton Community Farm was supported through pledges paid in advance by consumers at whatever rate they could afford, rather than paying fixed prices at harvest time. Its managers would publish the farm's annual budget and ask members to pledge whatever they could contribute to help the farm to meet its budget requirements.

Indian Line Farm, however, coined the term "community-supported agriculture" and designed the CSA model as it currently

Teresa Birtles, Heartland Family Farm

exists. The farmers who built Indian Line were advocates of sustainable farming, the idea that food should be grown and sold locally, and of strengthening the fading connections between farmers and consumers.

CSA programs have enjoyed an uninterrupted increase in popularity since the founding of the movement in 1986.

The US Department of Agriculture reports that more than 12,000 farms were operating on CSA models in 2012, up from about 1,000 in 1999.

CSAS ARE MAKE OR BREAK FOR FARMERS

It's CSA day at the Bloomington Winter Farmers' Market.

There are five vendors touting CSA programs. The basic facts are the same, table to table. You pay a flat fee now, and you receive a weekly batch of freshly harvested food for 18–25 weeks starting in May. The farmers talk about what they think sets their CSA apart from the competition.

"We offer both a standard and a flexible model for people who aren't always in town. We grow pretty much every vegetable you can imagine, and we have a big you-pick strawberry patch now, which will also feed into our CSA," says Michael Hicks of Living Roots Ecovillage.

"I specialize in European varieties, heirloom varieties," says Teresa Birtles of Heartland Family Farm. "I grow for flavor. Having chefs as customers, I have to have wonderful flavor."

"We are an organic farm. We're not certified organic. We grow a lot of greens, and a lot of times we have greens throughout the really hot, dry parts of summer. We have special techniques to grow them that most farms kind of give up on," says Jim Baughman of Freedom Valley Farm.

"And what you're doing is you're committing to focusing a good portion of your meat budget to one farm to ensure the survival of that farm, while getting the very best in terms of transparency, nutrient density, and the quality of the meat," says Larry Howard of Maple Valley Farm.

Birtles's table is packed with melons, three colors of cauliflowers, beans, broccoli, and berries. She admits she bought this food from the grocery store to illustrate the variety she offers through her CSA, but it seems to be causing as much confusion as excitement. "I've had some people who are not familiar with seasonality," she says. "So, they think, 'Do I get strawberries with my winter squash?' or 'Do I get tomatoes first thing in the spring?' So, the seasonality question has been a huge, huge question."

It's romantic to fantasize about fresh-from-the-farm vegetables when you're still wearing a winter coat and scraping your car off in the mornings. But for a farmer, the CSA can be an important part of the bottom line.

"It's make or break, it really is," says Larry Howard, whose meat CSA includes beef, lamb, goat, chicken, turkey, eggs, and pork. "I think everything with the small farms now, who are doing this, is make-or-break whether people realize it or not. We've been in this ten years, so we know what the numbers are. What we're trying to do is ensure that this is something truly sustainable." For him, sustainable means being able to pass a successful farm business down to his kids.

Howard is hoping for 50 members. He breaks down where the money goes—40 percent to salaries, 40 percent to sourcing the animals, and the rest for the risk management fund.

"What I fear the most probably, is that we have a bad growing year and we don't have much to put in there," says Baughman. "I'm not sure how well they would really accept that, and that's something I worry about." He says CSA membership dictates what he plants at Freedom Valley Farm. He had 40 members last year, and he wants to nearly double that this season. That's despite a stressful 2015 on his farm.

"Last year, it got really bad. We had a lot of rain early on. We had a lot of onions and carrots rotting in the ground. We had full-year disease problems, so it was a struggle. And I was at one point thinking, we're going to have to refund people. But somehow we managed through it, and actually we were able to give them their amount every week."

Kathy Curry is shopping around for CSAs today.

"It just sounds like a good thing to do. I've tried to raise my own gardens throughout the years and not had a lot of success," she says.

After two conversations with Hicks of Living Roots and Birtles of Heartland, "I'm ready to sign up, but I know that's not a wise thing to do. I'll think about that over the week."

She grabs flyers and takes one last look at the bounty on the Heartland table. She still has three more pitches to hear, and then she'll go home and see how a CSA fits into her food budget.

MINTY COUSCOUS SALAD vegan

SARA CONRAD

A couple of my friends and I decided to buy CSA shares this year. We are all in different cities and states, so it has been fun comparing what is in our boxes each week. We joke that sometimes we feel like we are on an episode of *Chopped*, and we wonder how we're going to prepare some of the ingredients.

My friend from Philadelphia contacted me asking for something to do with mint because she was drinking too many Mojitos. I was in the same boat, so I came up with this super simple couscous salad.

Ingredients:
- ■ 1 cup couscous, prepared according to box directions and cooled
- ■ 1 lemon, juiced
- ■ ¼ cup extra-virgin olive oil
- ■ 2 large tomatoes, cut into chunks
- ■ ½ English cucumber, cut into chunks
- ■ 1 bunch of mint, torn
- ■ salt to taste

Directions:
Combine lemon juice, olive oil, tomatoes, cucumber, and mint. Add to cooled couscous, toss and serve.

Carrot Top Pesto

NEW TO CARROT TOPS? THIS PESTO IS A GOOD PLACE TO START

Chef Arlyn Llewellyn sources carrots from farmer Jim Baughman of Freedom Valley Farm. "We were talking to him about carrots, and he said, 'Do you want to do anything with the tops because I've got a bunch of those,'" she says. Since she was new to cooking with carrot greens, creating a pesto seemed like a good place to start.

Pesto has a simple ratio of ingredients, which makes substitutions easy. "You can use almost any leafy vegetable for the basil, you can use almost any form of acid for the lemon juice, any form of nut for the pine nuts," she says. She made some other substitutions for this recipe—aged gouda instead of parmesan cheese and cashews instead of pine nuts.

Ingredients:

- 10 ounces carrot tops, chopped into 1-inch segments
- 5 cloves garlic, peeled
- 5 ounces aged gouda
- 7.5 ounces toasted cashews (5 minutes at 375°F; allow to cool before proceeding)
- 10 teaspoons lemon juice
- 1 ⅔ cups olive oil
- 1 ½ tablespoons kosher salt
- 1 tablespoon ground black pepper

Directions:

Add carrot tops, garlic, gouda, and cashews in a food processor. Pulse until combined.

Then add lemon juice, olive oil, and salt and pepper. Pulse until combined.

ONE HECKUVA SANDWICH

The sandwiches at Llewellyn's restaurant Function Brewing are intense. There's a lot going on between the two slices of bread.

She has a very specific way of constructing each of the sandwiches. With the Wood Nymph Panini, the carrot-top pesto goes on the bottom so it's the first flavor to hit your tongue after you bite through the bread.

"That's a nice thing about sandwiches," she says. "As a chef, you can control how the customer is going to experience it, whereas if you're putting things on a plate and they're just diving in with a knife and fork, they may not eat it in the sequence you want them to. In a sandwich, they're kind of forced to."

She spreads some raisin aioli on the other slice of bread. The veggies on this sandwich are roasted local carrots and braised collard greens; she uses two types of cheese—blue cheese and Havarti.

She puts the sandwich on a panini press for several minutes. Once she hears the sizzle and sees the cheese oozing out from the sides, she knows it's ready.

But before we bite into this monstrosity, she lets it rest. "Right now that bottom piece of bread is super hot so if you put it on a flat surface, it's going to steam up against the plate and the bottom piece will be soggy," she says. "We put it on that resting rack for a couple minutes to lose the most intense heat before we cut it and put it on a plate."

❧ Asparagus

Asparagus is one of the first vegetables to pop up in the garden in the spring.

"And it's always exciting to see those first little tips coming up," Chef Daniel Orr tells us. "It's amazing how they grow, because one day there will be nothing, and the next day there will be all these little asparagus tips coming up."

They grow haphazardly all over the garden; two stalks here, another one over there. "One of my old managers, when she first saw them growing, said 'I thought they grew in bunches.' She'd never seen them growing, so she thought they grew just like they did in the supermarket."

Once you've harvested your asparagus (or brought it home from the market) keep it upright in a glass of water and it will stay good for about a week in the fridge. When you're ready to cook it up, gently bend the stalk until it snaps. Use the top part in your cooking, but don't throw away the tough bottom half. You can make a soup by blending them with some cream and seasonings of your choice.

Sunny-Side Up Asparagus Salad

DANIEL ORR

Ingredients:

- new potatoes
- asparagus spears
- olive oil
- eggs
- salad greens
- goat cheese
- vinegar
- crusty bread

Directions:

Cut new potatoes into bite-sized pieces. Snap the tough ends off the asparagus. Boil asparagus and new potatoes in lightly salted water until cooked through.

In a pan with olive oil, crack the eggs. Cover the pan with a plate as the eggs cook.

Assemble a bed of spring greens and place asparagus and potatoes on top. Add some chunks of goat cheese.

Drizzle a little good extra-virgin olive oil and a little bit of your favorite vinegar. Serve with the sunny-side up eggs on top and some crusty bread.

Asparagus and Mushrooms on the Grill

Ingredients:

- asparagus spears
- portobello mushroom caps
- lemon juice
- olive oil
- salt and pepper

Directions:

Place asparagus and portobello cap on the grill. (Don't worry. We will be marinating the asparagus after it's grilled.)

Grill asparagus until it starts to blister and develop a little caramelization around the edges.

Remove from grill and marinate the asparagus in a simple lemon vinaigrette—one part lemon juice to two parts olive oil, adding salt and pepper to taste.

Stack several asparagus tips on top of the portobello cap and serve.

Easy Roasted Asparagus

NATALIE RAE GOOD

New York has begun its slow thaw. Last weekend, a meandering walk took me through the Brooklyn Botanic Garden where soft fuzzy buds have started to peel open. There are few seasons more anticipated than spring with its flowering trees and bright, sheer sun.

Asparagus is one of the first heralds of change, gracing us with tender shoots for a few short weeks between April and May.

There are many great ways to prepare the green stalks, but roasting is my favorite. Simply rub the trimmed shoots with olive oil and sprinkle with salt. I suppose you could get wild and add crushed red pepper flakes or cumin but I am a bit of a traditionalist here, seasoning with smoked sea salt, cracked pepper, and a squeeze of lemon.

These slender stalks were perfect alongside beet risotto and a dilly spring salad at brunch last weekend. You could also stuff them in savory crepes or layer in a sandwich with hummus and sun-dried tomatoes.

Ingredients:

- 2 pounds asparagus
- olive oil
- sea salt
- cracked pepper
- ½ lemon

Directions:

Preheat oven to 400°F.

Trim the asparagus by cutting off the tough ends (about 1 inch).

Place asparagus on a baking sheet and drizzle with olive oil. Sprinkle with sea salt and rub to combine. Roast for 15–20 minutes until softened and crisp on the ends. (Be careful not to let the stalks get too soft!)

Remove from oven and sprinkle with cracked black pepper and a squeeze of lemon.

Springtime Asparagus Pasta

SARA CONRAD

I love going to the farmers' market with my three-year-old son. We frequently have conversations about which foods are good for our bodies, which lettuces are the prettiest, and why we buy from farmers.

I feel like I am giving my son a connection to the foods he eats, which makes us both feel good.

We are both excited that with spring comes more green!

The growers have been bringing in the most beautiful asparagus spears the past couple of weeks. Grilled asparagus with olive oil is one of my favorites. But the nights have been chilly here lately, and what's better than steamy, starchy pasta to warm you up? How about a little heat from some red pepper flakes to really get the job done?

Ingredients:

- 1 bunch asparagus, chopped
- 8 ounces mushrooms, chopped, with woody ends removed
- 1 pound cooked pasta
- 4–5 cloves garlic
- 1 tomato, chopped
- ½ cup cheese
- a handful of kalamata olives
- 2 tablespoons olive oil
- ½ tablespoon Italian seasoning
- red pepper flakes, to taste

Directions:

Cook pasta according to instructions on box.

While pasta is cooking, sauté garlic in oil for 2 minutes.

Add mushrooms and asparagus, and sauté until tender. Toss with seasoning, add remaining ingredients (except red pepper flakes) and toss thoroughly until cheese melts.

Serve immediately and pass the pepper flakes around the table.

Miso-Glazed Tofu with Shiitakes and Asparagus

STEPHANIE WEAVER

Ingredients:

- 3 tablespoons rice vinegar
- 2 tablespoons white miso
- 1 tablespoon minced peeled ginger
- 1 tablespoon minced garlic
- 1 tablespoon soy sauce
- 1 ½ teaspoons sugar
- 1 tablespoon toasted sesame oil

- 1 14-ounce block of extra-firm tofu
- 4 ounces uncooked organic rice noodles
- up to 2 tablespoons canola, sunflower, or grapeseed oil, divided
- 6 ounces shiitake mushrooms
- 1 pound asparagus spears
- 2 green onions

Directions:

For the marinade, combine rice vinegar with sesame oil in a large serving bowl, stirring with a whisk.

Drain the tofu and pat dry with a clean towel. Slice lengthwise evenly into 16 long pieces. Add to the marinade and let sit at least 30 minutes. If possible, marinate the tofu overnight in the refrigerator.

Fifteen minutes before you are ready to eat, cook noodles according to package directions; drain and rinse. For these noodles, I simply poured near-boiling water over them in a heatproof bowl and let them soak for 10 minutes; then I rinsed and drained them.

Carefully remove the tofu from the marinade using kitchen tongs, allowing as much marinade as possible to drip back into the bowl. Remove half of the remaining marinade to use as a glaze. Combine noodles with the remaining marinade in the large serving bowl; toss to coat.

Heat a large nonstick skillet over medium-high heat. Add 1 tablespoon oil to pan; swirl to coat.

Add tofu to pan; cook 3 minutes on each side or until browned and crispy. Remove tofu from pan; add to the noodles. Pour a little of the reserved marinade over the tofu.

Remove the stems from the mushrooms; clean mushrooms with a damp towel if necessary. Slice thin. Wash asparagus and trim off the tough ends. Lightly peel the stalks to help them get tender. Cut into 1-inch pieces.

Add remaining 1 tablespoon oil to sauté pan if needed; swirl to coat. Add mushrooms and cook for 3–4 minutes. Add asparagus and sauté 4 minutes or until tender.

Add any remaining marinade to pan; toss to coat. Sprinkle with green onions and let the heat wilt them a little.

Add veggie mixture to the large bowl and toss.

Sugaring Season

There are several mature sugar maple trees on the grounds of the Hinkle-Garton Farmstead. Michael Bell, chair of the grounds committee at the farmstead, is tasked with tapping these majestic trees to collect sap and then boil it down for the farmstead's own maple syrup.

Bell is trying to be reasonably faithful to how they would have collected sap back in 1886 when the property was first settled. The old fashioned spile he's using is $\frac{7}{16}$ inch in diameter, with a hook from which the galvanized bucket and its lid will hang. The one update of the process is the electric drill he uses to create the initial hole in the tree.

Ideal temperatures for sap to start flowing are mid-20s at night to mid-40s during the day. During freezing temperatures, the tree draws in water from its roots. When the temperatures warm up, it expels sap. The freeze-thaw cycle will produce syrup-worthy sap until the tree buds. On days when these trees are really flowing, the four-gallon buckets will be completely full. "The old-timers call it 100 drips per minute, sort of a heartbeat rate," Bell says.

Trees must be a minimum of 10 inches in diameter to be tapped; a tree over 16 inches can be tapped twice. Bell is sure to select a spot 6–10 inches away from the previous year's tap sites because the sap flow won't be as great near the spots where the tree is healing. Once he's drilled a hole two inches into the tree, he hammers the spile into place. "You'll notice a distinct change in tone when it's seated," he says, "a dead sound, so you know you've got it all the way in." He hangs the bucket from the hook on the spile, slides the lid into place, and moves on to the next tree.

Bell spends much of his time these days huddled in a makeshift sugar shack in the backyard

CHEERS TO MAPLE SAP

Michael Farrell had never tasted real maple syrup until a pancake breakfast at State University of New York College of Environmental Science and Forestry. A graduate student at the time, he called it a lightning moment, and he knew he wanted to try to make the stuff himself.

He now taps 5,120 trees in New York and serves as director of the Uihlein Forest, Cornell's Sugar Maple Research & Extension Field Station in Lake Placid, New York.

He says that back in the 1800s, many Americans would tap trees and make sugar. Today, not only has technology made the process easier, but we also have more trees that could be tapped. "There's no reason why we can't produce and consume just as much maple sugar as we did back when people were really living off the land," he says.

When Farrell was a novice sugarmaker, he discovered a love of maple sap straight from the tree. "That's what I really loved every spring," he says, "tapping the trees and collecting and drinking the sap."

What does sap taste like? Well, water. After all, it only contains 2 percent sugar (along with various minerals). Simply put, it tastes like it came from a tree.

To this day, Farrell enjoys sap as a seasonal beverage. "It's what's bringing the tree to life in the springtime, and just like it's good for the trees, it's good for us," he says.

of the farmstead. He doesn't seem to mind the long hours, though. Once you get close enough to the bubbling pans of maple liquid, you can understand why. The smell is intoxicating!

His maple syrup evaporator is decidedly low tech. He fashioned it out of an old legal-sized filing cabinet. He cut the drawers and back out and fit it with a barrel stove conversion kit. The fire door is at one end, with an eight-foot smokestack at the other. "This is almost like a blast furnace," he says. "You want an awful lot of heat."

Forty gallons of sap will boil down to one gallon of syrup, "so you have an awful lot of boiling to do," says Bell. In addition to looking at color and consistency, he's constantly measuring the maple liquid to judge its progress. He knows he's reached syrup when it measures 66 percent sugar content.

One vat off to the side contains sap that's been only lightly boiled, giving it a golden hue. He grabs his hydrometer and dips it into the vat, pulling out a sample of the liquid. The weighted bulb bounces up and down and settles at 5 percent, which is almost twice as sugary as when it was collected from the tree.

"I've got a long way to go!"

Michael Bell of Hinkle-Garton Farmstead

BFFs: Rhubarb and Strawberries

Strawberry Rhubarb Pie vegan

NATALIE RAE GOOD

Since we're in the glorious narrow window of time when rhubarb and strawberries grow rampant, I filled up my co-op basket with pink and red.

This pie takes a few hours to set, so get started early. That way you can spend the whole day ogling it on the counter, or if you're impatient, sneaking sloppy spoonfuls out of the pan before it's ready.

Pie crust

Ingredients:

- 3 cups all-purpose flour
- 3 teaspoons sugar
- ¼ teaspoon salt
- 1 cup vegan margarine
- 3 tablespoons canola oil

Directions:

In a large bowl or food processor, mix the flour, sugar, and salt.

Using two knives or a pastry cutter, cut the margarine and oil into the dough until you get large crumbles. Slowly add the ice water, one tablespoon at a time, until a ball forms.

Work quickly and try to keep as many buttery chunks in the dough as possible.

Place in a covered container in the fridge for at least an hour while you prepare the filling.

Strawberry Rhubarb Filling

Ingredients:

- 4 cups rhubarb, trimmed and chopped into ½-inch chunks
- 3 ½ cups strawberries, trimmed and quartered
- ⅓ cup packed brown sugar
- ⅔ cup white sugar
- ⅓ cup cornstarch
- ½ teaspoon cinnamon
- 1 teaspoon lemon juice
- ¼ teaspoon salt

Directions:

Preheat your oven to 400°F.

Mix all ingredients in a large bowl until combined.

Roll half of your pie dough into a large circle and place in pan. Prick the crust with a fork and fill.

Roll out the remainder of the dough and slice into long strips for the lattice top. Sprinkle the lattice with coarse sugar and place in the oven for 1 hour, or until the edges of the crust are browned.

Let the pie sit until cooled and solidified.

Rhubarb Consommé with Strawberries and Mint

vegan

DANIEL ORR

Think of this recipe as a deconstructed strawberry rhubarb pie.

We start off by making a rhubarb consommé, which is basically a clear soup. This particular consommé will be more like syrup because it is sweet.

I like to utilize all parts of the plant if at all possible when I cook, but not with rhubarb. The stems are edible but the leaves are poisonous.

Ingredients:

- 5 pounds rhubarb, leaves removed and discarded, roughly chopped
- 4 cups dry white wine
- 1 vanilla bean, split lengthwise
- 3 cups sugar
- 2 sticks cinnamon
- ¼-inch slice fresh ginger, cut on a bias
- 1 ½ pints strawberries, sliced and chilled
- 10 to 15 mint leaves, cut into chiffonade
- 1 tablespoon orange zest
- 3 sprigs mint

Directions:

Place the rhubarb, wine, vanilla bean, sugar, cinnamon, and ginger in a large saucepan and bring to a boil. Reduce the heat to a simmer and cook for 10 to 12 minutes until the rhubarb has released its juices. Remove the pan from the heat and let the mixture steep for 10 to 15 minutes. Pour the liquid through a strainer.

Just before serving (not more than 1 hour in advance), place the cold strawberries in a metal bowl set over another bowl with ice. Reheat the syrup in a saucepan until it is just warm, pour the syrup over the berries, then set aside to cool. Add the chiffonade mint and orange zest.

To serve, ladle the syrup and berries into individual bowls. Garnish with the mint sprigs and serve ice cold.

No-Bake Rhubarb and Strawberry Tart

Ingredients:

- 3 ½–4 cups rhubarb
  (cut into ¼–½ inch pieces)
- ½ cup sugar
- fresh strawberries, quartered
- strawberry jam
- prepared pastry shells

Directions:

Cook rhubarb and sugar in a saucepan over medium heat for 15–20 minutes. The rhubarb will cook down and become tender, from a celerylike consistency to more of an apple-butter consistency.

Meanwhile, combine strawberries with strawberry jam.

To assemble the tart, spread rhubarb compote into a prebaked puff pastry shell. Top with strawberries.

Strawberry Rhubarb Cherry Pie

STEPHANIE WEAVER

My friend Jill recently moved to Rhode Island. When she mentioned on Facebook that she was having a bumper crop of rhubarb this year and didn't know what to do with it, I said I'd be happy to take some off her hands. Three days later a box of rhubarb arrived for me to play with! Jill is 100 percent responsible for this recipe, due to her willingness to ship rhubarb across the country.

You can use fresh or frozen strawberries, a can of water-packed sour cherries, and fresh rhubarb while it's still in season. If you have a ton of rhubarb now, prep it and freeze it so you can enjoy lovely pies later in the year.

Ingredients:

- 3 cups fresh rhubarb
- 2 cups fresh strawberries
- 1 ¾ cups canned sour cherries (water packed)
- ¼ teaspoon kosher or table salt
- 1 cup agave syrup
- ¼ cup tapioca
- zest of 1 lemon
- 2 piecrusts

Directions:

Prepare your piecrusts and set aside. Preheat oven to 400°F. Put the tapioca pearls into a blender and blend until they are very small.

Wash the strawberries and use a paring knife to remove the green leaves and the white bit around the stem. (This is called "hulling" strawberries.) Slice into quarter-inch-thick slices and set aside.

Wash the rhubarb, dry, and slice into half-inch-thick slices. Make sure you do not include any leaves, as they are toxic.

Drain the cherries, reserving the juice for another use. Mix all the fruit in a bowl with the zest from one lemon, agave syrup, salt, and the ground tapioca. Toss well to mix.

Put one piecrust into your pie dish. Pour in the filling. Put on the top crust and crimp well around the edges so it's completely sealed. Cut slits in the center to allow steam to escape.

Bake for 20 minutes, then turn down the oven to 350°F and bake for 20 minutes more. Check for doneness and to make sure the filling isn't boiling over. You can put a cookie sheet on the rack below to catch drips. Bake until the crust is golden and flaky and the filling is bubbling.

Cool on a rack at least 15 minutes before slicing.

Artist Leah Gauthier assembles a miniature sculpture out of parts of her Marshall strawberry plants

MARSHALL STRAWBERRY EXPLORES ITS ARTISTIC SIDE

Leah Gauthier is sitting in her studio looking through a bowl of plant parts she plucked from her garden. There's a green and orange leaf, a short red stem with a cluster of buds, a delicate white flower.

"I am intrigued the most with this little Marshall strawberry baby, just because this stem here is what used to be attached to the mother plant, and I just feel like I severed it. It sounds weird, but I feel like it should be bleeding a little bit right now."

She picks up her sewing needle and some red embroidery thread. She stitches the thread into the stem, looping it back onto itself. She then photographs this miniature sculpture to be included in her project *Mending Season*. Since the materials start deteriorating as soon as they're harvested, the photographs are her only way to share her work.

"I love that challenge of trying to let go," she says. "Things are always in motion, they are always changing. I wanted to be able to give myself that challenge of resolving something and being able to move on to the next idea."

While she constructs sculptures with a variety of plants from her garden, she has a special affinity for her Marshall strawberry plants. Known for its exceptional taste and firmness, the Marshall strawberry was once described as the finest eating strawberry in America. But after World War II, the plant was devastated by a virus and almost completely removed from commercial production because of its delicacy.

Gauthier discovered the Marshall strawberry on a list of endangered American plants. She not only wanted to taste the finest eating strawberry in the States, she wanted to bring it back to life.

"When I thought about trying to revive one little thing that was something I could do, it felt like I had some hope," she says.

In 2007, she requested a few runners from the only place that still grew the strawberries—the USDA's National Clonal Germplasm Repository in Corvallis, Oregon. She's been growing them ever since.

Now, Gauthier also sells Marshall strawberry starter plants. She calls it her ultimate art project. "I can't revive that strawberry by myself. It needs lots and lots of people to do it, and us doing it together to me is an art piece."

Once she's done creating the sculpture and photographing it, she dismantles it. She replants whatever she can and tries to nurse it back to life.

Strawberry Shortcake with Cashew Cream

NATALIE RAE GOOD

As a kid, I loved strawberry shortcake. In my family, the dish usually consisted of angel food cake topped with fresh cream and strawberries. I decided to try my hand at real shortcake biscuits and was pleasantly surprised!

The trick is to use a food processor to cut the cold vegan margarine quickly so that some buttery crumbs remain and to add the almond milk gradually while pulsing. The buttery bits will make the biscuits flaky and light, a perfect complement to the thick layer of cashew cream.

Cashew cream is naturally sweet, and so easy to prepare. Just be sure to allow a few hours for the nuts to soak.

Serve these shortcakes as a light finish to an evening of kebabs and corn on the cob. Yum!

Ingredients:

- 1½ cups flour
- ¼ cup sugar
- 2 teaspoons baking powder
- ¼ teaspoon salt
- 7 tablespoons cold vegan margarine
- ⅓ to ½ cup almond milk
- 3 to 5 cups fresh strawberries

Directions:

Slice 3 to 5 cups fresh strawberries and place in a bowl with 1 tablespoon of sugar. Set aside.

Preheat oven to 400°F.

In a food processor, pulse the flour, sugar, baking powder, and salt until combined. Add the margarine and pulse until the mixture consists of fine crumbs. Slowly add the almond milk while pulsing until the dough holds together.

Plop 6 to 8 spoonfuls onto a lightly greased baking sheet and bake for 20 minutes, or until golden. Allow to cool and prepare the cashew cream.

Cashew Cream

Ingredients:

- 2 cups cashews
- cold water

Directions:

Soak the cashews in cold water for a few hours.

Rinse and place in a food processor or high-powered blender. Cover the cashews with water (about 1 cup). Blend until very smooth, scraping down sides as necessary.

Add more water if you would like a thinner cream and add a few tablespoons of sugar if you want the cream to be a bit sweet. It's really up to you!

Slice the shortcake biscuits in half and cover with cream and strawberries. Enjoy!

A Fresh Take on Strawberry Shortcake

DANIEL ORR

Ingredients:

- 3–4 cups strawberries
- ½–¾ cup maple syrup, Grade B
- ½ lemon, juiced
- fresh mint
- pinch salt and freshly ground black pepper
- buttermilk biscuits (recipe follows)
- vanilla ice cream
- plain yogurt

Directions:

Prepare biscuits according to recipe. If you've prepared them ahead, warm biscuits in oven.

In a medium bowl, mix the maple syrup, lemon juice, mint, and salt and pepper with the strawberries. Toss to cover strawberries completely. Let macerate 10–15 minutes.

Cut the warm biscuits in halves. Place the bottom halves on a plate.

Top the warmed biscuit halves with strawberry mixture and then top that with the vanilla ice cream. Finish with another layer of strawberries and top with the remaining biscuit halves.

Dollop plain yogurt around the dish and garnish with extra mint leaves. Serve immediately.

Grandma's Buttermilk Biscuits

Ingredients:

- 2 cups flour
- 1 tablespoon baking powder
- ¼ teaspoon baking soda
- ½ teaspoon salt
- 1 teaspoon sugar
- ½ cup butter, cut into pea-sized pieces and chilled well
- ¾ to 1 cup buttermilk (Grandma used sour milk or fresh milk with a little vinegar in it when she didn't have buttermilk)

Directions:

Sift dry ingredients into a stainless steel bowl and chill in the freezer.

With a dough cutter, large fork, or in the bowl of a food processor cut the butter into the dry ingredients, being careful not to overwork the dough. The butter should remain visible in the dough.

Pour out the mixture and form a well in the center. Put three-quarters of the buttermilk in the well and quickly incorporate it. Add more liquid if needed until the dough holds its shape.

Press out to an even ½-inch thickness and cut into desired shape. Brush with a little buttermilk and chill until ready to bake.

Bake in a preheated 400°F oven for 10 minutes. Reduce heat to 350°F and bake until golden brown and light to the touch.

Simple Radish Sandwiches

DANIEL ORR

Simplicity is everything in good cooking. I like to say that 90 percent of being a great chef is being a good shopper, and 10 percent is not screwing up what you bought. These radish and butter sandwiches are about as simple as you get!

I made this recipe in the spring when my farm was producing more French Breakfast radishes than I knew what to do with. But there are plenty of varieties of winter radishes that would taste fantastic in this preparation. I suggest holding a radish taste test to see which variety—from very spicy to more mild—suits your taste buds.

We're going to fancy it up just a little bit. We're going to use my Grandma's Buttermilk Biscuit recipe. Slice those biscuits into chunks and put a nice slab of butter on each. Use a good unsalted creamery butter. This is not the dish on which to be stingy with your butter—slather it on!

Cut the radishes into julienne (little matchsticks). That makes them look pretty and easier to arrange on the biscuit chunks.

Finally, dust the radishes and biscuits with sea salt and a few sprigs of dill. Enjoy!

Spinach and Radish Sprout Salad with Strawberries

DIANA BAUMAN

Thinning seedlings is one of the most difficult parts of gardening. Some of us believe we'll be losing a good portion of the harvest, but thinning needs to be done in order to have a harvest at all.

Case in point: radishes need to be thinned in order to have room to form their peppery and spicy roots below the earth. In my garden, the radish sprouts were the first veggies I harvested this season.

I decided to make a salad featuring the radish sprouts and incorporating the best of what's in season: spinach, organic strawberries, and mint. Spring, I'm so glad you're here!

Ingredients:

- fresh spinach leaves
- radish sprouts
- strawberries
- feta cheese
- ⅔ cup fresh mint, chopped
- ½ cup extra-virgin olive oil
- ¼ cup white wine vinegar
- 3 tablespoons raw honey
- ½ teaspoon sea salt
- dash of pepper

Directions:

Mix mint, oil, vinegar, honey, and salt and pepper in a mason jar and shake. Refrigerate for at least two hours so the flavors can incorporate.

Combine radish sprouts and spinach. Top with freshly cut organic strawberries and sprinkle with feta cheese. Dress salad immediately before serving.

✎ Get to Know Spring Wild Edibles

Spring foraging is all the rage these days. Wet and warm weather has morel lovers putting on their boots and grabbing their mesh bags in the hopes of hitting it big in the woods.

But then there are people like Jill Vance. Maybe you can relate.

"I have never loved the taste of mushrooms," she says, "and I just don't have an eye for them either. I can step in a patch of morels and not see them."

Vance spends a lot of time in the woods looking for other goodies, most of which are easier to spot than camouflaged mushrooms. She's an interpretive naturalist at Monroe Lake and one of the wild edibles experts on staff at Indiana's Department of Natural Resources.

INTO THE WOODS

Spicebush

We meet up near the southwest portion of Monroe Lake. It's a damp day, and the woods are glowing bright green with new growth. We walk 20 paces in on the trail and she stops near a small shrub—spicebush. The stems arch over the trail, giving the shrub an umbrella shape. She crushes up a leaf to release the lemon aroma. "We get a variety of descriptions for what it smells like," she says. "My favorite one is that little kids will tell you it smells like Froot Loops."

Spicebush is a wild edible that foragers can enjoy year round. The leaves and twigs make a nice tea. Stuff them in a saucepan, cover

Jill Vance finds a spicebush

Violet wood sorrel has heart-shaped leaflets and a purple underside

We take a few big steps over downed limbs, duck under tree branches, and brush away some cobwebs. We come across a patch of dark green ground cover. At first glance, I incorrectly guess clover. Vance points to the heart-shaped leaflets, which indicate to her that this is wood sorrel. "This is probably one of my favorites of the wild edibles," she says, as she plucks two petals from the patch. She flips them over to reveal the bright purple undersides of the leaflets, which means this variety is violet wood sorrel. (Keep an eye out for another variety of sorrel that is green on both sides and produces a yellow flower.)

"These are for the people who like a little bit of a sour taste to their food," she says. Vance makes a few pitchers of "sorrelade" every year—like lemonade, but wilder.

Clover

Notice that the shape a clover leaf is rounder than that of wood sorrel. You'll also recognize the white flowers that grow in clover patches. Clover is a nice addition to a salad; Vance says the flavor reminds her of dill.

Ramps

A little further into the woods and halfway down a slope, we spot a darling of spring foraging—a type of wild leek called ramps. The patch is the size of an area rug, with the green leaves clustered in groups or six or eight. Cut a leaf and you'll immediately smell garlic and onions.

"Ramps are kind of a trend, and that's a good thing and a bad thing," she says. "It's good because it helps people appreciate what we have here naturally. It's bad because these things do not reproduce very quickly on their own, and a lot of wild populations have just been decimated by the trend seekers."

She digs up an entire ramp plant—stalk, bulb, and all. This is how most foragers sell

with water, bring to a boil, and then sweeten to taste. Later in the summer, look for little hard red berries on the spicebush. Dry them, crush them into a powder, and use that as a substitute for allspice.

Wood Sorrel

We leave the trail, which Vance says is okay in an Indiana State Recreation Area—but don't assume that's okay everywhere. She says it's important to know the rules of the place you'll be visiting. All it takes is a quick phone call to the manager of the land to make sure you're doing everything by the book.

ramps to chefs and at farmers' markets. But removing the bulb from the ground means ramps struggle to rebuild their population. "And there's no reason you have to take the bulb," she says. Instead, harvest a portion of the leaves only—10 percent of any one patch—to sustainably enjoy the flavor of ramps.

Then, Vance tucked the ramp bulb back into the ground.

BACKYARD ADVENTURES

We've stepped out of the woods and are now exploring the land that surrounds the parking lot—what Vance calls the edge areas. She says these areas tend to contain more diversity of plant life than the middle of a forest.

You might recognize some of these plants from your backyard, and you might call them weeds.

Dandelions

"I know people who like beautiful perfect lawns hate dandelions, but you should get to love them," she says. Except for the stem, every part of the dandelion is edible. The roots can be dried and used as a tea. The flowers can be dipped in batter and fried. And the greens can be eaten any number of ways. (Yes, you can eat dandelion greens raw, but be sure to pick them in the early spring when they're still young and tender.)

"These were carried all over the world by our ancestors as they migrated, because they're one of the very first plants to send out leaves and flowers," Vance says. During a mild winter in southern Indiana, we can see dandelions bloom as early as late December. "And that's very beneficial if you don't have a lot of fresh food available, which our ancestors wouldn't at that time of year," she adds.

While dandelions are not native to southern Indiana, Vance says they are not

A FORAGING FOODIE'S SPRINGTIME TREASURE: RAMPS

For Chef Bob Adkins, fishing is about more than just what's happening in the water.

"I always keep my eye on the dry part of the creek to see if I can spot these bright green objects," he says.

He's talking about ramps, or wild leeks. He found a big batch of ramps near an old riverbed growing in some sandy soil.

He was surprised to have been successful in his foraging so early in April—normally ramps aren't harvested until early May. They like wet conditions with daytime highs in the 60s and overnight lows in the 40s. Maybe that week of temperatures in the 70s encouraged some early growth.

Ramps are pretty unassuming unless you see them out in the wild. The lime-green color sets them apart from other plants he sees this time of year. "If you're outside enough and you've seen enough of the native plants, these are as emerald as the Emerald City in *The Wizard of Oz*," Adkins says.

He's tight lipped about his foraging spots because he wants to preserve them for seasons to come. "I've found numerous patches and gone back the next year and they haven't been there," he says.

considered invasive because they don't push anything else out of the way. They grow mostly in lawns and waste areas. "And if you think about it, the grass that most people have in their lawns isn't native grass anyway," she says.

Greenbrier

Growing amid a patch of poison ivy is a vine called greenbrier. In early spring, it produces curvy tendrils along with its leaves. Both taste like spinach and make a nice addition to a salad. But beware of the thorny stem. This plant earns its name!

Autumn Olive

Look at the leaves on an autumn olive shrub and you'll see silver spots on one side and a shimmering sheen on the other. You'll have to wait until summer for the red berries to grow, but if you harvest several cups worth, you can make wine from them. Vance plans to make autumn olive and wild grape jelly this year.

This is the first invasive plant we find near Monroe Lake. Vance says these shrubs were purposely planted around the area in the 1970s. What officials didn't know then is how much the birds would love those little berries. "With the help of the birds, it has invaded a good portion of our natural areas, and has proven to be next to impossible to get rid of once it's established," she says.

Violets

Tiny purple flowers help violet plants stand out in a mess of greenery. You can also look for the heart-shaped leaves with jagged edges. Add the leaves to a salad, and if you can find enough, Vance suggests collecting a couple cups of flowers and making violet flower sugar.

SUSTAINABLE FORAGING

There is one plant that we don't want to come back. We want to harvest every last bit and remove it from the ecosystem entirely. Wild garlic mustard greens, I'm looking at you.

"That's a highly invasive, really nasty plant," says Vance. It was brought to this area in the 1700s as a culinary herb and has done very well for itself—a little too well, if you ask Vance. "It's my personal nemesis plant, and I can't find a single one here. So, go figure."

Isn't that the way with foraging.

Wild Garlic Mustard

RULES FOR FORAGING:

- Make sure you have permission to harvest.
- Know what you're harvesting.
- Know how to harvest it and how to prepare it.
- Only forage in areas that have not been treated with chemicals.

Just as important, she adds, is to harvest sustainably. "If you enjoy these things, you should want them to return."

KNOW BEFORE YOU GO FORAGING

It's important to take one or two identification books with you when you look for wild foods. Vance owns dozens of plant identification books, which she breaks down into three categories:

General Plant Identification Books

- *101 Trees of Indiana: A Field Guide* by Marion T. Jackson
- *Newcomb's Wildflower Guide* by Lawrence Newcomb

Wild Edibles Identification Books

- *A Field Guide to Edible Wild Plants: Eastern and Central North America* by Lee Allen Peterson
- *Wild Food Plants for Indiana & Adjacent States* by Alan J. McPherson and Sue A. Clark

Recipe Books for Wild Edibles

- *Cooking with Wild Berries & Fruits of Kentucky, Indiana and Ohio* by Teresa Marrone
- *Edible Wild Foods from Dirt to Plate* by John Kallas

HUNTING FOR MORELS   DIANA BAUMAN

It's the middle of morel season in Iowa, and foragers are scrambling to hit all the local state parks and personal spots in hopes of taking home hundreds of the prized mushrooms.

For many years now, I've found myself right in the mix, hoping to find the jackpot. I've realized there's so much more to foraging morels than just searching in the woods—there is strategy.

Since seasoned pros are generally pretty tight lipped about their methods, you are going to have to figure a lot of things out for yourself.

Here are a few tips to get you going:

- Start looking wherever there are elms, especially dead elms. Bark falling off the defunct trees nourishes the ground below. Morels love this.
- The best time to go out hunting is after a good rain, when temperatures hover around 70 degrees.
- There are different kinds of morels. The first to appear are small and gray. Later you'll see larger yellow ones.

- Search low and slow. Use a stick and get down on your knees.
- They tend to cluster in packs. If you find one, you'll usually find more around them, so be careful where you step.
- Don't forget to return to the same place the next day. New mushrooms can pop up literally overnight.
- It takes time and patience to find morels. Many newbies go out expecting to just walk into the woods and find pounds of them. In reality, though, some days you can go out and not run into any. It takes practice to learn to "see" them. You have to get out there more than just once per season.
- Of course, when you *do* find a good spot, take care of it. Always use a mesh bag to collect your morels, which will allow the spores to fall back to the earth. This translates into more morels in the same place next year.
- Most importantly, keep the location secret!

DANIEL ORR

Redbud Flowers for Dessert

Morel hunters see the blooming of the redbud trees as an indication that their coveted mushrooms are now in season. But these beautiful little pink flowers aren't just nice to look at—you can also eat redbuds.

They're a member of the legume family right along with beans and peas. They have little pods that are especially delicious if you pick them when they're still young and tender.

Ingredients:

- meringue cookies (recipe follows)
- plain yogurt
- fresh berries (whatever is seasonal; we used blueberries and blackberries)
- local honey
- your favorite berry preserves
- redbud flowers (rinsed)

Directisons:

Place meringues in the middle of a plate (make a few large flat ones the base for your dessert). Top meringues with plain yogurt and some fresh berries.

Drizzle with local honey and berry preserves. Top with a little more yogurt and sprinkle the flowers over the top.

Meringue Cookies

Ingredients:

- 3 large egg whites
- ¾ cup superfine sugar
- food coloring (optional)

Directions:

Preheat oven to 200°F. Line a baking sheet with parchment paper.

In an electric mixer, beat egg whites until they hold soft peaks.

Add sugar a bit at a time until the egg whites hold stiff peaks and the texture is no longer gritty (the sugar should be fully dissolved).

Form meringues using spoons or a pastry bag and then bake for 1 ½ to 1 ¾ hours, rotating the baking sheet halfway through to ensure even baking. Leave meringues in the oven to finish drying overnight and then store in an airtight container.

Dandelion Greens with Potatoes and Sausage

Spring is the best time to pick dandelions to be eaten raw in salads. They tend to have a milder flavor when the weather is cooler. I like the raw greens tossed in walnut oil or warm bacon drippings with some mild vinegar and a poached or fried egg on top.

Once the summer heat hits, these greens really do have a lion's bite. Find them in a shady corner of the yard or garden and they can remain tender throughout the summer. These more mature greens tend to be bitter and should be blanched and cooked. Some folks blanch them two times to make them less bitter, but this also leaches out the vitamins.

Make sure you wash your greens well in room-temperature water with a spoonful of white vinegar. This helps get the dirt off and any critters out.

Ingredients:

- 1 gallon dandelion greens— washed well and spun dry
- ¼ cup olive oil
- 1 Spanish onion—sliced thinly
- 4 cloves garlic
- 1 pound local Italian sausage— cut into bite-sized pieces
- 6 small red potatoes, diced
- 2 cups water, chicken stock, or vegetable stock
- 4 tablespoons vinegar
- salt and ground black pepper to taste
- hot sauce or chili flakes, butter (optional)

Directions:

Roughly cut dandelion greens in 3-inch pieces.

Preheat a heavy-bottomed stainless steel pot over medium heat and add oil, onions, garlic, and sausage. Cook until lightly browned.

Place dandelion greens on top of sausage mixture and add water or stock.

Top with potatoes. Bring to a boil then reduce heat. Simmer, covered, for 25–30 minutes until greens and potatoes are tender.

Remove cover and reduce the liquids by half. My grandpa called this nectar the pot liquor. Add 4 tablespoons of vinegar (and a little butter if desired) and season to taste with salt and pepper.

Petits Pois à la Française

Generally this classic preparation includes lettuce, but I'm using the invasive wild garlic mustard greens.

Ingredients:

- 3–4 cups blanched peas
- ½ cup chopped bacon (I prefer pepper-crusted bacon)
- 2 big handfuls wild garlic mustard greens (or lettuce)
- 1 teaspoon olive oil
- 1 ½ tablespoons butter
- juice of 1 lemon
- ¼ teaspoon salt
- 1 teaspoon sugar
- ½ cup scallions
- 1 teaspoon minced garlic
- 1 teaspoon lemon peel (finely diced)

Directions:

Add 1 teaspoon olive oil to a hot pan, then add 1–1 ½ tablespoons of butter to the pan, allow the butter to melt (adding the oil to the pan first will keep the butter from burning).

Add the chopped bacon and scallions. Then add the greens. Cook until the greens are wilted.

Add the peas, lemon juice and peel, sugar, salt, and garlic. Cook just until the peas are warmed through.

✍ All in the Allium Family

Onions, scallions, leeks, garlic, chives, ramps—all members of the allium family—along with some 850 other species!

A tip when foraging for members of the allium family: use your nose. Any plant that smells like onions is edible and not toxic to humans. Also, rodents and deer don't like plants in the allium family. You can plant onions or garlic in your garden as a form of natural pest control.

Spring Buttermilk Dressing

Ingredients:

- 2 poached (or boiled) eggs
- 1 tablespoon mustard
- ¼ cup domestic chives (chopped)
- ¼ cup wild chives (chopped)
- ¼ cup garlic chives (chopped)
- 3 cups loosely packed herbs (fennel and chervil)
- 1 teaspoon lemon brunoise (lemon zest finely diced)
- 2 teaspoons chopped garlic
- 1 teaspoon salt
- 1 teaspoon sugar
- 1 cup buttermilk
- juice of ½ lemon
- 1 cup olive oil

Directions:

Blend the eggs, mustard, herbs, chives, lemon brunoise, garlic, salt, sugar, and buttermilk.

Add oil and lemon juice and blend again until smooth.

Garlic Scapes Garlic Salt

Garlic scapes are the stems of the garlic plant, the things that would turn into flowers if left alone. Breaking off the scapes allows the garlic plant to strengthen its bulb, so you're helping out the plant in the process. You can cook them like scallions (in stir fries, pestos, etc.).

Garlic scapes do not have the same heat as regular garlic cloves or a mature garlic plant. So you can use them chopped up in stir fries and eat the whole thing, and not worry about overcooking them.

Ingredients:

- 10–12 garlic scapes
- 2 pounds kosher salt

Directions:

Preheat oven to 250°F.

Roughly chop garlic scapes and combine with kosher salt. Add mixture to the food processor and run until you no longer see chunks of garlic. Spread garlic salt on a cookie sheet. Bake until garlic salt has dried out.

Remove from oven and pulse garlic salt in a food processor once more.

Put the salt in jars and enjoy it as seasoning for your food throughout the winter.

Ramp Pesto

Ingredients:

- a handful of ramp leaves, blanched
- olive oil
- 2–3 garlic cloves
- ½ cup parmesan cheese (finely grated)
- crushed red pepper flakes (to taste)
- pinch of salt
- your favorite hot sauce (to taste)

Directions:

Blanch the ramp leaves by dropping them into boiling salt water and cook until tender. Plunge ramps into an ice bath to stop the cooking. This sets their color and tenderizes them, making it easier to process them in the blender.

Coarsely chop the blanched ramp leaves and add to a high-powered blender with the garlic, salt, red pepper flakes, and about ¼ cup of olive oil.

Start blending, adding ¼ cup oil to every 2 cups of blanched ramps you add to the blender. The result should be a nice thick puree.

Adjust seasoning and add hot sauce to taste. If you're going to freeze the pesto, this is the point where you'll want to stop, put it in small containers (or an ice cube tray), and freeze it.

If you'll be enjoying the pesto immediately, add parmesan cheese and blend a bit more to finish.

Sautéed Fish Wrapped in Ramps

Take the ramp greens, blanch them in boiling salted water, and shock them in ice water. Wrap the ramps around little pieces of cod and sauté them, being sure to not overcook the fish. It should be translucent in the center and opaque on the outside. Present the sautéed, ramp-wrapped cod on a plate with a bit of ramp pesto and a little red wine sauce. Drizzle with fresh lemon juice and garnish with fresh herbs.

summer

Tempura Green Beans

BOB ADKINS

Deep frying has gotten a bad rap.

Think about it like this. You're immersing your food in a really hot environment and steaming it from the inside out. This recipe will help you do it right, so your fries won't hold on to too much excess oil.

Green beans are getting the deep-fried treatment today. This tempura batter is so light that you'll be able to see an outline of green in the finished fries.

Ingredients:

- vegetable oil, for frying
- 1 pound of green beans
- ½ teaspoon salt
- ¾ cup unbleached flour
- additional 1 cup flour in a separate bowl
- ½ cup cornstarch
- 2 tablespoons sugar
- 1 cup ice-cold beer (or soda water)
- 1 egg, beaten

Directions:

Snap the stem ends off the beans.

Combine salt, flour, cornstarch, sugar, and beer for batter. Mix with your hands just to combine. The batter should be thinner than pancake batter but thicker than crepe batter. If it's too thin, add more flour little by little. If it's too thick, add a touch more beer or water.

Heat oil to 350°F.

Drop the beans into some flour. Then submerge them in the beaten egg, and then into the batter.

Drop the battered green beans into the oil one at a time to prevent them from clumping together. Fry until crispy, 2–3 minutes.

Drain on paper towels and season with salt while the beans are still hot. Serve straight away with your favorite dipping sauces.

THE MEANING OF A "FARMERS' MARKET"

Local food works best when both growers and customers claim ownership over it, according to Jennifer Meta-Robinson, the author of *The Farmers' Market Book: Growing Food, Cultivating Community.* Although the apostrophe in "farmers' market" is an important detail, she says, because it puts growers at the center.

"We want people who are extending the possibilities of what it means to live close to a place and be really part of a place and help others to connect to where they live through what they eat," she says.

Meta-Robinson has noticed the phrase "farmers' market" popping up in unusual places, like the produce section in the supermarket. She sees this as an opportunity for true farmers' markets to be more transparent, as a way of educating their consumers.

"Markets could start to develop terms and publicize them, to make clear that this is a producer/vendor market. That's an ongoing education, because especially in a college town, every time there's a turnover of population, you would want to say, 'Here's our market and this is what we have. This is who's there,'" she says.

Green Gazpacho with Cucumbers

DANIEL ORR

Ingredients:

- 6 cucumbers, diced
- 2 garlic cloves
- 1 tablespoon ginger
- 5 scallions
- 1 cup assorted herbs (basil, dill, chives, mint, parsley, etc.)
- ½ cup olive oil
- ½ cup yogurt
- salt and pepper to taste

Optional Garnishes:

- ½ cup cucumbers, diced
- ½ cup herbs, roughly chopped
- ½ cup sweet potatoes, diced
- ½ cup scallions, chopped
- 1 tablespoon green chilies, minced
- 1 cup crab or shrimp

Directions:

Combine the cucumbers, garlic, ginger, scallions, herbs, olive oil, and yogurt in a blender and puree until smooth. Season to taste with salt, pepper, and hot sauce. Chill well. Fold in remaining ingredients just before serving and adjust seasoning.

Garnish bowls with cucumbers, yogurt, herbs, and other condiments of your choice.

Raw Okra Salad

Ingredients:

- 8–12 small okras, sliced in half
- ½–1 cup tomatoes (variety of colors and types), chopped
- ½–1 cup red onions, sliced
- ½–1 cup tomatillos, chopped
- 1 teaspoon garlic, minced
- 2–3 cayenne pepper rings
- lemon zest
- 3 tablespoons vinegar
- 2–3 tablespoons olive oil
- salt and pepper to taste

Directions:

Choose small, young okra. They get more fibrous and are less ideal for raw dishes as they get larger. Combine all ingredients in a bowl and toss. Serve immediately.

❧Eggplant

Eggplant is like a sponge. It wants to soak up liquid. To avoid greasy, gross eggplant, do a little work with it before you broil it up. You can slice it and dry it out in the oven to create a seal. You can also soak it in salt water and squeeze the liquid out of the eggplant.

I like to work with medium-sized eggplants or fairy tale eggplants (also called Asian eggplants). These tend to have denser flesh and fewer seeds. If you have a large eggplant, consider making a dish that requires processing all the ingredients in a blender, like baba ghanoush.

Broiled Miso Eggplant

DANIEL ORR

earth eats

Ingredients:

- 4 Asian eggplants
- ½ cup soy sauce
- ¼ cup honey
- 3 tablespoons Chinese 5-spice powder (a combination of cinnamon, cloves, star anise, fennel, and peppercorns)
- 1 teaspoon freshly ground pepper
- 1 teaspoon toasted sesame oil
- 1 tablespoon Asian chili paste
- 2 large cloves garlic, minced
- 1 tablespoon minced fresh ginger
- 1 lemon, juiced

Directions:

Preheat oven to 425°F. Cut eggplant on a bias into ½-inch thick ovals.

Place remaining ingredients in a sauce pan, bring to a boil, and reduce to a glaze. Taste and adjust the seasoning as you like.

Brush eggplant with glaze. Broil eggplant until well caramelized; turn and do the same on the other side. Finish in the oven for 8–10 minutes, until tender.

Squeeze juice from the lemon over the top and serve.

Eggplant Caviar

This is my take on baba ghanoush, but I like to give it a fancy name. Look toward the bottom of the ingredients list and you'll see anchovies. Don't turn back! These little fish add a certain something to this dish that elevates it to a new level of delicious. Add as many (or as few) anchovies as you like. Your palate should rule the recipe.

Make it a completely homemade appetizer by toasting your own pita chips to serve alongside. They are especially tasty if you toast them immediately before serving.

Ingredients:

- 6 eggplant (salted, rinsed, and squeezed out)
- 5 branches thyme
- 3 branches rosemary
- 1 tablespoon white pepper
- 2 tablespoons fennel seeds
- 4 cups white wine
- 10 garlic cloves
- 1 cup olive oil
- 1 tablespoon sea salt
- touch of curry
- anchovies
- juice of one lemon
- lemon zest
- chives
- parsley

Directions:

To roast the eggplants: Rub them with olive oil. Roast in 350–375°F oven for 30–40 minutes until they collapse and become very soft to the touch.

For the dip: Coarsely chop roasted eggplants (skin and all) and puree with all remaining ingredients in food processor.

Finish with a bit of olive oil, fresh herbs, and lemon. Serve with toasted pita or pita chips.

Chipotle-Marinated Eggplant Tacos

ARLYN LLEWELLYN

Plan ahead before you make this recipe. You'll need to let the eggplant marinate for 1 or 2 days. Peel the eggplant to take away the bitter edge to the taste, then slice it into long strips. It will save you time when flipping it on the grill.

Ingredients:

- 4 cloves of garlic
- 1 tablespoon kosher salt
- ½ cup red wine vinegar
- 1 teaspoon black pepper
- 2 tablespoons dried oregano
- 1 teaspoon sugar
- 3 tablespoons ancho chili powder
- 1 chipotle pepper from can of chipotles in adobo sauce
- 1 ½ tablespoons adobo sauce from chipotle can
- 2 tablespoons water
- 2 small eggplants, peeled, sliced into 1-inch-thick rounds

Directions:

Blend all ingredients (except eggplant) in a blender until a paste forms.

Peel eggplant and slice into long strips. Arrange the eggplant slices in a large bowl and pour marinade over them. Toss by hand (gloves recommended) until all pieces are evenly coasted. Transfer eggplant slices and marinade into plastic bags or other suitable container and allow to marinate for 1 to 2 days in the refrigerator.

When ready to prepare, take eggplants out of fridge and allow them to come to room temperature. Drain marinade off of eggplant slices and grill over medium heat. Once grilled, slice eggplant rounds into ½-inch strips.

Serve these in crunchy taco shells with shredded cheese and creamy cilantro lime slaw.

Creamy Cilantro-Lime Slaw

Ingredients:

- 8 scallions (white and green parts), chopped
- 2 ounces fresh cilantro, chopped
- 1 tablespoon Dijon mustard
- 2 garlic cloves, minced
- 2 teaspoons kosher salt
- 2 tablespoons lime juice
- 2 teaspoons freshly ground black pepper
- 1 cup mayonnaise
- ½ cup sour cream
- ½ cup buttermilk, shaken
- 1 ⅓ pounds green cabbage, finely sliced
- 4 scallions, finely chopped

Directions:

Pulse scallions, cilantro, and garlic in food processor, scraping down sides periodically, until mixture is as finely minced as food processor allows. Add mustard, lime juice, mayonnaise, sour cream, buttermilk, and salt and pepper. Pulse to combine.

Combine cabbage and scallions in a large bowl. Pour 1 ½ cups dressing over vegetables and toss until well combined. Refrigerate for at least 2 hours before serving.

Eggplant Fries

DANIEL ORR

Ingredients:

- 1 medium eggplant, sliced into ¼ inch-by-4 inch slices
- salt
- 1 egg
- ¼ cup milk or nondairy milk
- ⅓ cup cornmeal
- ⅓ cup sorghum and sweet rice flour (combine the two)
- ½ teaspoon salt
- dash smoked paprika
- dash Italian seasoning
- dash garlic powder
- dash black pepper

Directions:

Peel and slice the eggplant. Then set it in a colander in the sink. Sprinkle the slices with salt, toss around, and then leave them for 30 minutes to sweat. Sweating is important when preparing eggplant. The salt helps extract the water.

After 30 minutes, rinse the eggplant off with water, and then spread on a paper-towel-covered plate. Pat dry with paper towels. In one bowl, beat the egg into the milk. In another bowl, combine the cornmeal, flour, and seasonings.

Heat the oil in a shallow pan on high heat. Dredge the eggplant in the egg mixture, then in the flour mixture. Carefully fry the eggplant for 3 minutes on each side, or until golden brown and crispy. Serve hot.

🌿 Day-to-Day Job of a Gardener

DIANNE VENETTA

No matter how you "till it," maintenance comes with the job of gardening—I mean the *joy* of gardening.

THE WEEDS HAVE IT

Weeding. Gasp. Did I say that out loud? The horror!

It's true. A veritable fact of nature. If given the chance, weeds will crowd out your plants in the span of one sunny afternoon, and some weeds don't even need sun. It's actually an amazing feat when you stop to think about it!

I have had several weeds growing underneath my weed paper, no kidding, but I do still recommend using the stuff. Most weeds will succumb underneath the layer of protective paper. Line your rows with weed paper. Line your walkways, line your borders and by all means cover any unused beds with paper. If you don't have weed paper, a heavy layer of mulch will work—hay, pine, straw, or bark are a few examples. If left for long enough it will decompose, and this will add compost to the garden. I do like a multitasker.

IT'S ALL ABOUT THE WET STUFF

Watering is your first step to success in the garden. It's so important that it's worth taking water needs into account when you're planning the design and layout of your garden. Without a good watering system, your plants are toast—literally.

I'M ONLY HAPPY WHEN IT RAINS

Steven Janowiecki is a gardener with an itch for engineering.

A few weeks after he bought his house in Bloomington, Indiana, the first improvement he made was to build a dozen raised beds for his garden. The next step was to find an easy way to water the plants.

This astronomy graduate student purchased six 55-gallon rain barrels for $5 each, constructed wooden frames to hold them four feet above ground, "and then just played with PVC pipe until it worked."

This experiment in elementary engineering has resulted in a watering system for his garden that takes only five minutes to execute.

An elaborate maze of PVC pipes runs through Janowiecki's garden. While he could have buried the pipes, the aboveground system allows him to spot problems and fix clogs more easily.

There is about 1,500 square feet of collecting area on the roof that drains into the barrels by way of the gutters. His barrels have a total of 300 gallons of storage, and they fill up completely with ¼ inch of rain. "The barrels have not been dry since the beginning of March because we've had so much rain lately," he says.

But the rainy weather will not continue indefinitely. He says full barrels will last him one week of regular watering.

Don't waste it. Water is a precious commodity and spraying it willy-nilly through the air via your sprinkler is not ideal. It's much better to incorporate a drip line or soaker hose within your garden.

Perhaps your space is small and not worth the effort of installing an irrigation system. Then you may want to consider the use of an old-fashioned watering can. They work!

If you must resort to a sprinkler system of some kind, be sure to water in the early morning hours or late afternoon or evening. This will reduce the amount of water lost to evaporation. In the spirit of beauty sleep and busy schedules, you'll also want to utilize a timer. After all, a timer never forgets.

Form a well around your plants to collect and direct as much water as possible to the base. Focus, people. We're aiming for the roots!

When determining how much water to apply, consider the thirstiness of your various plants. Garlic and okra don't require as much water as squash or eggplant. You know this by the makeup of the vegetable itself. Juicy means it needs lots of water, while dry veggies don't need as much. Simple! Some other plants vary in their water needs depending on their stage in the growing cycle. For example, beans require low water at planting, medium amounts at flowering, and heavy watering during harvest when they're in full production mode.

If you're faced with a difficult watering schedule, choose to water deeply and less frequently. Deep watering encourages deep roots and deep roots make for strong plants that are able to produce big fruits.

GOOD GUYS VERSUS BAD GUYS

When you're an organic gardener, you face challenges that conventional gardeners don't, especially when it comes to bugs. While

others may be content with a chemical spritz from their spray bottle, or a toxic toss of their powders, you refuse such tactics. You are not going to add potential hazards to your otherwise healthy garden. Choosing organic methods requires you to be smarter than the bugs and quicker than the beasts.

It's up to you to be vigilant and determined. In other words, to be a successful organic gardener you must become skilled in the Battle of the Bugs.

You can combat pests the old-fashioned way—by plucking them off one by one. Keep your eyes peeled for hornworms and caterpillars. They're easy to catch and pull from the vine.

Lure slugs and snails away from your plants with a small glass of beer. It seems that they have an affinity for the stuff, and it's easier for them to get in than it is to get out.

You can plan ahead by referring to your handy-dandy list of companion plants and organize your garden with pest control in mind. Rosemary deters cabbage moths. Dill *attracts* hornworms. Lavender nourishes a host of beneficial insects. Marigolds are a great flower to plant in and around your garden. Not only do they repel many insects, they deter underground nematodes that can contribute to the destruction of your plants by root rot.

You can also invite some friends to your garden. Did you know that ladybugs love aphids, while frogs consume crickets and spiders like they're going out of style? Then there are dragonflies that make a feast of mosquitoes and flies. Cardinals apparently feed grasshoppers to their young. This is good news, because grasshoppers can prove to be a horrible nuisance in the garden. Anything that keeps them on the run receives an extra star in my garden journal.

DISEASE CONTROL, THE ORGANIC DILEMMA

Disease control in an organic garden begins with prevention. When planting seeds, be sure to maintain proper spacing between them. When they grow up into adult plants, they'll benefit from the airflow that comes with space.

Then, be aware of your watering techniques. Problems like powdery mildew and root rot occur because of moist conditions. In humid areas it's an even bigger problem, because moisture hangs in the air. I know what you're thinking: How do you prevent humidity? You don't. What you can do is water your plants with a concoction of compost or manure tea. Not only is this mixture a great source of plant food, it can also help fight off many plant diseases by inoculating plants with beneficial organisms.

A little spritz of neem oil will help control disease, particularly early blight and rust (those red, yellow, and orange spots on your leaves). Baking soda spray is another old-fashioned remedy that has proven successful in prevention. Keep in mind that disease can spread fairly quickly, so you'll want to pluck off affected leaves immediately to prevent further infection.

Some diseases can linger in the soil and affect next season's crop, harming your plants before they ever get going. That's why rotating your crops from planting to planting and season to season is so important. In between seasons, consider solarizing your soil. Cover your beds with plastic paper and allow the sun's heat to penetrate and warm the soil to temperatures that will kill pests and disease. It takes a good six weeks under the hot summer sun to achieve optimum results.

ALL-NATURAL DEER REPELLENT | DANIEL ORR

Deer will eat just about anything. I learned that the hard way this season. A group of them decimated the leaves on my newly planted apple, pear, and plum trees one night.

But I'm fighting back!*

I grow my plants organically, so I was motivated to find an all-natural way to deter pests. At first glance, this repellent looks edible—almost like a Green Goddess dressing—but let it sit out in the sun for a few days to "brew." The buttermilk will go rancid and the heat from the peppers will tickle your nose. You'll understand why deer won't want to be anywhere near this stuff. With that said, don't use this on the trees and plants near your front door. You want to repel deer and other pests, not your houseguests.

Ingredients:

1 egg
2 whole spicy chilies (habanero or Scotch bonnet)
¼ cup buttermilk
1–2 garlic cloves
handful of garlic chives
1 tablespoon salad oil
3 quarts water

Directions:

Combine first 6 ingredients in a blender. Add 1 quart of water and blend.

Pour mixture into a jug and add 2 more quarts of water. Let it sit out for a couple days to develop a pungent odor.

Strain the mixture and put it in a squirt bottle. Apply to the bark of trees, around plants, and wherever pests go for a snack.

*No deer were harmed in the making of this repellent.

EVEN THE PROS PULL WEEDS

Stranger's Hill Organics in Bloomington, Indiana, has been fighting the good fight—the war against weeds—for a long time. According to farm manager Rachel Beyer, weeds (more politely called non-crop competitors) are probably the biggest challenge to organic farmers.

Beyer talks about three ways to remove weeds:

- Cultivating manually with a hoe, or pulling the weeds by hand.

- Using black plastic mulch—She says some organic farmers have a problem using this because it's a petroleum-based product that gets thrown away at the end of the season. "But it's a major savings in terms of labor, which otherwise you would be spending a lot of money on."

- Mulching deeply with cardboard and wood chips—That stuff will break down in the soil and you don't have to worry about removing it before you till. You're also adding organic matter while controlling the weeds at the same time. Of the three options, this is the most labor intensive.

The parsley and thyme patches at the farm are being overrun by ragweed and a variety of grasses. The worst weed of all, however, is vine weed. This especially pernicious weed wraps itself around the plants, suffocates them, and takes their nutrients. Ben Smith, the CSA manager at Stranger's Hill, advises gardeners to make sure to remove the root or else it will just grow back.

Luckily, the benefits of removing the weeds from the beds are obvious. The plants that have had their non-crop competitor neighbors removed are lusher and a darker shade of green. "They probably taste better, too, because they have all the nutrients they need," says Smith.

"Sometimes you find yourself doing the funniest things for organic farming," says Smith. "On conventional farms, you could just spray some Round Up on everything and it'll take care of the problem," but the organic mindset is to do what's best for the entire environment.

He explains that spraying chemicals kills not only the bad plants but also the beneficial organisms that live in various parts of the ecosystem. "Even weeds can be good in a way," he adds. For instance, the farm has a colony of bees. If they were to remove all the plants they didn't specifically put into the ground, there wouldn't be a whole lot of pollen for those bees to gather.

After the weeds are removed, organic material will be applied to the land to create rich topsoil that is ideal for plant growth.

After the deep mulching procedure, Beyer explains, they will apply compost made from vegetables that have rotted in the fields or that were not sold at market.

Smith is hopeful that after all this work, the parsley and thyme will bounce back.

"It's going to be the best-tasting thyme and parsley you've ever had."

IT'S HARVEST TIME!

DIANNE VENETTA

Harvesting can be tricky. Without experience, it's hard to know when to harvest those onions and garlic you've been salivating over since fall or the potatoes you planted this spring. Each vegetable has its own time for picking.

Let's begin with garlic and onions. Both require months and months to reach full maturity, and both have slender green points for leaves. Ultimately, these tops yellow and fall over. Don't worry, they're not dead. They're finally mature! Pull them gently from the ground and lay them out on a screen in the sun to "cure." Give onions one week, garlic two weeks, unless the days are extremely hot. Then you'll want to lay them in light shade to prevent sunburn. When the onion exteriors are papery and the garlic necks are tight, they are ready to store in a cool dry place. I like to braid those long stems and hang them in a dark corner of the kitchen or pantry.

You'll know your potatoes are ready for prime time when their tops die back. When they do, gently dig them up (called "swimming for potatoes") and lightly brush the dirt from their skin. Cure in the potatoes in humid conditions at around 55°F for about two weeks. Then store them for the long haul in a root cellar (about 40°F). Be careful—if you store them in a light area or near apples, your potatoes will be on the fast track to sprouting. No longer good to eat!

Carrots can be harvested when you spot their orange bodies poking through the soil's surface. It will be obvious they're of good size and ready to devour. For storing, cut off the greens to within an inch of the body and lay the carrots in a box of damp sand or sawdust, preferably in a root cellar. They'll keep like that for weeks. Don't have a root cellar? You can also store them in cold water in your refrigerator.

Vegetables like broccoli, cabbage, and squash are easy to harvest. You simply pluck them when they look ready. If your broccoli blooms with pretty yellow flowers, toss them in a salad.

Tomatoes can be picked at the first sign of red. Then set them by a sunny window to fully ripen. Why not allow them to ripen on the vine? Because pests could attack, or an impending freeze might speed up your harvest date. Either way, it's good to have options. The same goes for green peppers. For a sweeter version, leave them on the branch until they turn red.

Okra gets a bad rap for being slimy, but if you pick it young (about 1–2 inches in length) and consume fresh, there's no slime in sight.

Corn is a bit trickier. As the first silk appears, count your days. It will take somewhere between 12 and 18 days for your silk to brown. When it's still slightly green near the husk with brownish ends, twist that cob free and call the neighbors—it's picnic time! Some say to pick corn in the morning and refrigerate until suppertime. I say pick right before you plan to eat, because once pulled from the stalk the sugar in corn begins turning to starch.

Then there's my favorite: lettuce. Salads are delicious, but keeping lettuce fresh long enough to enjoy more than once is tough. Try this: Wash and rinse your leaves, pat dry and then roll them in a damp paper towel. Place the lettuce inside a sealed bag and store in the refrigerator. You will be amazed at how long your greens stay crisp and tasty!

Old-fashioned green beans are easy—you simply harvest when their pods are plump. Shelling beans, on the other hand, turn colors as they mature. When green turns tan, you know you've got some beauties inside. In the case of Black Turtle black beans, they turn a gorgeous deep eggplant in color.

❧ Tons of
Tomatoes

A LIFE WITH TOMATOES

It's tomato season in Midwest gardens. Jeff Mease's tomato patch at Loesch Farm is bursting with color. "I'm a pizza man, so tomatoes sort of come naturally," he says.

Mease is a restaurateur, a businessman, and a gentleman farmer. Before he opened a series of restaurants in Bloomington, Indiana, he was growing food. "I used to grow a lot of tomatoes when I was young, even though I really didn't like them. Like, I would never eat a tomato. And still, to sit down and eat a whole tomato is not that appealing to me," he says.

We took a walking tour of the 70-acre farm. One small plot of land is a maze of vines and stakes. This had been home to some of his pigs. They tilled and fertilized the soil, which made the area perfect for 800 tomato plants. He sells the tomatoes at wholesale to his restaurant, Lennie's.

He sees a bigger purpose in this hobby than helping his restaurants stay on budget. "It's more about raising something that's unique to your place, unique to the area. Something that, say, only is available at your restaurant, so that there's a story behind it," he says.

His story started in 1982. He had worked as a delivery guy for Domino's Pizza and thought he could open a local business that would give the corporate guy a run for his money. The original Pizza X location is right next to the Indiana University–Bloomington campus. He opened the casual dining restaurant Lennie's in the same complex in 1989.

Today, he operates One World Enterprises, which consists of five Pizza X carry-out locations, a craft brewery, a catering business, and Lennie's. Mease also operates a kitchen share program out of the One World commissary. Small food businesses rent space in the commercial kitchen while One World employees prepare the day's pizza dough.

He admits that the majority of food his businesses sell comes from nonlocal sources, but what makes his business different is that *he* is local. He's able to communicate the value of those local tomatoes to the customers.

"If I'm going to dine this way, I want meaning. I want understanding. I want to know that you, the restaurateur, are giving me your best through the value chain, not just making it 'gourmet.'" And that, he says, is the core of the farm-to-table movement.

Back in the tomato patch at Loesch Farm, the plants look like grape vines. The style of trellising is called the Florida weave.

"What we've done is sink ⅝-inch rebar 10-foot stakes every 10–12 feet and plant double rows of tomatoes down in between them," he says. The rows are set 12 feet apart so they can pull a cart in between the plants. On the ground, there's a lush covering of clover, which Mease says is a nitrogen fixer. "Much better to do this than to just leave the ground bare," he says.

Mease imagines it will likely take another handful of years before his farm is able to grow production to the point of commercial sale. "Just slowly, kind of organically, letting the vision for what we're going to do out here take shape," he says. "We want to do it once and do it right."

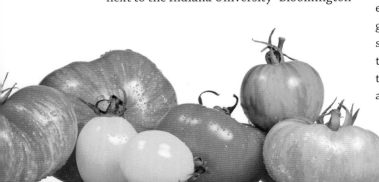

Vine-ripened tomatoes are one of my favorite foods to preserve. There is nothing that brings you back to summer faster than using preserved tomatoes during the winter. The sweetness and the acidity will complement all of your winter stews and chili. You can even use them to make salsa and gazpacho that taste just as fresh as summer.

Tomato Ice Cubes

Freezing tomatoes is hands down my favorite way to preserve tomatoes. It doesn't require me to spend time canning them in a hot water bath. In order to freeze tomatoes, all you need to do is rinse them off, then put them in a plastic bag and into the freezer. Really, it's that easy! Tomatoes do not need to be blanched before being frozen. When you are ready to use them, all you need to do is let them thaw out, and when they start to defrost, their skins slip right off.

Canned Tomato Salsa

Canned tomato salsa is a recipe I was a little hesitant to share. Tomatoes do have just enough acid to can, but some say they may not have enough to kill food-borne pathogens. In order to remedy this (and for my own sanity), I add extra lemon juice to increase the acid level.

Ingredients:

- 10 cups peeled, cored, chopped tomatoes
- 6 cups seeded, chopped jalapeno peppers
- 4 cups chopped onions
- 1 cup lemon juice
- 1 cup chopped cilantro
- 3–4 teaspoons salt

Directions:

This process is set up to move one batch at a time. Boil your tomatoes 12 at a time for 45 seconds. Remove tomato skins by immediately plunging them into a bowl filled with ice water. The skins should slip right off. Chop up the first batch of tomatoes and place them in a colander over a bowl to reserve the juices.

Squeeze out as much juice as you can from the tomatoes in the colander. Place the tomatoes in a large bowl. Pour the juice into a large pot. Bring the tomato juice to a boil, lower the heat to medium, and simmer. As you boil, remove skins and chop more tomatoes; continue to add more juice to the pot. While the sauce is still simmering and thickening, chop the peppers, onions, and cilantro. Add to the large bowl of tomatoes. Add the lemon juice and salt. Once the tomato sauce on the stove has thickened, add the contents of the large bowl and mix. Bring to a boil, lower the heat, and simmer for 15–20 minutes.

Sterilize your canning jars by running them through one cycle in the dishwasher. Or, hand wash them inside and out and then submerge them in boiling water for 10–15 minutes. Ladle salsa into sterilized jars, leaving ½-inch of headspace. Process in a hot water canner for 15 minutes at 0–1,000 feet altitude, 20 minutes at 1,001–6,000 feet, or 25 minutes above 6,000 feet.

Burst Cherry Tomatoes

Cherry tomatoes are bite-sized flavor bullets that are just as good straight from the garden to your mouth as they are cooked with pasta.

We walked all over Daniel Orr's expansive garden in Columbus, Indiana, picking tomatoes here and there, along the chain-link fence and next to a flowerbed. They tend to spread themselves all over the place from season to season. This makes cherry tomatoes volunteers in the garden.

They grow quickly, so it's easy to get overwhelmed with all the tomatoes you suddenly have waiting to be eaten. "When you have a whole lot of tomatoes right out of the garden, you need to use them up somehow," he said.

Ingredients:

- 2 pints cherry tomatoes
- ½ cup olive oil
- ½ tablespoon minced garlic
- 1 teaspoon freshly ground pepper
- ½ teaspoon crushed red pepper
- ¼ cup grated parmesan cheese
- ½ cup roughly chopped parsley
- salt and pepper to taste

Directions:

Heat oil in a large sauté pan and remove from heat. Remove stems from tomatoes. Add tomatoes. Cover to prevent splattering.

Return to heat and add garlic. Cook just until the skins split.

Season with remaining ingredients and toss carefully. Best served at room temperature.

Pour over a tart shell. Sprinkle with parmesan cheese. Or serve over pasta, meat, or fish. Add to vegetable plate.

Millet Caprese Salad

DANIEL ORR

We're going to eat some birdseed today! No, really. Millet is a common ingredient in commercial birdseed. But for humans, especially those of us who are gluten free, millet is also a great choice.

My suggestion when trying new ingredients is to incorporate them into existing recipes that you know you love. One of my go-to recipes to tinker with is a traditional caprese salad—perfect for cherry tomato season!

I didn't include proportions for this recipe, so I encourage you to make it your own. A few more cherry tomatoes here, a generous splash of caper juice there. Taste as you go and adjust the proportions accordingly.

Ingredients:

- cherry tomatoes, cut in half
- basil, roughly chopped
- mozzarella, cut into cubes
- jalapeño, diced
- capers
- cooked millet
- brussels sprouts
- salt and pepper to taste
- splash of sherry vinegar
- splash of caper juice
- extra virgin olive oil (use the good stuff!)

Directions:

Use a 1:2 grain-to-water ratio when cooking millet. Bring water to a boil, reduce heat, and add millet. Cook for 15 minutes, then let sit for 10 minutes. Fluff with a fork and let cool before adding it to the salad.

Combine first six ingredients in a large bowl. Cut open the brussels sprouts and sprinkle the raw leaves into the salad. Add sherry vinegar, caper juice, and salt and pepper to taste. Finish with a drizzle of olive oil for shine.

Panzanella Salad for Your Forgotten Bread

I love Italian cooking because it lets the ingredients speak for themselves, and there are many ingredients in this recipe that have a lot to say.

Select the freshest tomatoes and cucumbers you can find, and then scavenge for stale bread in the back of your pantry. (Hopefully you haven't tossed it in the compost just yet!)

I start by baking chunks of bread into croutons, seasoned with parmesan cheese, olive oil, and salt and pepper. Then before I assemble the salad, I mix them with ¼ cup of hot water to moisten them up.

Three different types of tomatoes add the color in this recipe—globe tomatoes, cherry tomatoes, and sun-dried tomatoes. Do your guests a favor and cut the cherry tomatoes in half. No one enjoys chasing tomatoes around their plate with a fork.

One final tip before you get started: after you chop the garlic, take the side of your knife and smash it into a paste. You'll taste the difference!

Ingredients:

- 2 cups globe tomatoes, diced into large chunks
- 2 cups cherry tomatoes, sliced in half
- 4 cups day-old (somewhat dry and hard) crusty bread, cut into chunks the same size as the tomatoes
- 1 cucumber, skinned and seeded, cut into chunks
- ½ red onion, chopped
- 1 bunch fresh basil, torn into little pieces
- 2 balls fresh mozzarella cheese, cut into chunks
- ¼ to ½ cup good olive oil
- salt and pepper to taste
- handful of sun-dried tomatoes, chopped
- dash of herbes de Provence (a combination of savory, marjoram, rosemary, thyme, oregano)

Directions:

Mix everything together and let marinate, covered, at room temperature for at least 30 minutes, up to 2 hours. Do not refrigerate or you will destroy the texture of the tomatoes!

Serve at room temperature.

The World's Best BLT

Ingredients:

- 2 slices 7-grain bread
- 1 ½ ounces goat cheese
- 2 ounces ripe avocado, sliced
- ½ ounce greens
- 1 ounce vine-ripe tomatoes
- ⅛ ounce basil leaves
- 1 tablespoon green herb mayonnaise (or basil wasabi mayo)
- 4 pieces cooked pepper bacon
- fresh lemon juice, sea salt, and black pepper to taste

Directions:

Rub garlic on two slices of lightly toasted bread. Layer with goat cheese, tomatoes, basil leaves, and bacon.

Toast in a 350°F oven for 4–5 minutes.

Then spread one slice of bread with green herb mayonnaise. (We used basil wasabi mayonnaise, which is exactly what it sounds like: add minced basil and wasabi to regular mayo.)

Layer the toast with avocado. Season with a bit of lemon juice and salt and pepper. Top with greens and serve immediately.

Fried Green Tomatoes

At the end of the season, pick all your tomatoes, even if they're still green. Wrap them in newspaper, and store them in a box in a cool dark place or in the bottom of your refrigerator. They'll keep for a long time. Or you could fry them up and enjoy them right away!

Ingredients:

- 4 large green tomatoes
- 3 eggs, beaten
- ½ cup buttermilk
- 1 ½ cups cornmeal
- ¼ cup parmesan cheese
- 1 teaspoon granulated garlic
- 1 cup all-purpose flour
- salt and pepper
- oil for frying

Directions:

Core and slice tomatoes.

In one bowl, whisk together eggs and buttermilk. Fill another with flour and salt and pepper. In the third, mix cornmeal, parmesan, and garlic.

Dredge tomato slices through a standard breading procedure: drop them in the flour. Then submerge them in the egg mixture. Finally, toss them in the cornmeal mixture until coated.

In a heavy-bottomed pan, add oil to halfway up. Heat the oil to 350°F. Add breaded tomato slices and fry until brown and crispy.

Tuscan-Flavored Roast Tomatoes

I'm using Italian plum tomatoes because they are meaty and have few seeds. If you were to roast a juicy variety of heirloom tomato, for instance, it would fall apart in the oven. I love fresh oregano, basil, and other Tuscan-flavored herbs on my roasted tomatoes. I also love garlic—lots and lots of garlic! This recipe features eight cloves of garlic, but feel free to add as much or as little as you prefer. If you want to add a little spice to your tomatoes, chop up some jalapeños. Some cooks put some sugar or honey on roasted tomatoes to intensify their sweetness. If you want some additional acidity, throw in a couple teaspoons of white vinegar.

Ingredients:

- 5–6 Italian plum tomatoes
- ¼ cup oregano
- ¼ cup basil
- 8 cloves garlic
- 2 jalapeños (optional)
- 1 teaspoon salt
- 1 teaspoon pepper
- 2 tablespoons olive oil
- 2–3 teaspoons honey or sugar (optional)
- 2 teaspoons white vinegar (optional)

Directions:

Preheat oven to 375°F. Slice tomatoes into quarters. Chop herbs finely and remove large stems. Dice jalapeños. Toss tomatoes with herbs, jalapeños, salt and pepper, and oil. (Add honey, sugar, or white vinegar to this mixture if you choose.) Spread seasoned tomatoes on cookie sheet. Roast tomatoes for 15–20 minutes until they start to caramelize.

Roast Tomatoes and Snow Peas

Ingredients:

- 4 cups blanched pea pods
- 3 cups roasted Roma tomatoes
- olive oil
- 1 tablespoon chopped garlic
- 1 teaspoon lemon zest
- handful roughly chopped herbs (e.g., basil, mint, cilantro, scallions, chervil, dill)
- salt and pepper to taste

Directions:

To roast the tomatoes, slice them in quarters. Toss them with olive oil, garlic, salt and pepper, and herbs. Put them under the broiler to let them caramelize.

To blanch the snow peas, cook them in boiling salted water until they're tender but still crisp (6 to 8 minutes). Drain the peas and plunge them into a bowl of ice water to chill quickly.

Add tomatoes and snow peas to a bowl. Combine with just enough olive oil to coat, lemon zest, and additional herbs. Toss together and add salt and pepper to taste.

Bacon-Wrapped Roasted Garlic

While you have the oven fired up, toss in this recipe.

Ingredients:

- 1 bunch of garlic
- 1 slice of peppered bacon
- pinch salt and pepper
- drizzle of olive oil

Directions:

Preheat oven to 325°F.

Slice off the top third of the bunch of garlic, revealing the tops of the cloves.

On a sheet of foil, place the garlic bunch in the middle of a slice of bacon. Season with salt and pepper and a drizzle of olive oil. Wrap the bacon around the garlic and cover with foil.

Roast the bacon-garlic package for 45 minutes or until very soft and light brown. When fully roasted, you should easily be able to squeeze the garlic out of its shell. If you're a fireplace owner, you could do this overnight. When the fire has died down, tuck these aluminum foil packages next to the coals. You'll wake up to wonderful roasted garlic to spread on your bagels.

Salsa Verde with Fresh Tomatillos

Tomatillos are called ground cherries or husked tomatoes. The last time we planted tomatillos was 10–15 years ago, and they're still going strong.

Along with onions, a chili pepper, and a healthy portion of garlic, I'm roasting the tomatillos to develop a caramelized flavor. This will also evaporate some of the moisture and will give us a thicker salsa.

Ingredients:

- 15–20 tomatillos, sliced
- 1 white onion, chopped
- lemon zest
- 1 chili pepper, chopped (keep seeds for extra heat)
- 2 tablespoons olive oil
- 1 cup basil
- salt and pepper to taste

Directions:

Mix the chopped vegetables with lemon zest and olive oil. Roast the vegetables in an oven-proof pan under a broiler. The vegetables will cook down and become caramelized.

After broiling the vegetables, add the basil and an additional clove of chopped garlic. Pulse the mixture in a food processor. At this point, you can add raw vegetables, like red onions or more tomatillos. Feel free to add whatever flavors you especially enjoy.

Choose a chili pepper that will provide the heat and flavor you're looking for (serrano, jalapeño, habanero, etc.). Add remaining ingredients and pulse in food processor until desired consistency is reached. Add salt and pepper to taste.

Salsas

CLARA MOORE

I lived in Mexico for a spell a few years ago. It was one of the greatest times of my culinary life. I learned so much from the ladies I worked with. They were patient and sweet, and they liked to explain things to me in very simple terms.

The greatest skill I picked up there was salsa making. These ladies had about 60 different salsa recipes cataloged in their brains. These are two I smuggled out of the country.

Salsa Mexicana

Ingredients:

- 5 firm Roma tomatoes, finely chopped
- ½ large white onion, finely chopped
- 2 serrano peppers or 1 jalapeño pepper, finely chopped
- juice of 2 limes
- ⅓ cup cilantro, finely chopped
- salt to taste

Directions:

Combine all ingredients in a bowl and enjoy immediately.

Salsa Verde

Ingredients:

- 5 large tomatillos
- 2 jalapeño peppers
- 3 unpeeled garlic cloves
- ¼ cup white onion, diced
- ⅓ cup cilantro
- juice of 1 lime
- salt to taste

Directions:

Turn on oven broiler, or begin to heat griddle.

Husk and wash the tomatillos. Place tomatillos, unpeeled garlic, and peppers on cookie sheet in the broiler or on the warmed griddle. Rotate often to char all sides. Once vegetables are charred on all sides, remove from pan. Once cool to the touch, remove garlic cloves from their skins and remove seeds and stems from peppers. (That is, unless you want a *very* spicy salsa. In that case, leave the seeds intact.)

Place all ingredients in a blender or food processor. Process to your desired consistency. Enjoy warm or chilled.

Mango Nectarine Salsa

STEPHANIE WEAVER

I can't remember when I first had mango salsa but it's been a favorite ever since. You can make this as mild or as spicy as you like. The fresh lime provides the perfect zing to the creamy avocado, fruit, and vegetables. You can make it chunky (great for dipping) or cut everything much more finely and use it as a sauce for shrimp, fish, or chicken.

Ingredients:

- 1 large or 2 small nectarines (or apples, pears, or plums)
- 1 mango
- 1 lime
- 1 bunch cilantro
- 1 jalapeño
- 1 red pepper
- 1 avocado
- ½ teaspoon sea salt
- ½ teaspoon white pepper

Directions:

Cut the nectarine in half and remove the pit. Cut into small or medium-sized pieces and place in a medium-sized bowl. Try to make all the other items the same size. If you want a chunky-style salsa, use larger pieces. If you want the salsa to be more refined, you can cut things pretty small. Cut up the mango. Juice the lime and add to the bowl.

Halve the jalapeño and the red pepper, removing the ribs, stem, and seeds. Cut up and add. Cut up the avocado and add the salt and pepper.

Mix well, making sure the avocado gets coated with juice to prevent it from browning.

You can serve it immediately or place it in the refrigerator for several hours so the flavors meld.

summer

Sun-Dried Tomatoes

DIANNE VENETTA

I had never wondered how sun-dried tomatoes were created. I figured the name said it all. I imagined them splayed across specialty terra-cotta baking stones in Italy or California sunning until they reached crispy, crunchy, chewy perfection.

It wasn't until I witnessed Mother Nature's first sun-dried tomatoes in my garden that it dawned on me. (Actually, it was the scorch of summer and my lack of attention that did it, but who's checking?) I planted these gorgeous Romas this spring and they dried by summertime all by themselves. For all of you cringing right now thinking, "Please no, tell me you didn't actually eat those rotten things," rest assured: I didn't. Who knows what may have tainted those shriveled beauties? I don't eat anything from my garden without full certainty of its wholesome goodness.

So how does one sun-dry tomatoes? Easy—the same way you dry the herbs from your garden.

Directions:

Preheat your oven to 150–200°F. Cut a variety of tomatoes into quarters. Remove the seeds or keep them in, it's up to you. Spread the tomatoes across a baking sheet. I used a vented sheet for more even drying. Bake tomatoes for about 4–5 hours, depending on the size of your tomatoes and the heat strength of your oven.

Monitor them throughout the process, turning when necessary. After about 4 hours, my small batch was perfectly dried.

Sun-Dried Tomato Bonbons

DANIEL ORR

When I invite guests over for dinner, I want to prepare something simple ahead of time to keep them occupied while I cook. These savory bonbons fit the bill perfectly. They are a play on the little sweet chocolate treats you usually enjoy after dinner.

Ingredients:

- 12 sun-dried tomatoes
- ½ pound soft, fresh goat cheese
- ¼ cup chopped herbs of your choosing (like scallions and basil)
- ½ clove of garlic, minced
- salt and pepper to taste

Directions:

Soak the sun-dried tomatoes in warm water until they are very tender. Remove from water and pat dry. Place on a sheet tray, cut side up.

Mix goat cheese with the herbs and garlic. Season with salt and pepper.

Place a spoonful of seasoned cheese on each of the tomatoes and fold over. Chill until served.

earth eats

HOT DAYS, COOL CHICKS

JANA WILSON

When winter's on the horizon, many chicken owners I know ask the same question: how will I keep my chickens warm in cold weather?

Actually, chickens have more problems right now, during the hottest months of the year. Their built-in down coat is to blame. A covering of feathers makes getting rid of body heat much more difficult for chickens than for other animals with less covering.

If you find your hens panting with their beaks wide open, you can be sure they're getting hot. Here are a few ways to ensure your backyard birds are cool as cucumbers.

Make sure your coop is well ventilated. Windows covered in wire mesh small enough to keep out nocturnal predators are a good way to ensure airflow. By positioning your coop in a way that takes advantage of breezes in your area, you'll be adding some natural air conditioning. If you have the space and an electrical source, you can try a fan. Just make sure your coop is kept as clean as possible, to keep dust to a minimum.

Be sure to provide your birds with shade. If there aren't trees near your run, rig up a tarp or other covering above the ground.

Just like you, chickens are thirstier than usual during the summer. It's extremely important for your birds to have plenty of water. Beware of the things that can grow in water dispensers, and make sure you clean them out thoroughly at least a couple of times a week.

Try freezing small plastic bottles filled with water and putting them in your birds' cages. I've seen chickens drape their bodies over icy bottles in county fair poultry barns.

For a special treat, I like to give my birds a piece of cold watermelon or cantaloupe.

The First Eggs Are Here . . . I Think?

As the days get longer, you'll see more eggs appearing in your coop. Chickens need 14 to 16 hours of sunlight per day to lay eggs on a regular basis.

If you got your chicks in the late spring, your young pullets (female chickens under a year old) should have just laid their first eggs. But to the first-time chicken owner, it can be somewhat dismaying to see how small that first egg is. Fear not! The first eggs laid by pullets often are smaller than they will be later on. Early eggs can also have softer shells. I've found many eggs that were actually pliable when I picked them up. As young pullets continue to grow, so will the size of their eggs. Usually eggs will reach full size by the hens' second laying season.

I make a point of visiting my chicken coop a couple times every day during the summer to collect eggs. The less time eggs spend in the nesting box, the less chance they have of getting dirty.

You may find that every chicken wants to lay eggs in the same nesting box. Even so, you need to offer one nesting box for every three to four chickens so the hens will be encouraged to lay there instead of, say, outside in the mud or rain. Hens like their nesting boxes to be dark and private so that they feel safe while laying eggs.

Eggs covered in small amounts of dirt and debris can be cleaned off with some fine sandpaper or emery cloth. Wash the eggs in water that is almost but not quite too hot to put your hands in. Use unscented soap. Let the eggs dry completely before packing them into an egg carton.

Brooding Season

And then, sometimes your chickens stop laying eggs altogether. This time of year, brooding is the likely culprit.

Brooding happens when a hormone causes female chickens of egg-laying age to stop laying and instead sit on whatever eggs are already in the nest. This behavior is great if you have some fertile eggs that you want to hatch. After all, there is no better incubator than a real live chicken.

However, if you have a flock of backyard birds and have no intention of hatching eggs, you'll have to take action. Many broody hens stop eating or drinking and can get overheated inside the coop on especially hot days. Not to mention that while they're sitting, you're not getting any fresh eggs!

The best thing to do is to remove your hen from the nest as soon as you notice brooding. Put her in a new space, like a dog crate or separate coop. She will fuss at first, but the new surroundings should interrupt the hormonal cycle. Expect to have her back with the flock anywhere from a few days to a couple of weeks.

PRACTICE YOUR POACHING WITH A BREAKFAST SALAD

Zachary Eve is staring into a pot of slowly swirling, simmering water. At FARMbloomington, he's the guy in the kitchen in charge of poaching eggs.

He's already added a couple of tablespoons of white vinegar to the pot and a pinch of salt. He cracks an egg and gently drops it into the liquid, where it's picked up by the current. "You'll notice as soon as you throw it in there, the whites wrap around the yolk and form a nice little ball," he says. The key to success, he adds, is to add enough vinegar to the pot.

These poached eggs will be served to brunch customers in a couple days. Zach is doing the prep work now to streamline service on Saturday and Sunday. "If we're busy, probably about 12 dozen eggs, and then we burn them up all weekend," he says. Yes, you can poach eggs a couple days ahead. Zach says to store them in water in the fridge and then revive them with warm water right before serving.

He tosses the eggshells into the kitchen's compost bucket.

Gardener's Breakfast

DANIEL ORR

This recipe is a nod to my Grandma Kolb's favorite breakfast during garden season.

I like using arugula, romaine, and Napa cabbage leaves, but you can use whatever greens you have on hand. The dressing is as simple as can be—olive oil, sea salt, freshly ground pepper, and a dash of fresh lemon juice.

Ingredients:

- 4 poached eggs
- 2–4 lettuce leaves (arugula or spinach)
- 2–4 romaine leaves
- 2–4 Napa cabbage leaves
- several basil leaves

- ½ cup ricotta cheese
- 1 large tomato, cored and sliced
- 1 tablespoon olive oil
- ½ teaspoon garlic salt
- freshly ground black pepper, to taste
- lemon juice, to taste

Directions:

Lay the lettuce, romaine, and Napa cabbage leaves on the plate and top with ricotta, tomato, and poached eggs. Drizzle olive oil over everything and season with garlic salt and pepper.

OMELET 101 WITH CHEF DIDI EMMONS

Didi Emmons fell in love with cooking when she was 12 years old after making applesauce in a home economics class. "Soon after, I mastered the omelet and made my parents breakfast in bed more Sundays than they really expected or wanted."

Emmons lays out her method for preparing a basic omelet:

Start with a well-seasoned pan. Nonstick would be fine, but even better would be to have a special pan that you never wash and only use for making omelets. (Season the pan with a generous pinch of sea salt. Add 1 inch of vegetable oil. Let it sit for 12 hours at room temperature. Then, warm the pan over moderately low heat so the oil begins to smoke. Wipe the oil out of the pan and it's ready to use.)

Get your pan nice and hot.

Add butter and heat it so you hear the fat sizzling. You need to hear a *major* sizzle when you add the eggs.

After the eggs hit, stir quickly for 30 seconds, then turn the heat off and let it set. Incorporate whatever add-ins you like. Fold it in half. Enjoy!

French Sailor Omelet with Salmon and Brie

DANIEL ORR

When you think of an American omelet, it's cooked all the way through and even browned a little bit—in other words, overcooked!

In a French-style omelet, the eggs are a little bit runny. To get them that way, keep the eggs moving in the pan, almost as if you were cooking custard. You want your eggs to come up to temperature as a whole. You'll end up with a much smoother consistency, not scrambled eggs with stuff in them.

Ingredients:

- 4 eggs (equaling 8 ounces)
- smoked salmon
- scallions
- brie
- whipped cream cheese

Directions:

Beat the eggs before dumping them into an omelet skillet.

Over a medium flame, constantly keep the eggs moving. Break up any large chunks of eggs. Scrape the bottom of the pan often, as that is where the eggs cook the fastest. Eggs should stay somewhat runny. Be careful not to overcook!

Add salmon, scallions, brie, and whipped cream cheese. Finish it in a broiler or oven for a fluffier, lighter omelet.

SOUTHERN INDIANA'S LOST CRAFT—OAK-ROD BASKETS

Jon Kay came into the Earth Eats studios carrying a basket. "This is a basket that my great-great grandmother used to both feed the chickens and gather eggs in," he says.

It's an oak-rod basket. His great-great grandmother lived in Heltonville, Indiana. You can imagine her resting the basket in the crook of her arm as she did chores around the farm.

This family heirloom was the inspiration for Kay's latest research project, looking into the history and eventual disappearance of oak-rod basket making in southern Indiana.

"This was the type of craft where someone would farm during the day and in the evening make four or five baskets," he says. "Lots of times making baskets all winter long with the hope of being able to sell a barnful of baskets come spring or come fall."

He traced the practice back to three men—and this was a craft practiced almost exclusively by men. Henry Hovis brought the tradition to Brown County in 1848. George Bohall taught his five sons how to make baskets. That family was so famous, oak-rod baskets were often called Bohall baskets. A bit later, Reub Morgan and his family got into basketry.

Kay combed through historic photographs and discovered that these baskets were part of everyday life. "They would have carried these baskets full of food to important family gatherings when they went."

That was in the 1920s and 1930s. Demand went up when tourists started visiting Brown County and wanting these baskets as souvenirs. But after World War II, traditional baskets lost favor to more decorative versions imported from Kentucky and Tennessee. And it made more sense for locals to use plastic buckets rather than oak-rod baskets for farm work. The grandsons of Hovis and Bohall made baskets through the 1980s, but that was the generation that didn't pass the skill onto their kids. It's hard to pinpoint exactly when the craft stopped. Kay says it just faded away.

Record of the Past

There isn't a handbook or how-to guide for making oak-rod baskets. For his research, Kay had been planning to measure every last inch of his great-great grandmother's basket to learn as much as he could about the makers' process. But then he started asking around.

"I actually went to talk to Clyde Morgan, Reub Morgan's son, who made one basket when he was a kid. He's probably the last of the makers, you might say, even though he says he's not a basket maker," he says.

Kay asked to see the place where Reub Morgan did his work at the turn of the century. "We went to the barn. On the wall, on the door jamb, on the posts of the walls of his barn, he has all the materials written out—what lengths, how many rods, what length of rod they needed to be, what pattern you start with for each one of his baskets. The recipes, you might say, right there on the wall of the barn," he says.

Jackpot. He snapped pictures so he could analyze Morgan's process and write up his recipes. The current owners say Kay got there just in time. They had been thinking about putting a fresh coat of paint on that wall.

Jon Kay, director of Traditional Arts Indiana, with his great-great-grandmother's oak rod basket

Fruity Summer Meringue

DANIEL ORR

Grab your mixing bowl and hand beater (or whisk, if you want some exercise) and let's talk meringues.

To start, be sure your egg whites are completely fat free. If your whites aren't forming foam as you whisk them, stray yolk might be the culprit.

Then, let your egg whites and the bowl reach room temperature. (You want cold cream and a cold bowl for making whipped cream, but just the opposite for making a meringue!) It will take several minutes of whisking to fully dissolve the sugar into the egg whites. You'll know it's ready to go when you lift the mixers and a stiff peak forms.

As for the fruit, I used what was in season at the time—strawberries and raspberries. Perhaps you have some melons or apples instead. Those would be just as delicious!

Ingredients:

- 8 strawberries
- 1 ½ apricots
- several raspberries
- 1 cup egg whites, lightly beaten
- 1 ½ cups granulated sugar
- ½ teaspoon Chinese 5-spice powder (a combination of cinnamon, cloves, fennel, star anise, and peppercorns)
- 4 sprigs mint
- 4 tablespoons bitter orange coulis

Directions:

Wash the fruit in tepid water to remove any sand that covered it. Place on towels and allow to dry at room temperature.

Preheat broiler to high with rack near the top.

In a room-temperature mixing bowl, whisk egg whites. (Egg whites should also be room temperature.) Add sugar and continue whisking. Your meringue is ready when the sugar has completely combined and the mixture comes to a sturdy peak—approximately 5 minutes.

Treat oven-safe gratin dishes with nonstick spray. Add fruit and spoon meringue on top.

Place the gratin dish on the lower level of the broiler. Cook until the meringue caramelizes and turns brown. This will happen quickly—3–4 minutes.

Garnish with bitter orange coulis and fresh mint, and serve with candied orange slices.

Malt Vinegar Pickled Eggs

BOB ADKINS

Ingredients:

- 30 eggs
- 1 large Spanish onion, sliced
- 2 jalapeños, sliced
- ¼ cup fennel seeds
- ¼ cup kosher salt
- 40 whole black peppercorns
- 1 tablespoon dried oregano
- 3 sprigs fresh rosemary
- 6 sprigs fresh thyme
- 2 tablespoons crushed red chili flakes
- 4 bay leaves
- 4 cloves garlic
- 8 cups malt vinegar

Directions:

To cook the eggs, cover them with 2–3 inches of water and bring to a boil on high heat. Remove from heat, let stand 10–15 minutes, then shock them with cold water.

While the eggs are simmering, combine the brine ingredients in a large pot and bring to a boil. Turn down the heat and simmer for a few more minutes.

While the brine is simmering, remove the shells from the eggs. Then, slice an X pattern in each egg, down to the yolk, to allow the brine to seep in. Combine eggs and brine. First combine the two in a boilproof bowl (like stainless steel) and then transfer to jars for storing in the fridge once the liquid has cooled. The eggs should soak for a minimum of two days, but a week or more is best. The eggs will get better and better the longer they soak in the brine.

Homemade Root Beer Syrup

John Allen Flynn's table at the Bloomington Community Farmers' Market is divided in two parts. "Basically this side of the table is foraging, and this is gardening." The result is a really diverse offering—blackberries, broccoli, zucchini, peppers, walnuts, and sassafras bark. "I have numerous sassafras trees on my property, and I just sell it to people and some people will try to make root beer out of it."

Jackie Howard came across Flynn's table one Saturday morning. She shops at the farmers' market all the time for local fruit to incorporate into her soda recipes. She's a co-owner of Bea's Soda Bar. Sassafras bark is usually hard to find, she says, so she knew she found something special with Flynn. She immediately started playing with root beer recipes to see what could work for her food truck.

"You could take it and ferment it, similar to actually making beer," she says. "What we do is make a syrup and combine that with club soda." That way, it's easier to transport because they don't have to bottle or keg it. They can also use the syrup in other preparations. (Root beer shot in your coffee, why not!)

Ingredients:

- 9 ½ cups water
- 1 bundle sassafras bark
- 2 ½ tablespoons wintergreen
- 5 teaspoons burdock root
- 5 teaspoons sarsaparilla root
- 5 teaspoons cherry bark
- 1 star anise
- 1 cinnamon stick
- 1 cup brown sugar
- ½ cup turbinado sugar
- ½ cup cane sugar
- 3 tablespoons molasses
- 1 tablespoon freshly-ground coffee
- 2 vanilla beans
- splash of lemon juice

Directions:

Combine all the ingredients in a large pot. Bring mixture to a boil, then reduce heat. Let it steep on low heat for about an hour, or until it has reduced by ⅓.

Serve over ice. Use a 4-to-1 ratio of club soda to root beer syrup. Fold the syrup into the club soda with a spoon or straw, using an up-and-down motion. (This way you won't lose the fizziness of the soda.)

Peach Mojitos

HEATHER TALLMAN

Ingredients:

- 3 cups ripe peaches, peeled and coarsely chopped
- 1 teaspoon lime zest
- 1 cup fresh lime juice (about 4 limes)
- ¾ cup agave syrup
- ½ cup packed mint leaves
- 2 cups white rum
- 4 cups club soda, chilled

Directions:

Place the peaches in a blender and puree until smooth. You can pass the puree through a sieve to strain out the solids, but I don't always do that. I like to be reminded that I'm eating a pureed fresh fruit.

Combine zest, lime juice, sugar, and mint in a tall pitcher. Use a wooden spoon to crush the mixture. Add peach puree and rum to the pitcher, stirring until well combined.

Stir in the club soda. Best served over crushed ice with a mint sprig.

Silky Strawberry Smoothie

DANIEL ORR

This smoothie includes tofu, but you'd never know it. This protein source is important to avoid the sugar rush that comes from eating fruit by itself.

This recipe takes only a few minutes to make—the hardest part of it is cleaning the blender.

Ingredients:

- ½ cup strawberries
- 2 ounces silken tofu
- 1 cup orange juice
- 1 scoop ice

Directions:

Combine ingredients in blender. Blend until smooth and silky.

Pour into chilled glass. Serve with a straw and garnish with a strawberry and a slice of orange.

Tea Powered by the Sun

You don't have to heat up the kitchen to enjoy a freshly brewed cup of tea. We're using the power of the summer sun for this recipe.

I grabbed a bunch of fresh herbs from the garden, whatever suited my fancy.

Ingredients:

- pineapple sage
- lemongrass
- lemon basil and white basil
- fennel
- chamomile, both the flowers and greens

Directions:

Fill a jar to the brim with water. Add several lemon wedges and fresh herbs, and let the tea steep in the sun for a couple hours. Cool it off in the fridge for another couple hours. If you can't wait, you can pour it over some ice cubes.

For sweet tea drinkers, add some simple syrup, agave nectar, or honey. Enjoy!

Watermelon Puree

When fruit is perfectly ripened and freshly harvested, you don't need to do a lot with it to make it delicious. I'm taking a beautiful watermelon and pureeing it into a juice. The only other addition is a few mint leaves.

If you want to jazz up this recipe, serve the juice in salt-rimmed glasses—just like a margarita. You can freeze the leftover puree into watermelon ice cubes.

Ingredients:

- 1 cup watermelon
- 2–3 tablespoons water
- several mint leaves

Directions:

Peel the watermelon and discard the rind. Cut the watermelon in half. You'll notice that the seeds grow in a circle. Remove the seeds with a knife.

Place the watermelon flesh in a blender. Add water and blend until pureed.

Slice the mint leaves into thin ribbons and place them at the bottom of frozen glasses. Pour watermelon juice over top.

Elderberry Syrup

DIANA BAUMAN

It's the season of elderberries. Clusters of berries grow heavily on bushes that can reach up to 10 feet tall. Many people grow these bushes at home, while others forage for the berries in the wild.

If you do try your hand at foraging, make sure you harvest ripened berries. Bring a plant identification book with you to make sure you know what you're picking.

These berries are not as sweet as raspberries or blueberries. They share a mild sort of sweetness similar to that of wild mulberries or marionberries.

Elderberries can be used in many ways—baked in pies, crumbles, and tarts, or frozen and mixed in sorbets, ice cream, and slushies. Homesteaders like to process elderberries into jams and sweet syrups.

The use that I have found most intriguing is as a cold and flu remedy. What I especially love about this treatment is that the syrup is as sweet as candy and something children will actually enjoy taking.

Ingredients:

- 1 cup fresh, ripened elderberries
- 2 cups water
- ½–1 cup raw honey

Directions:

Remove stems from the berries. In a saucepan, add 1 cup berries to 2 cups water. Bring to a boil, reduce the heat, and simmer for 30 minutes.

Once the berries have simmered for ½ hour, mash them with a potato masher.

Strain through a jelly bag or cheesecloth to separate the juice from the skins and seeds.

Add ½ cup elderberry juice to 1 cup raw honey. Stir well and store in a mason jar in the refrigerator. This should keep for 2–3 months.

Blackberries Get the Cordial Treatment

DANIEL ORR

When my brother came up from Texas recently, we revisited our childhoods by doing a little blackberry picking. Several years ago, they cleared out the greenery at our favorite foraging spot, and now it's filled with blackberry plants. We cleaned up!

These tiny berries are too tart for your cereal or yogurt, but they will be perfect in a fruity liqueur called a cordial.

Choose your most beautiful decanter for this recipe and display it in your kitchen or dining room while it steeps.

Ingredients:

- 2 cups blackberries
- 1 cup simple syrup
- 3 cups vodka (or any clear liquor)
- ½ cup Chambord

Directions:

Wash the blackberries, then combine all ingredients in a decanter.

Muddle blackberries in the decanter to jump-start the maceration process.

Let the cordial sit for at least a month. It will turn a dark purple.

❧U-Pick, U-Cook Berries Adventure

SARAH OSTASZEWSKI

Nothing says summer like picking berries. I visited farms throughout northwest Indiana and Michigan, picking (and tasting) the freshest berries I could find.

STRAWBERRIES

My maiden voyage to a U-pick farm was Johnson's Farm Produce in Hobart, Indiana, to pick strawberries.

I learned quickly that this would be back-breaking work! Since the bushes grow low to the ground, we had to stoop down and sift between leafy foliage for ripe fruit. Much of the ripest fruit droops on the vines, making contact with the soil and then quickly developing mold. And thanks to a wet spring, much of the field was mushy or underwater, so we had to wade through puddles.

I learned to look at all angles of the fruit to make sure the strawberry wasn't hiding any moldy spots. While I'm all for eating blemished fruit, I am more careful when U-picking to avoid moldy fruit becoming part of my taste testing out in the field.

When you do find a ripe strawberry, use proper picking technique so as to not harm the bush or fruit. Place your index and middle fingers around the strawberry stem. Place your thumb on the strawberry and tug gently. If the fruit is ripe it should pull away easily; underripe fruit would require a bit more tugging.

My family ate nearly the entire two buckets of strawberries before the day was done. I reserved two cups of the leftovers to make this Strawberry Chia Jam.

First, I macerated the fruit in its own juices, placing it in a pot over medium heat. Next, I added one tablespoon of honey to the strawberries and stirred. When it developed a jam-like consistency, I poured the contents into a jar with about ¼ cup chia seeds. I stirred the mixture and then let it sit. After the jam cooled a bit, I placed it in the fridge to enjoy for the next day's breakfast.

RASPBERRIES

Up next were raspberries at the U-pick farm The Extraordinary Berry in Benton Harbor, Michigan. We went with red raspberries in mind but we discovered gold raspberries in the process.

Raspberry bushes grow about waist high, but much of the fruit is lower, hiding underneath dense leaves.

After collecting three baskets of red raspberries, we moved to the gold. These are more difficult to spot on the bushes, and they taste less acidic than their red counterparts.

BLUEBERRIES

Save the best for last, they say.

Jones Berry Farm in Bridgman, Michigan, consists of 10,000 acres and 20,000 berry trees, all neatly pruned and in great condition. Although many of the smaller trees produce berries, U-pickers may only harvest from larger trees that have been growing and producing for four to six years.

My back liked blueberry U-picking the best.

The trees are taller, so we didn't need to hunch over the plants. We also noticed that the fruits grow in small clusters. One swipe through the leaves will give you six or more berries.

The blueberries, sweet and juicy as they were, went into my mouth almost as often as they went into my basket. Occasionally one blueberry would taste tart. As with raspberries, the fruit on any one plant doesn't ripen all at once. Multiple harvests are necessary to find the ripest fruit.

I collected five pounds of blueberries, and I'm already dreaming about a cobbler for later.

Pick Your Own Berries, Make Your Own Cobbler

HEATHER TALLMAN

My younger son joined me at the grocery store last week. He stopped me in my tracks by asking why I was buying berries at the store when it was berry season and we could pick our own. Sometimes his insights shock me—he made a good point!

That day I hopped online and found out that 25 minutes from my house there was a berry farm that was open for business. I planned our little road trip south for the next day.

We could have picked all day. We employed the "eat one, save one" method. After two hours of picking, we came home with three gallons of fresh handpicked berries. Our family outing was not only economical but also memorable. I heard them whispering just last night about those ripe, juicy berries. We plan on heading back down there this weekend to see if the blackberries or red currants are ready.

The best part was coming home and making this tasty cobbler. I must admit it didn't last long.

Ingredients:

- 2 ½ cups fresh blackberries and raspberries (I used half and half)
- 1 cup sugar
- 1 cup all-purpose flour
- 2 teaspoons baking powder
- ½ teaspoon salt
- 1 cup milk
- ½ cup butter, melted
- 2 tablespoons turbinado sugar (optional)

Directions:

Preheat oven to 375°F.

In medium bowl, stir together berries and sugar. Let stand about 20 minutes so the mixture macerates a little.

In large bowl, stir together flour, baking powder, salt, and milk. Stir in melted butter until blended.

Spread batter in a lightly buttered 8-inch square pan. Spoon berry mixture on top of the batter. I like to add a sprinkle of turbinado sugar to the top of my cobbler before I bake it.

Bake 45 to 55 minutes or until dough rises through the berries and is golden. Serve warm with whipped cream or ice cream.

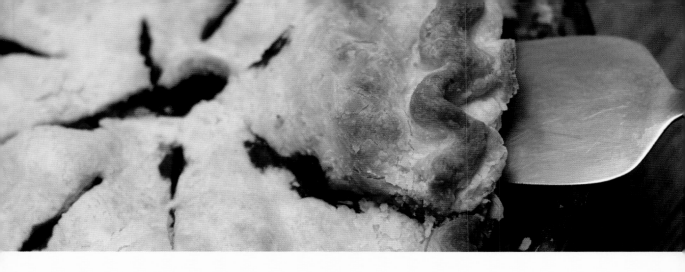

Classic Blueberry Pie

STEPHANIE WEAVER

Blueberry pie is one of my favorite summer treats and the first thing I make when blueberries come into season. My mom was a wonderful pie baker, and I've always loved pie more than cake. It showcases the luscious beauty of summer fruit.

When I lived in Chicago, my friend Douglas used to organize blueberry-picking parties every summer. We'd drive over to Michigan and spend the afternoon picking, then come home and make pies and ice cream. While I can't pick blueberries here in Southern California, I do love to buy a batch when they're in season and make at least one pie.

Ingredients:

- 24 ounces blueberries
- ¼ cup honey or agave syrup
- ½ fresh lemon, juiced
- 1 teaspoon cinnamon
- ¼ cup tapioca flour or pearls
- 2 piecrusts, with crust tops

Directions:

Wash the blueberries and drain well. If you are using tapioca pearls, put in the blender and blend until they are as fine as you can get them. Mix the tapioca and the cinnamon. Juice the lemon and add to the dry mixture, stirring until well mixed. Add the honey and stir. Put the blueberries in a large bowl and pour this mixture over them. Let sit for 15 minutes.

Preheat the oven to 375°F. Pour the berries into the piecrust(s). Put the crust top on. Crimp the edges together using a fork or your fingers. Trim off the excess. Cut a few slits in the top to allow steam to escape. Bake for 35 minutes. Check after 35 minutes. If it's light golden brown and you're starting to see the filling bubble up, pull it out. Place on a wire rack to cool completely. The filling will firm up the longer it sits and will get very firm on day three—if the pie lasts that long!

Blueberry Sweets vegan

HELEN COBB

My hometown is Alma, Georgia. It had one red light, hundreds of dirt roads, and millions of blueberries. As a child, my lips and cheeks were perpetually purple from eating blueberries.

Now I live in Atlanta, but my family still keeps me supplied. Most berries go into the freezer to be used in smoothies for breakfast, but I decided to use some of the blueberries to make one of my absolute favorite childhood desserts—blueberry cobbler.

Fruit cobblers are a quintessential Southern dessert, and every southerner knows we bake two versions. These recipes came from my mother, who learned them from my grandmother.

Blueberry Cobbler Cake

Ingredients:

- 4 tablespoons margarine
- 3 cups fresh blueberries
- 1 cup flour
- 1 ¼ teaspoons baking powder
- ⅓ teaspoon salt
- ⅔ cup soy milk
- ¾ cup agave nectar
- 1 teaspoon vanilla
- 1 tablespoon turbinado sugar

Directions:

Preheat oven to 350°F. Melt the margarine and pour into a 2-quart baking dish. Add the blueberries to dish.

In a separate bowl, blend the flour, baking powder, and salt. Then add the milk, agave, and vanilla to form a batter. Pour over berries.

Bake for 30 minutes. Sprinkle with sugar during the last ten minutes of baking.

Note: I replace the sugar in my baked goods with agave nectar. However, you can use sugar; simply increase your liquid by one half, and your sweetener by one third.

Blueberry Sorbet vegan

Ingredients:

- 4 cups blueberries
- 1 banana
- 3 tablespoons agave nectar
- ½ cup coconut milk
- 1 teaspoon vanilla

Directions:

Process all ingredients in the food processor until smooth. Occasionally scrape the sides of the bowl with a spatula.

Pour in a shallow pan and freeze. Just before serving, process again until very smooth, about 5 minutes.

Blueberry Cobbler 'N' Dumplings

Ingredients:

- 4 cups blueberries
- ¼ cup water
- 3 tablespoons agave nectar
- thin flour dumplings (recipe follows)
- a top pie crust (recipe follows)
- a little soymilk and lemon (to glaze)
- 2 tablespoons turbinado sugar

Directions:

Bring the blueberries, agave, and water to a low simmer until a good amount of liquid has cooked out of the berries. Drop in the dumplings, making sure they're submerged in the juice, and simmer on low for twenty minutes. Pour the berries and dumplings into a baking dish of your choice. For a soupier dumpling cobbler, choose a deep dish. If you prefer more crust with your cobbler, choose a larger, shallower dish.

Roll out the pie crust on a floured surface, and use a pastry cutter to cut into ribbons, or top the dish with one solid sheet (if using one solid sheet, be sure to cut slits with a fork). For a traditional dumpling dessert, the crust does not hang over the edges of the dish as in a pie, but instead rests on the fruit mixture, barely touching the edges of the dish. Use a pastry brush to glaze the crust with a little milk and lemon. Sprinkle with turbinado sugar.

Bake in a 350°F oven for 45 minutes (if your crust starts to brown too soon, cover the edges with foil, but the timing should work perfectly).

Thin Flour Dumplings

Ingredients:

- 1 cup flour
- ½ teaspoon salt
- 6 tablespoons ice water

Directions:

Blend flour and salt. Add ice water and mix with a fork until dough forms. Roll out on a floured surface as thin as you can. Cut into 1×2 inch squares.

Pie Crust

Ingredients:

- 1 cup flour
- ½ tsp salt
- 2 tablespoons shortening
- 6 tablespoons cold margarine
- 6–7 tablespoons ice water

Directions:

Blend four and salt. Use fingers to quickly blend shortening and cold margarine into flour, until the margarine and shortening form tiny balls in the flour. Add ice water slowly, until dough forms. Dust with flour, wrap in plastic wrap, and refrigerate for 30 minutes or until ready to use.

Summer Berry Grunt

DANIEL ORR

Ingredients:

- 1 cup sugar
- ¼ teaspoon plus a pinch ground cinnamon
- ¾ cup all-purpose flour
- ¾ teaspoon baking powder
- ⅓ cup whole milk, at room temperature
- 2 tablespoons unsalted butter, melted
- 2 tablespoons minced fresh ginger
- 3 pints fresh berries (blueberries, blackberries, or raspberries)
- 2 tablespoons fresh lemon juice
- 2 tablespoons lemon zest
- 1 tablespoon fresh lemon thyme leaves
- salt and pepper as needed
- vanilla ice cream, sour cream, or top cream (the heavy cream that forms on top of fresh milk) for drizzling

Directions:

Make cinnamon sugar. Stir together 2 tablespoons sugar, ¼ teaspoon cinnamon, and a pinch of salt and pepper in a small bowl; set aside.

Make dumplings using a standard drop biscuit dough. Whisk together flour, 2 tablespoons sugar, the baking powder, a pinch of salt, and the ginger in a medium bowl. Stir together milk and butter in a small bowl. Stir milk-butter mixture into the flour mixture. Set batter aside.

For the berry mixture and finishing, place ¾ cup sugar, fresh ginger, lemon juice, zest, lemon thyme, and a small pinch of salt and pepper in the skillet with 2 tablespoons water and bring to a boil.

Add berries and stir to combine.

Bring to a boil and top with 8 equal portions of drop biscuit dough and sprinkle with cinnamon sugar mix.

Cover the pan tightly and simmer over medium heat until dumplings are cooked through and juices have thickened into a rich sauce, 20–30 minutes. Be careful not to burn the bottom. Reduce heat during cooking if needed.

Serve warm with cream of choice; garnish with lemon thyme sprigs.

Gojju:
Blackberries in Sweet and Sour Gravy vegan

RAMA COUSIK

Gojju is a favorite South Indian dish. It usually features okra or potatoes, white or yellow pumpkin, or eggplant.

This summer, I spotted a blackberry bush full of fruit at the far end of our backyard. The berries had a slightly tart and sour taste—perfect for Gojju!

Ingredients:

- 2 cups blackberries
- 1 teaspoon fenugreek seeds
- 1 tablespoon coriander seeds
- 1–4 red chilies
- 1 cup garbanzo bean flour
- 1 teaspoon turmeric
- 1 tablespoon tamarind paste (can substitute lemon juice or vinegar)
- 1 ½ teaspoons salt
- 2 tablespoons brown sugar

Directions:

Wash blackberries and cover with water. Add turmeric and ½ teaspoon salt. Cook on medium heat for 5–6 minutes. Be careful not to overcook.

Roast fenugreek seeds, coriander seeds, and red chilies on medium heat for a few minutes, until the fenugreek is slightly brown. Remove from heat and combine with garbanzo flour. In a food processor, grind to a fine powder. Add this to the berries and mix well, taking care to break any lumps.

Add 3 cups water, tamarind paste, remainder of the salt, and brown sugar. Stir well. Cook for another 5 minutes. (Add 1 more cup of water if you want more sauce.)

114

earth eats

Spicy Peanut Sauce with Vietnamese Summer Salad Rolls

vegan

NATALIE RAE GOOD

I am in love with the summer. My diet during these hot days relies heavily on fresh vegetables and fruits—raw rules! These Vietnamese summer rolls are fabulously versatile and can be altered to include any fresh veggie of your choice. They are a favorite of mine for a light dinner after a long hot day. Serve alongside a spicy homemade peanut sauce.

   If you have never worked with rice paper wrappers, they can be a bit difficult, so be patient. The package comes with tons of wrappers, so don't worry if you tear a few and have to toss the ripped skins aside. The wrappers start off brittle and become pliable when you soak them in hot water.

Spicy Peanut Sauce

Ingredients:

- 1 cup peanut butter
- ⅓ cup water
- 1 teaspoon sugar
- 2 limes, juiced
- 2 tablespoons soy sauce
- 1 teaspoon apple cider vinegar
- 1 teaspoon hot sesame oil
- 1 tablespoon hot chili garlic sauce or Sriracha
- 1 clove garlic, crushed and mashed

Directions:

Combine all ingredients in a bowl and stir. Add more lime, hot sauce, or vinegar to taste.

Vietnamese Summer Salad Rolls

Ingredients:

- 1 package medium-sized rice paper wrappers
- 1 package rice noodles
- 1 head lettuce, shredded
- 4 carrots, shredded or sliced into thin strips
- 1 cucumber, sliced into thin strips
- 1 avocado, sliced
- 1 ripe mango, sliced into thin strips
- 1 bunch mint or cilantro

Directions:

Place the package of rice noodles in a large bowl and cover with hot water. Cover with a lid or baking pan and let sit undisturbed for 7–10 minutes, or until the noodles separate and become pliable. Drain the noodles and set aside. Prepare each of your vegetables and set up an area to work. Fill a pie pan or similarly sized dish with hot water and soak a wrapper until pliable. Place on a very clean dishtowel and pat dry. Arrange noodles, vegetables, and herbs in a small mound and wrap carefully like a burrito. Try to make the rolls as tight as possible.

Sweet and Sour Pumpkin Sauce

RAMA COUSIK

The yellow pumpkin is used in home kitchens in traditional Indian cuisine during festivals. My mom cooked it with either pigeon peas or split mung beans. I remember her telling me that the yellow pumpkin had a cooling effect on the body.

This summer, several pumpkin plants started to grow from seeds I had disposed of in our compost pit. There are about 8 to 10 pumpkins in our garden now, slowly turning golden yellow—they will be ready to harvest within the week!

Ingredients:

- 2 cups pumpkin, cubed
- ¼ teaspoon mustard seeds
- 1 cup water
- 1 teaspoon olive oil
- 1 teaspoon salt
- 2 tablespoons brown sugar (or to taste)
- 2 teaspoons tamarind paste (can substitute lemon juice or vinegar)
- ½ teaspoon chili powder
- 1–3 springs cilantro, chopped

Directions:

Cook pumpkin until it's well done. Puree and set aside. Heat oil in a pan and add mustard seeds. After they pop, add pumpkin puree and the rest of the ingredients (except cilantro) and cook for 5 minutes. Garnish with cilantro.

Green Goddess Dressing for Iceberg Salad

DANIEL ORR

Ingredients:

- 3–4 salted anchovies
- 3 scallions—thinly sliced
- 2 tablespoons tarragon
- 2 tablespoons minced chives
- ¼ cup minced parsley
- 2 cups mayonnaise
- ¼ cup sour cream
- 4 tablespoons tarragon vinegar (or your favorite)
- Tabasco (to taste)
- water as needed to thin
- 1 head iceberg lettuce
- 1 cup assorted edible flowers (see page 20)

Directions:

Combine all ingredients except lettuce and flowers in food processor. Blend until smooth and season to taste. Cut the iceberg into 4 wedges and remove the stem core. Place each wedge on a plate and dress with Green Goddess dressing. Just before serving, sprinkle with flowers.

Simple Syrups Meet Your Herb Garden

When you think of herbs, you probably think of savory dishes, but they're also great seasonings for simple syrups. We're going to make two different sweet toppings that you can use for breakfast or throughout the whole day.

Both of these sauces start with simple syrup made with 1 cup of sugar and 1 cup of water. Bring this to a boil on the stove and allow the sugar to dissolve. Then you're ready to infuse the syrup with herbs and other flavors.

Mint and Orange Syrup over Raspberries

Ingredients:

- simple syrup (see above)
- 1 small bunch peppermint
- zest of one orange
- juice of ½ orange
- pinch of salt

Directions:

Turn down heat on the simple syrup once sugar has dissolved. Add peppermint, zest, orange juice, and salt. Let simmer for 10–15 minutes.

Remove big pieces of peppermint and drizzle over raspberries. Garnish with a mint sprig.

Thyme and Lime Syrup over Melon

Ingredients:

- simple syrup (see above)
- ½ bunch thyme (still on twigs)
- zest of 1 lime
- juice of ½ lime
- pinch of salt

Directions:

Turn down heat on the simple syrup once sugar has dissolved. Add thyme, zest, lime juice, and salt. Let simmer for 10–15 minutes.

Remove big pieces of thyme and drizzle over melon. Garnish with a thyme sprig and gooseberries.

Harrison Lake Garden Burger

I threw these together with my brother Dave on the Fourth of July, 2002, at our family home in Indiana. You can add all types of stuff to these, from corn kernels to sautéed zucchini or eggplant. Garden burgers are a great way to use up those lonely veggies in the crisper.

    I like to offer my guests the choice of chipotle ketchup or beet vinaigrette.

Ingredients:

- 2 cans white beans, drained and rinsed
- 3 egg whites
- ¼ cup olive oil
- 2 boxes falafel mix
- 1 ½ cups water
- 1 jalapeño, diced fine
- 1 cup cooked wheat berries
- 1 cup cooked green lentils
- 1 cup cooked portobello mushrooms (diced in ¼-inch cubes and roasted or sautéed)
- 1 cup toasted sunflower seeds
- 5 scallions, chopped fine
- 2 tomatoes, diced fine
- ½ cup chopped herbs (e.g., basil, coriander, parsley, and oregano)
- salt and pepper to taste

Directions:

Place the beans, egg whites, and olive oil in the bowl of a food processor and blend until smooth. Add the falafel mix and water and pulse until mixture is bound.

    Place the jalapeño, grains, mushrooms, scallions, tomatoes, and herbs in a large bowl and fold in the bean mixture. Add water or some whole wheat flour to bind or moisten as needed. Taste and adjust seasoning as needed. Form into patties and chill until ready to grill.

    Spray with olive oil nonstick spray and grill, sauté, or broil until cooked through (about 5 minutes a side depending on heat and thickness).

    Serve open-faced on grilled garlic toast with cucumber and yogurt sauce, chickpea salad, red onion slices, and sliced tomatoes.

Chipotle Ketchup

Ingredients:

- 1 ½ teaspoon cumin seeds
- ¾ cup ketchup
- 2 teaspoons chopped chipotle peppers in adobo sauce (or to taste)
- 1 tablespoon adobo sauce from chipotle can
- 2 tablespoons of molasses or sorghum
- 2 tablespoons balsamic vinegar
- 1 tablespoon garlic powder
- 2 tablespoons fresh lime juice
- 2 tablespoons tequila
- salt and pepper to taste

Directions:

Toast the cumin seeds in a small heavy-bottomed saucepan over medium heat until they smoke lightly and are fragrant. Transfer to plate and cool. Grind seeds in spice grinder or with mortar and pestle. Set aside.

Combine remaining ingredients in the same saucepan and add the cumin back to it.

Simmer over medium-low heat until ketchup thickens slightly, stirring occasionally, about 5 minutes.

Beet and Honey Vinaigrette with Orange

Ingredients:

- 1 inch peeled and roughly chopped ginger
- 3 strips orange peel
- juice of 1 orange
- 2 medium roasted beets, peeled and roughly chopped
- ¼ cup white balsamic vinegar
- 2–3 cups salad oil
- salt and pepper
- ¼ cup honey
- ¼ cup water
- 2 cloves garlic

Directions:

Combine all ingredients in a blender and puree until very smooth. Taste and adjust seasoning as needed.

Asian-Inspired Mint Pesto

DANIEL ORR

The word "pesto" comes from a mortar and *pestle,* as you grind up your ingredients into a paste, but life is much easier these days with food processors.

People think of pesto as being basil, pine nuts, parmesan cheese, olive oil, and garlic. But there's no reason you can't use other herbs in your pestos.

A jalapeño pepper in the pesto? If you're not fond of too much heat in your food, cut out the white membrane and the seeds before adding it to your food processor. That's where the dynamite is!

This easy and tasty recipe can be used on top of vegetables, smothered on a filet of fish, or added to some stewed zucchinis and tomatoes.

Ingredients:

- 5–6 cloves of garlic
- 1 teaspoon lemon zest
- 1 tablespoon ginger
- ½ jalapeño pepper
- 3–4 cups of mint (no stems)
- 1 ½–2 cups of extra virgin olive oil
- pinch of salt

Directions:

Grind all the ingredients in a food processor.

If you are planning to eat the pesto immediately, add cheese and nuts as you like.

If you are freezing the pesto, do not add cheese and nuts until just before serving.

Herb Oil Becomes Pumpkin Seed Pesto

This recipe begins with something I like to have on hand in the restaurant—different sauces with which to paint my plates. For a green hue, I like to bring out the squirt bottle of herb oil. This is a basic recipe using basil, parsley, and baby arugula.

To start, blanch the greens quickly in boiling salted water, then shock them in an ice bath. Don't worry about squeezing all the water out of the greens before putting them in the blender. A little extra liquid is a good thing.

A suggestion about the oil: I use 1 cup salad oil and ½ cup olive oil. The salad oil is a more neutral flavor, which is important for a recipe like this that is packed with tasty ingredients. Save your fancy olive oil for recipes where its flavor can truly shine.

Ingredients:

- 2 bunches of basil, baby spinach, or arugula
- ½ bunch parsley
- 1 small clove of garlic, minced
- 1 teaspoon cracked black pepper
- 1 cup salad oil
- ½ cup olive oil
- salt and pepper to taste
- For pesto: 1 cup pumpkin seeds

Directions:

Blanch the basil (or greens) and parsley in heavily salted, boiling water until just tender. Shock to room temperature.

Place greens in blender with remaining ingredients and puree until very smooth and green. Adjust seasoning, chill quickly, and top with a little extra olive oil to keep from discoloring. Add pumpkin seeds to blender if you want pesto. Stir well before serving.

Store in refrigerator. Bring to room temperature before serving. You can freeze the leftovers.

Black Walnut Vinaigrette

DANIEL ORR

Ingredients:

- 1 cup salad oil
- ¼ cup black walnuts, finely ground
- ½ cup red wine vinegar, highest quality
- ¼ cup fresh lemon juice
- 4 tablespoons scallions, chopped
- ½ teaspoon fresh garlic, minced
- 1 teaspoon Dijon mustard
- 3 tablespoons honey
- 1 teaspoon salt
- 1 teaspoon black pepper, freshly ground
- 1 cup olive oil
- 4 teaspoons fresh thyme, minced

Directions:

Heat salad oil and black walnuts in a saucepan until they are lightly browned and oil is infused with the walnut flavor. Remove nuts and set aside.

Cool the black walnut oil to room temperature.

Whisk vinegar, lemon juice, scallion, garlic, mustard, honey, salt and pepper, and olive oil together.

Slowly add the black walnut oil. Stir in nuts and thyme.

Make 2–3 hours before using for flavors to marry and bloom. Then adjust seasoning if necessary.

Curry Vinaigrette for a Kohlrabi Papaya Salad

I can understand the hesitation with kohlrabi. It's a weird-looking veggie! You can treat it like broccoli or cauliflower, which makes it much less intimidating.

We are only using the bulb for this dish, but reserve the leaves and cook them like kale or collard greens.

Before you get cracking on this recipe, take care to remove the skin on the kohlrabi bulb. With a sharp knife, grab hold of the skin at the base and pull up. It will remove the tough exterior along with any celerylike strands.

Ingredients:

- ¼ cup shallots, chopped
- ½ tablespoon garlic, finely chopped
- 2 tablespoons curry powder
- ½ tablespoon turmeric
- ¼ cup cider vinegar
- 1 tablespoon honey
- 1 cup vegetable oil
- ½ tablespoon salt
- 1 teaspoon pepper
- juice of 2 lemons
- zest of ½ lemon
- 3 medium kohlrabi, cut into bâtonnet (1 ½ inches long and ¼-inch thick)
- ½ cup minced red onion
- ½ papaya, diced into ¼-inch cubes
- ¼ cup chopped cilantro
- whole lime, juiced

Directions:

Heat vegetable oil in a heavy-bottomed saucepan and add the shallots and garlic. Cook slowly until transparent but uncolored. Add curry powder and turmeric and continue to cook to bring the flavors together.

Deglaze with cider vinegar. Add honey, salt and pepper, and juice and zest from lemons.

Transfer dressing to blender and puree until smooth. Thin as needed with hot water. Season to taste.

Then for the salad, combine kohlrabi, red onion, papaya, and cilantro and mix with hands.

Add lime juice and ¼ cup curry vinaigrette. Mix with hands and serve.

Chili Herb Lime Vinaigrette with Barley Salad

Ingredients:

- 10 asparagus spears
- 1 yellow squash
- ¾ cup barley
- 2 tablespoons olive oil
- 1 tablespoon cider vinegar
- ½ teaspoon chili powder
- juice of 1 lime
- 1 teaspoon lime zest brunoise
- juice of ½ lemon
- salt
- freshly ground pepper
- ¼ cup diced sweet red pepper
- ¼ cup diced yellow pepper

Directions:

To make the vinaigrette, whisk together the oil, 1 tablespoon water, the vinegar, chili powder, lime juice and zest, lemon juice, and salt and pepper to taste.

Blanch the asparagus spears in boiling water for 5–7 minutes; drain and chill. Cut off and reserve 3-inch tips and cut the stems into thin rounds.

Cut the yellow squash into small sticks, blanch briefly, drain, and chill.

Rinse the barley thoroughly under cold running water and drain. In a medium-sized saucepan cover the barley with 3 ½ cups cold water. Bring to a boil, then reduce the heat to a simmer and cook for 35–45 minutes until the barley is tender and no longer raw, but is chewy to the bite. Rinse the barley under cold water and drain.

In a large bowl combine the chilled barley, asparagus rounds, squash, red and yellow peppers, and the vinaigrette; toss well and adjust the seasoning as necessary. Top with the asparagus tips. The salad will keep, tightly covered, in the refrigerator for 2–3 days.

Hoosier Sugar Cream Pie

HEATHER TALLMAN

There are many things Indiana is known for: basketball, corn, pork tenderloin sandwiches, and the Indianapolis 500. We need to add the Hoosier Sugar Cream Pie to that list. Go to any potluck or church pitch-in, and you are bound to see this pie on the dessert table.

Some say that to have a true sugar cream pie you have to make your own crust using lard. I'm not ashamed to admit that I use a frozen piecrust. It's up to you!

Ingredients:

- 2 cups white sugar
- ¾ cup all-purpose white flour
- 1 ½ cups heavy whipping cream
- 1 cup milk
- 1 teaspoon pure vanilla extract
- 3 tablespoons unsalted butter
- whole nutmeg (or powdered)
- 1 egg, beaten
- 1 piecrust

Directions:

Preheat oven to 450°F. Add all ingredients, except for nutmeg, butter, and egg, in a mixing bowl and combine using a whisk. Pour into piecrust.

Drop small pieces of butter on top of the batter and then grate fresh nutmeg evenly over the top of the pie. (I prefer to grate fresh whole nutmeg but use what you have.) With a pastry brush, brush the crimped edge of the crust with the beaten egg.

Bake for 10 minutes. Reduce the heat to 350°F and bake for 30 minutes. Refrigerate and serve chilled.

Caribbean Coleslaw

DANIEL ORR

Ingredients:

- ¼ cup honey
- ½ cup cider vinegar
- 1 lemon, juiced
- 1 tablespoon cumin seeds, toasted in a dry sauté pan until lightly smoked
- 1 tablespoon curry
- ½ cup olive oil
- ½ jalapeño, minced
- ½ head red cabbage, cut in thin ribbons
- ½ head savoy cabbage, cut in thin ribbons
- 2 large carrots, cut julienne (in thin strips)
- 1 red onion, minced
- 1 bunch cilantro, very roughly chopped, including stems
- salt and cracked black pepper to taste

Directions:

Whisk first seven ingredients together. Toss with cabbage, carrot, and onion, and marinate for at least 2 hours. Just before serving, add cilantro and season to taste.

Raw Walnut Tacos

BOB ADKINS

Ingredients:

- 4 ounces walnut halves
- 1 teaspoon garlic powder
- 2 tablespoons fresh chili powder
- 2 teaspoons freshly ground cumin
- 2 tablespoons olive oil
- pinch salt and pepper
- 8 Napa cabbage leaves
- fresh pico de gallo
- fresh cilantro
- tofu sour cream (optional)

Directions:

Add walnuts, seasonings, and olive oil in a food processor. Pulse the contents until it becomes crumbly, just like taco meat.

Scoop walnut mixture into Napa cabbage leaves.

Add a spoonful of pico de gallo, tofu sour cream, and a fresh sprig of cilantro to each taco boat.

Pralines

DANIEL ORR

Ingredients:

- 1 cup chopped pecans
- ½ cup pecan halves
- 1 ½ cups sugar
- 1 ½ cups packed light brown sugar
- ⅛ teaspoon salt
- 3 tablespoons dark corn syrup
- 1 cup evaporated milk
- 2 tablespoons butter
- 1 teaspoon pure vanilla extract
- 1 teaspoon Chinese 5-spice powder (a combination of cinnamon, cloves, star anise, fennel, and peppercorns)

Directions:

Preheat oven to 400°F. Place chopped and halved pecans on a cookie sheet and toast in oven until lightly browned and smelling toasty. Remove from oven and set aside.

Butter the sides of a heavy 2-quart saucepan. Put the sugars, salt, corn syrup, milk, and butter in saucepan. Over medium heat, stir mixture constantly with a wooden spoon until sugars have dissolved and mixture comes to a boil. Continue to cook until the mixture becomes a soft ball (approximately 236°F on a candy thermometer). Note: If you do a cold water test, drizzle a drop of candy into a glass of cold water. The ball of candy will flatten between your fingers when you take it out of the water. Stir in the vanilla, spices, and toasted nuts and beat with a spoon by hand for approximately two minutes or until candy is slightly thick and begins to lose its gloss. Quickly drop heaping tablespoons onto waxed paper. If the candy becomes stiff, return pan to the stove and carefully reheat. You may also add a few drops of hot water. Store in an airtight container for up to a week.

No-Dairy-Necessary Corn Chowder

HEATHER TALLMAN

Corn is a little bit like zucchini. If you grow it, there will be a time every year when you have it coming out your ears. I know that a few times over the summer we bring in a huge haul of ears to shuck. We eat some of it right away and freeze the rest for later.

One of our family favorites has always been corn chowder. Last summer, I decided to make my usual recipe, except this time I left out the milk and cream, most of the flour, and almost all of the butter. The result was still rich and delicious. The base of this soup has an intense corn flavor that I got from using what most would throw out: the boiling water and the cobs.

Ingredients:

- kernels from 8 large ears of corn, cooked
- boiling water from corn (keep hot)
- 1 cob (after kernels have been cut off)
- 4 cloves of garlic, minced
- 1 medium sweet onion
- drizzle of olive oil for pot
- 1 cup chicken stock
- 2 tablespoons butter
- 2 tablespoons flour
- 1 bunch chives, chopped
- salt and pepper to taste
- optional garnish: cheese, sour cream, hot sauce, fresh veggies, blue cheese, lobster, crab, or other meats

Directions:

Cook the ears of corn in boiling water. Once tender, remove the kernels. Reserve the boiling water and one of the cobs.

In a heavy soup pot add the olive oil, onions, garlic, and a pinch of salt. Sauté until translucent. Add the butter and flour to form a light roux. When incorporated but not yet brown, add the stock. Stir until it is a nice base.

Add all but a handful of the corn kernels to the pot. (I reserve some to throw in at the end for texture.) Add the cob to the pot as well. (It will help make the soup creamier.)

Add two ladles of boiling water from the corn pot. Let this simmer on a low setting for a while.

Remove the cob. Puree the soup in a food processor. Add the extra kernels and any amount of boiling liquid you feel you need to get the desired consistency. Just before serving, add the chopped chives and any other garnishes you like.

fall

🌱 Reclaiming the Old Ways: Fermentation

Sandor Katz eats savory vegetable sourdough pancakes almost every day, and he regularly makes sauerkraut, yogurt, and kefir. He says eating and preparing fermented foods has become a staple of his life. "At certain times my kitchen looks like a mad scientist zone."

His book *The Art of Fermentation* is a massive tome that could seem overwhelming to a novice, but he stresses that the basic process of fermentation is really very simple.

"My mission in fermentation revival is to empower people with tools to reclaim these ancient processes that our ancestors have been doing forever," he says.

IT ALL STARTED WITH A GARDEN

"When I moved from New York to Tennessee I got involved in keeping a garden. Suddenly all of the cabbage was ready at once and that was a little bit of a surprise to me. So I decided to figure out how to make sauerkraut.

"There are always seasonal overabundances of certain things, and then there are always seasons where there's very little food available. So fermentation developed as a survival strategy, depending on what was abundant."

ADVICE FOR FIRST TIMERS

"The realm of fermentation that I think makes the most sense for people wanting to explore this for the first time in their kitchens is fermenting vegetables. It's incredibly simple:

1. All you do is take some vegetables, chop them up, shred them.

2. Salt them lightly to taste.

3. Spend a few minutes in a big bowl with your hands just squeezing them, bruising the vegetables until they get really wet.

4. Once the vegetables are nice and wet, stuff them into a jar. Press really hard so they're submerged under their own juices.

5. Allow them to ferment for a few days or a few weeks."

NEW FLAVORS: ACARAJÉ

"One of my new favorites that I learned about in the course of working on *The Art of Fermentation* is called *acarajé*. It's an Afro-Brazilian ferment of black-eyed peas:

1. Soak black-eyed peas.

2. Try to remove the hulls of the peas as much as possible. I do that manually by rubbing them with my hands and fingers after they've soaked.

3. Blend black-eyed peas into a batter. I let that batter ferment for a couple of days.

4. Then I use a whisk and I beat it. Just like other kinds of proteinaceous things— whether we're talking about cream or egg whites—the beating stiffens it.

5. This stiffened black-eyed-pea fermented dough is typically deep fried in Brazil. I pan fry it and make little pancake fritters out of them.

"This really illustrates how most ferments are actually extremely simple. The act of adding water is what initiates the fermentation because microorganisms are present, but they are latent as long as it's dry. All life requires water. As soon as you add water, it initiates this microbial process that transforms the food."

FROM GOURMET TO EVERYDAY

"If you walk into a gourmet food store and look around and think about the nature of the foods that you see there, almost all of the foods we elevate to that gourmet status are products of fermentation.

"If you ask people what they had for breakfast, I would bet 75 percent of them had something that's fermented—if they had bread, cheese, coffee, they started their day with some product of fermentation."

FEAR NOT, FERMENTATION ROOKIE

"There's a lot of fear of microorganisms that many people in our culture share. They wonder, 'How do I know I'm going to get the right bacteria growing? How do I know I'm not going to make my family sick?' I like to remind people that these are ancient rituals that our ancestors have been doing forever without insights into microbiology, without microscopes, without thermometers, and really we don't need a lot of training or expertise or special equipment.

"With a little bit of information and tools that are already in our kitchens, we can do a lot of this ourselves."

Pickled Peppers

DANIEL ORR

You can stick these pickled peppers in a pot of rice to give it a nice perfume without too much heat. You can also use them throughout the winter to make ceviche and marinades. I like to throw some into barbecue or pasta sauce.

Ingredients:

- habaneros, banana peppers, Tabasco peppers (leave whole)
- 2 cups white vinegar
- 2 teaspoons salt
- ¼ cup sugar
- 1 cinnamon stick (2 ½ inches in length, broken in half)
- 2 slices of ginger
- 3 star anise

Directions:

Stuff whole peppers into a sterilized mason jar. Do not pierce the peppers or they will become super, super hot!

Prepare the brine by combining vinegar with the remaining ingredients in a pot on the stove. Bring to a boil, and stir so the sugar dissolves.

While brine is hot, pour into jar with the peppers. Screw lid on jar, and shake to disperse the spices.

Process jar in a hot water bath or store in the refrigerator until ready to use.

Quick Pickled Green Beans

Ingredients:

- green beans, blanched
- 2 cups white vinegar
- 2 teaspoons salt
- ¼ cup sugar
- ¼–½ teaspoon red pepper flakes
- 1 cinnamon stick (2 ½ inches long, cut in half)
- 1–2 star anise
- 1 teaspoon mustard seed
- 1 teaspoon coriander seed
- 5–6 whole cloves
- 4–5 cloves of garlic, sliced

Directions:

Blanch the green beans. Stuff beans into a mason jar.

For the brine, combine vinegar with the remaining ingredients in a pot on the stove. Bring it to a boil, and stir so the sugar dissolves. While brine is still hot, pour into jar with green beans. Screw lid on jar, and shake to disperse the spices.

Process jar in a hot water bath or store in the refrigerator until ready to use.

Pickled Brussels Sprouts

Of all the different types of pickles, from cucumbers to watermelon rinds, Chef Sasha Divine's favorite is pickled brussels sprouts. "You wouldn't think it, but they are phenomenal," he says. "The earthiness of the brussels sprouts really comes through." At No Coast Reserve, they don't blanch the sprouts before putting them up to pickle. They simply pour the brine on top and slide them into the fridge.

Is this proof that you can pickle just about anything? Yes . . . almost.

"If you try pickling a soft-boiled egg, it tastes like mayonnaise. It doesn't work out," says Divine.

Ingredients:

- 2 pounds brussels sprouts
- 6 cloves of garlic, sliced thin
- 3 whole dry cayenne chilis
- 5 cups cold water
- 5 cups white vinegar
- 7 tablespoons kosher salt

Directions:

Pour vinegar and cold water into separate pots. Add garlic, cayenne, and salt to the vinegar. Simmer until the salt is dissolved. Pour the vinegar mixture into the cold water to cool the brine.

Remove the core from each of the brussels sprouts with a paring knife. Place the sprouts in a 6-quart container and pour the vinegar mix over the top.

Cover the sprouts with a gallon plastic bag ⅓ filled with water to submerge the veggies. Put a lid on the container.

Label and date the pickles. Let them sit for at least three weeks refrigerated.

Taqueria-Style Pickles with Carrot, Onion, and Jalapeño

No matter how you take your tacos, a little topper of these taqueria pickles would enhance them.

These are a home-style refrigerator pickle with big chunks of rustic-cut veggies. Devastatingly hot? Not even close. These will taste light and mildly spicy and be very refreshing.

Chef Seth Elgar explains that they don't pressure can any of their pickles at No Coast Reserve and they often don't even cook the veggies ahead of time. "We're pouring brine over raw or blanched vegetables." This way, the vegetables maintain their integrity and last a lot longer on the shelf.

earth eats

Ingredients:

- 1 pound of carrots, peeled
- 2 onions (white or yellow), peeled
- 5 serrano chilies, sliced in half with stems and seeds removed
- 7 cloves of garlic, sliced thin
- 2 teaspoons dry oregano
- 4 bay leaves
- 1 tablespoon peppercorns
- 2 teaspoons kosher salt
- 3 cups white vinegar
- 4 ½ cups cold water

Directions:

Bring vinegar, bay leaves, peppercorns, and salt to a boil. Kill the burner, then let sit for one hour to infuse. Add the thinly sliced garlic to the vinegar mix. Leave for 10 minutes to cook, then add the water.

To prepare the vegetables, cut the carrots into ¼-inch-thick coins. Cut the onions in half, remove the woody core, and then cut into 1-inch wedges. Break them into petals. Slice the deseeded serrano chili halves in half once again.

In a large mixing bowl, toss the carrots, onion, and chilies with the oregano. Then transfer the veggies to 2-quart jars.

Pour the brine over the top of the veggies, screw on the lids, and refrigerate the jars.

Let them pickle for 7 or more days before serving. Agitate the jars regularly.

DIY Sauerkraut

STEPHANIE WEAVER

Sauerkraut is a naturally fermented raw salad that's easy to make at home with very few tools. This batch is made from green cabbage, carrots, and fennel fronds for extra flavor.

Ingredients:

- 1 green cabbage
- 3–4 large carrots or the equivalent in baby carrots
- 1 large bunch of fennel fronds
- 2 teaspoons kosher or sea salt

Directions:

Wash the vegetables. Set a large bowl on the counter, with the salt next to it.

Remove any wilted outer leaves, then cut the cabbage in quarters and remove the hard core. Using a sharp knife, or a food processor fitted with a shredder disk, shred or slice the cabbage finely. Shred or grate the carrots. Remove any hard stems from the fennel, and then chop finely.

As you add the shredded vegetables to the bowl, sprinkle each layer lightly with salt. Mix everything together thoroughly. The salt draws the water out of the vegetables and creates natural brine.

Pack wilted cabbage into a suitable vessel, using a flat-bottomed cup to mash each layer flat, removing any air. Once you have all the vegetables in there, press them down with a plate or cup to release more liquid. (You should already have a fair bit of brine.)

The liquid must rise above the level of the plate or cup so the vegetables are not in contact with air. Otherwise you will get mold, not fermented veggies. This usually happens within a few hours. If it hasn't happened overnight, make 1 cup of salt water by mixing 1 teaspoon of salt with 1 cup of filtered water and pour it in.

Put a clean kitchen towel over the crock or jars. This keeps insects and dust out. Place it in a cool dark place. I check it after 3 or 4 days, and skim off any foam that has formed. I taste it after 5 days, sometimes 7 if I forget. Putting a sticky note on my kitchen calendar helps me remember when I started it.

DIY Refrigerator Pickle Relish

Warning: Once you start making your own condiments you'll never go back to store-bought.

You'll save money in the long run, and you'll keep those pesky chemicals and preservatives out of your food. Not to mention the homemade stuff just tastes better!

Ingredients:

- 12–16 ounces pickling or persian cucumbers
- 6 tablespoons kosher salt
- ½ cup apple cider vinegar
- ¼ cup agave syrup
- 1 stick cinnamon
- 1 teaspoon whole cloves

Directions:

Add the salt to the water in a large, clean jar or bowl and stir to dissolve. (Congratulations, you have now made brine!)

Peel the cucumbers, take off the ends, and slice lengthwise. Use a spoon to scoop out the seeds. Dice into small cubes. Add to the brine and stir. Let it sit overnight. (This can sit out on the counter.)

The next day, start by preparing your pickle jar. Wash both the jar and the lid inside and out. Bring water to a boil in a pot large, enough to immerse the jar and the lid. Use tongs to gently place the room temperature jar and lid into the hot water (I turn it down to just under boiling). Immerse for 10 minutes.

In another pan, mix your pickling solution: the vinegar, agave syrup, and spices. Heat just to boiling.

Put the drained cucumbers into the jar. Pour the pickling solution over them. Seal the jar. Allow to cool to room temperature, then refrigerate.

Check after one week to see if you like them. These last about six months in the fridge. Make sure to continue to submerge the pickles in liquid.

Persimmons

'Tis the season for persimmons!

There are two varieties of persimmons grown in the United States; Japanese persimmons are common in California, and the Hoosier fruit was first found in Virginia.

If you want to venture into the woods to do your own foraging, look for persimmons that are mushy, with their skins nearly falling off. Eating an underripe persimmon is not a pleasant experience.

Save yourself the trouble of picking the seeds out by hand and invest in a food mill. By passing your persimmons through a food mill, you remove all the seeds and create the puree in one motion. Then you can freeze the puree in small containers and use it over the next several months.

Before you toss the seeds and skins into the compost heap, teach your kids this old wives' tale:

Take a persimmon seed and crack it in half with your teeth. Inside, you'll see a sliver of white in the shape of a spoon, fork, or knife. The spoon will catch a lot of snow flakes, which means a snowy winter. The tines of the fork will catch some snow, but not a lot. And if it looks like a knife—which it did in this year's batch of persimmons— the snow will fall right past the blade and we will have a light winter.

You can try this trick with any of the seeds from this year's batch of persimmons. They should all look the same.

Persimmon and Raisin Bread Pudding with Ginger Orange Rum Sauce

DANIEL ORR

Ingredients:

- 4 eggs
- pinch kosher salt
- ½ cup sugar
- ½ cup sorghum
- 2 cups heavy cream
- 1 teaspoon vanilla
- 2 cups local persimmon puree
- 8 cups sourdough bread, cut into 1-inch cubes
- ½ cup golden raisins
- 2 teaspoons lemon zest
- ½ teaspoon nutmeg
- ½ teaspoon cinnamon

Ingredients for the sauce:

- ⅔ cup orange juice
- ½ cup rum
- ⅓ cup light brown sugar
- 1 tablespoon butter
- 1 tablespoon minced ginger
- 1 pinch salt
- 1 tablespoon cornstarch

Directions:

For the pudding, combine eggs, salt, sugar, and sorghum in a large mixing bowl. Stir in cream, vanilla, spices, and persimmon puree. Mix well to incorporate. Add bread, raisins, and lemon zest; toss to coat well, and let stand at room temperature 30 to 60 minutes.

Preheat oven to 400°F.

Butter a 9-by-13-inch baking pan or similar-sized pan or 8–10 individual-portion ramekins. Distribute bread pudding mixture evenly. Put pan or ramekins into a larger pan that contains enough hot water to come halfway up the sides of the bread pudding dishes.

Bake about 40 minutes or until a knife comes out clean. Ramekins will take about 25 minutes. Cool until warm to touch.

While pudding cools, combine orange juice, rum, butter, ginger, and salt in a small saucepan. Bring to a boil then reduce to a simmer.

Combine cornstarch with ½ cup water. Add to the orange-juice mixture. Stir until thickened.

Serve bread pudding warm, cut into 8 even portions. Drizzle each with about 2 tablespoons of warm sauce.

Persimmon Jam

Ingredients:

- 5 cups pureed persimmon
- 3 cups sugar
- ¼ cup fresh squeezed lemon juice (or 1 ½ lemons)
- ½ teaspoon orange zest
- pinch Chinese 5-spice powder (a combination of cinnamon, cloves, fennel, star anise, and peppercorns)
- 6 mason jars

Directions:

Run the persimmons through a food mill to remove the seeds and create the puree.

In a large saucepan over medium heat, combine persimmon puree, sugar, lemon juice, orange zest, and spice blend. Boil for 30 minutes or until slightly thickened. (Your goal is not to reduce the mixture, just to thicken it.)

Pour into sterilized jars and seal. (Leave one inch of empty space at the top of the jar to allow room for expansion.) Store in freezer. Remove one hour before use to allow the jam to thaw.

Persimmon Panna Cotta

In Italian, *panna cotta* means cooked cream, but the persimmon puree outshines the cream in this dish. This recipe is especially delicious if you're looking for something light for the end of your meal. Since it is thickened with gelatin and not eggs, it's lighter than a custard or crème brûlée.

Ingredients:

- 3 cups heavy cream
- 1 ½ cups persimmon puree
- ¾ cup sugar
- ½ teaspoon cinnamon
- ¼ teaspoon Chinese 5-spice powder (a combination of cinnamon, cloves, fennel, star anise, and peppercorns)
- pinch salt and pepper
- 1 tablespoon plus ¼ teaspoon gelatin powder
- ⅓ cup water

Directions:

Heat heavy cream, persimmon puree, sugar, cinnamon, sweet seasonings, and salt and pepper together. Bring mixture to a boil then remove from heat. Strain persimmon cream mixture through a chinois or mesh strainer.

Meanwhile, allow gelatin powder to bloom in water for approximately 5 minutes. Then warm gelatin mixture over warm water. Add to persimmon cream, whisking to make sure gelatin is completely incorporated. Portion into individual cups and place in refrigerator to set.

THE GIVING TREE

Louise Briggs has a beautiful patio behind her house. It's a tidy space except for a pair of Adirondack chairs that are stacked with 10-gallon plastic bins and their lids. She and I are sitting at a table in the early evening. Her dogs are roaming around the yard. We rotate to face the 60-foot persimmon tree in the middle of the yard that's been casting an imposing shadow over the patio. A net propped up with 6-foot poles surrounds the footprint of the tree.

Louise sounds like a proud parent when she talks about her Giving Tree. "It's silent once it hits the net. The adorable sound is it hitting leaves and it goes down," she says. "My persimmon pinball machine."

She smiles and points at fruit way at the top of the tree, like a strand of orange Christmas lights. Those will fall soon enough.

Louise and her husband Bob moved to southern Indiana in the winter of 2010. After renting for a bit, they found a house that was perfect. "And the realtor said to me, 'Oh and there's a persimmon tree in the backyard, too.' I'm from Boston. What do I know from persimmons, you know?"

They purchased the home, made the move, and got settled in. When spring rolled around, she decided to start learning about persimmons. She knew to look for tile-shaped bark. "I went from tree to tree, and I looked at the big one in the middle of the yard, and I thought surely not that one." But indeed, the tallest tree on the property had that distinctive bark pattern, just like the pictures in her book.

That fall, the persimmons came quickly. "We knew we had to net them because over the course of a few weeks, my little dog became a pudgy little dog," she says.

She spent hours every day collecting freshly fallen persimmons from the net and pulling the caps off the fruit. When she had accumulated 60–70 pounds of fruit, she would devote her weekends to processing the fruit into pulp with two motorized food mills. During that season, she produced 200 2-cup portions of persimmon pulp.

This fall, when the fruit started dropping, she was in the midst of a home improvement project. It was the week before Labor Day. "The persimmons came early and they came fast," she says. "I was behind the eight ball." What she needed was a group of persimmon lovers to adopt her tree this year. "Because I had really decided I didn't want to do it this year. I really wanted a year off."

She put a call out to the Bloomington, Indiana, community—free persimmons to anyone who wanted to do the work! A dozen people answered the call, from professional bakers to curious home cooks. Louise taught them how to pull the persimmons from the net and clean and decap the fruit. Then it was up to them to process the pulp in their kitchens. Every day for the next several weeks, someone from the community will take her persimmons away.

This is the first year she's enjoyed the simple pleasure of watching persimmons drop from the tree. In previous seasons, the only thing this tree meant to her was a lot of work. "I won't say that I haven't had moments," she says, when she thinks about her life without the Giving Tree. "But no, I would miss it. I would really miss it."

And then swish-swish-swish goes another persimmon pinball plummeting from the tree down to the net.

Stuffed Acorn Squash with Quinoa and Persimmons

STEPHANIE WEAVER

Ingredients:

- 1 acorn squash
- ½ cup red quinoa
- 2 small persimmons (about ¾ cup chopped)
- ½ cup Swiss chard
- ¼ cup pine nuts

- 1 cup water or vegetable broth
- ½ cup dairy-free cheese or parmesan
- 3 fresh sage leaves (or ½ teaspoon dried sage)
- ½ teaspoon sea salt
- ¼ teaspoon chipotle chili powder
- ¼ teaspoon cumin
- ¼ teaspoon white pepper

Directions:

Preheat the oven to 350°F.

Wash the squash and slice off each end. Cut in half. (It's a little easier to cut them in half lengthwise, but the finished dish looks more like an acorn if you cut it crosswise.) Scoop out the seeds. Put the seeds in a small bowl of water.

Place the squash cut side down in an oiled baking pan. Bake 30–40 minutes until soft. Leave the oven on.

While it is baking, remove all the stringy bits of the squash from the seeds and rinse them clean. Place in a small saucepan with a cup of filtered water and 2–3 teaspoons of sea salt. Bring to a boil, then simmer for 10 minutes. Drain.

Rinse and drain the quinoa. Then add 1 cup water or vegetable broth. Bring to a boil, then turn down and simmer for 15 minutes on low. Turn off and let sit, then fluff with a fork.

Chop the chard and place in a large bowl. Core the persimmons and chop into about ½-inch dice. (Be careful to remove any seeds!) Add to the bowl. Mince the sage leaves. Add the pine nuts, cooked quinoa, cheese, and spices. Stir to mix.

When the squash is cooked, put the baking pan on your work counter (on a towel or hot pad) and flip the squash right side up. Using a fork to hold it steady, scoop out the cooked squash with a spoon, adding it to your filling bowl. Be careful not to poke through the skin. Leave about ½ inch of flesh inside.

Mix the squash evenly into the filling. Taste and adjust seasoning if needed. Pack it into a rounded 1 cup measure and invert it into the squash halves. Put the squash seeds in one corner of the pan, adding a small amount of olive oil and some smoked paprika. Stir to coat the seeds.

Bake for 15–20 minutes until the filling is hot and the cheese is melted. Top with the toasted seeds and a drizzle of garlic olive oil.

Cranberry Jalapeño Persimmon Chutney

Ingredients:

- 12 ounces cranberries
- 1 Asian pear
- 2–3 persimmons (or one large apple)
- 2 jalapeños
- ½ red onion
- 1 orange
- ½ cup agave syrup (or maple syrup or honey)
- ¼ teaspoon black pepper
- ¼ teaspoon cumin
- ¼ teaspoon cardamom seeds or ground cardamom

Directions:

Wash the cranberries, fruit, and peppers.

Finely chop the onion and put in a medium-sized saucepan. Add the cranberries. Core the fruit and chop. You can leave it in larger pieces for a chunkier sauce, or chop it finely if you want a smoother sauce.

Remove the core and seeds from the jalapeños and mince finely. Grind the cardamom seeds in a nut grinder or mortar and pestle.

Zest the orange into the pot, then cut in half and juice it. Add all the remaining ingredients.

Bring to a boil, then simmer for 30 minutes.

Fall Favorites: Paw Paws

PAW PAWS ARE STILL MORE AT HOME IN THE WOODS THAN ON FARMS

A paw paw is green on the outside and custard yellow on the inside. Everyone seems to describe its taste the same way—like a cross between a mango and a banana. We Hoosiers often refer to it as the Indiana Banana.

Author Andrew Moore says it tastes tropical, and that's saying something for a food native to Midwest America. "It's related to these other tropical fruits, like guanábana, cherimoya, soursop, sweetsop, fruits that have this wonderful custardlike texture," he says. "You can't grow any other fruits like this in the temperate north and get this kind of culinary experience. There's nothing else you can grow like it."

Moore is the author of *Paw Paw: In Search of America's Forgotten Fruit*. The paw paw is a soft fruit with a short shelf life, so that could be why the best place to find it is in the woods and not in the grocery store. But there are other fragile fruits that Americans have found a way to produce and sell on a large scale. Think raspberries and figs, says Moore.

"You have to pick them when they're ripe and you either have to get them to customers' hands or you have to process them rather quickly. So, it's not that it can't be done." It's just that growers are still working on it.

Thanks to evidence from fossilized fruits, we know paw paws have been growing wild from New Jersey to Mississippi for 56 million years. Growers started talking about domesticating paw paws after the Civil War. In 1888, the American Horticulture Society, headquartered in Greencastle, Indiana, called the paw paw the most promising native fruit for commercial development.

It's fitting, then, that a Hoosier stepped up first.

In 1905, James A. Little wrote a 22-page treatise on paw paws, a blueprint for growing the fruit's popularity. "He wanted folks to set paw paws out in orchards, grow from seed, observe the fruit, and find the better ones." He predicted that would be done, because at that time many of the wild paw paw patches were being converted to agricultural land.

Little had good reason to be optimistic. Around 1916 paw paws and blueberries occupied the same place in America's food culture, wild foods that scientists wanted to grow commercially. Take one stroll through a grocery store fruit section and you'll see how that worked out—blueberry cultivation took off and paw paws were left behind.

Fast forward to the next paw paw champion—"Johnny Paw Paw Seed" Neal Peterson. He has been working with paw paws since 1975, tracking down lost cultivars, conducting breeding experiments, and planting an orchard, just like Little had hoped. Peterson has produced several varieties of paw paws, all named after rivers—Susquehanna, Potomac, Wabash, and Shenandoah.

The process of cultivation is still very closely tied to original varieties. "These paw paws are sometimes two steps removed from the wild," says Moore. "They're just really good paw paws that the fruit explorers took

IN SEARCH OF WILD PAW PAWS

If you want to search for your own paw paw patch, look up. Paw paw leaves droop off the branches. They're long, large, and shaped sort of like a football.

The fruit grows in clumps and might be hard to spot against the green leaves.

You can bring a knife and spoon with you and enjoy some paw paws in the raw. That's what I imagine Bobbi Boos of Sundry Farm does while she's foraging.

"A part of it is that it's so fun to just take a walk in the woods for a change instead of in the field," she says.

Boos has been collecting paw paws for more than 10 years. She sells them at the Bloomington Community Farmers' Market alongside the vegetables she grows on her farm. But the season is brief—only about three weeks in the fall.

To ensure that she's gathering only the ripest paw paws, she shakes the tree in order to jar the ready-to-eat fruit off the branches. "And the animals love them," she adds, so you'll need to be quick. "If they fall, they're somebody else's dinner."

the time to know and propagate, and since then the paw paw community has recognized as really good paw paws."

But in the beginning of Peterson's work, it was a lot of sitting around and waiting. He started his orchard in 1990. It takes eight years for paw paw trees to bear fruit. He then selected the best trees to graft onto stumps and grow again. "Then he had to wait another six years to evaluate the fruit again," says Moore. "In terms of commercial cultivation, all of this takes time."

While commercial success for paw paws still seems a long way away, Moore says there's excitement around the fruit these days. He hints that James A. Little's prediction could come true.

"There are paw paw orchards everywhere from Indiana to Maryland. You're seeing people set them out by the dozens, hundreds, and in a few cases there are even orchards of a thousand paw paw trees, so it is happening," he says. "Whether the fruit will transition into an agriculture product is to be seen."

No matter what happens, we'll still be able to enjoy a good old-fashioned walk in the wild paw paw patch.

PAW PAW RECIPES

Paw Paw and Apple Salad

DANIEL ORR

Ingredients:

- paw paws
- apple slices
- lime juice

Directions:

Pull out the seeds and then mash the paw paw meat. Add a splash of lime juice to bring out a unique flavor in the paw paws. Toss the apples in the paw paw mash, coating the apples thoroughly.

Garnish with a sprig of Thai basil. Serve with sorbet or ice cream for a tasty dessert, or serve as is to start the morning.

Paw Paw Cookies

I remember my grandma and grandpa singing "Way Down Yonder in The Paw Paw Patch" when I was a kid growing up in southern Indiana. Back in that time, they didn't have all the candies we have now, and they lived out in the country. So when the paw paws ripened up, they would eat these until they got sick!

I grew up foraging for these fall treats. I don't have as much time now, so thanks to the local forager who provided us with the paw paws for these recipes.

When you slice the paw paw open, you'll see several large black seeds. I use a food mill to remove the seeds and pulverize the fruit into a puree, but you can do this by hand if you'd rather.

Ingredients:

- ½ cup raisins
- ½ cup dried dates
- 1 cup water
- ½ cup butter
- 1 cup oatmeal
- ¾ teaspoon baking powder
- ½ teaspoon baking soda
- 1 cup flour
- 2 eggs
- ¾ cup paw paw puree
- ½ cup toasted walnuts
- ¼ teaspoon salt
- ¼ teaspoon Chinese 5-spice powder (a combination of cinnamon, cloves, fennel, star anise, and peppercorns)

Directions:

Combine raisins, dates, and water. Boil for 3 minutes to soften the dried fruit. Add softened butter. Mix together oatmeal, eggs, flour, baking soda, baking powder, and walnuts. Add paw paw puree and the fruit and butter mixture. Blend all ingredients and refrigerate overnight.

Bake dollops of cookie dough on a cookie sheet in a 350°F oven for 10 minutes.

GARY PAUL NABHAN'S FAVORITE APPLES

Gary Paul Nabhan is the author of a number of books, including *Where Our Food Comes From*, and he's also been called the Father of the Local Food Movement. "We ought to promote the notion of good keepers as something that we want in our community again whether they're people or apples," he says.

At one time, Americans had access to 16,000 different varieties of apples: sour ones and sweet ones, red ones and yellow ones, tear-shaped ones and lumpy ones. Ones that were good for making cider, others for pies, others for fritters, others for pancakes and sauces. Now, Nabhan says, 90 percent of the apples eaten in North America are from just 12 varieties. "And most kids can only name two or three different apples if that, so a Red Delicious becomes all that a child thinks an apple can be."

But there are still unique varieties of apples being grown in orchards all over the country. Nabhan describes some of his favorites.

For fresh eating: "I love something called the 'Kandil Sinap,' which is a crisp, pale-fleshed apple that's sort of teardrop shaped. It's from Crimea and Russia and Turkey originally but has been grown in the United States for over a century. It's just unlike any apple I've ever seen. It looks like this translucent globe of light hanging from a tree, it's like candles were put in a tree. It has a pale yellow skin. And it just has a crispness and freshness and a kind of vanilla and cinnamon aftertaste that are just stunning."

For baking pies: "It depends where you make the pie. In the south, people tend to like tart apples for pies, and in the north they like sweets. So it's from what kind of pie tradition that you've emerged. If you like tart apples, some in the range of Granny Smith—I'm not promoting Granny Smiths alone—but that kind of tartness or bite to them is nice. But there are apples like Magnum Bonum and Gloria Mundi that are old apple varieties that make terrific pies. I like a lot of the Winter Pearmains for pies, good keeping apples that then you can use a month or two after they've been picked and still have great apple pies."

DANIEL ORR'S TOP PICKS

I like to use these varieties for my baking projects.

Braeburn

These apples have been imported from New Zealand, but Americans can get them closer to home now, from Washington state. They are great baking apples because they maintain their shape well. Think Granny Smith.

Empire

If a McIntosh and a Red Delicious had an apple baby, this would be the result. The Empire is much better as a baking apple than either of those. This sweet-tart apple's skin turns pink when cooked.

Honeycrisp

Sweet but mellow is the way to describe the flavor of this crisp, red-yellow apple. It is a descendent of the Macoun, Golden Delicious, and Haralson varieties.

Jonathan

These are not the best for baking because they don't hold their shape quite as well as some other varieties, but the sweet-tart flavor might be enticing enough to cook them anyway.

Rome

These apples are large, which is always a plus when baking. The skin can split and become rough after cooking, but if you're looking for a tart taste, try experimenting with this variety.

153

fall

Old-Fashioned Baked Apples

DANIEL ORR

These apples perfume the kitchen as they bake. The juices result in a sweetly spiced sauce. Add a scoop of ice cream for dessert or have them plain for breakfast. Even better—smother them with leftover eggnog.

Ingredients:

- 6 large (7–10 ounces each) baking apples, such as Braeburn, Empire, Honeycrisp, Jonathan, or Rome
- ½ cup apple juice
- 2 teaspoons fresh lemon juice
- ½ teaspoon vanilla extract
- ¼ cup raisins
- ¼ cup old-fashioned rolled oats
- ¼ cup breadcrumbs
- 6 tablespoons packed light brown sugar
- 3 tablespoons maple syrup
- 1 ½ tablespoons unsalted butter, at room temperature
- ¼ teaspoon cinnamon

Directions:

Preheat the oven to 350°F. Adjust the oven rack to the middle position.

Using an apple corer or a small, sharp paring knife, core the apples. (The center cavity should be no more than 1 inch in diameter.) If necessary, trim a thin slice from the bottom of each apple so it stands upright.

Using a vegetable peeler or a sharp knife, peel away a 1-inch ring of skin from around the top of each apple. Using the tip of a paring knife, make four small slashes about ½-inch deep around the equator of each apple. (These steps aid the release of steam, which helps the apples remain intact rather than collapsing.)

Place the apples in a baking dish just large enough to contain them, such as a 9-by-9- or 7-by-11-inch baking dish.

In a bowl, combine the juice, lemon juice, and vanilla, and pour the mixture around the apples. In the same bowl as you used for the juice mixture, combine the raisins, oats, breadcrumbs, sugar, maple syrup, butter, and spices. Divide the mixture evenly among the apples, spooning it into the cavity.

Bake the apples, basting occasionally with the pan juices, until they are tender when pricked with the tines of a fork, 45–65 minutes, depending on the size and variety of apple. If they begin to darken, cover with foil and continue to bake until tender. Set the apples aside to cool for at least 15 minutes before serving. (May cover and refrigerate for up to several days and reheat until warm, but not hot, before serving.)

To serve, spoon the apples into individual bowls and spoon the warm juices over and around them.

Grandma's Apple Pie

Ingredients for the crust:

- 2 cups all-purpose flour, plus extra for rolling
- ½ cup finely ground blanched almonds
- ½ pound lard or butter
- 1 teaspoon salt
- 1 heaping teaspoon brown sugar
- 3 to 6 tablespoons water, very cold

Ingredients for the filling:

- ⅔ cup sugar
- 3 tablespoons all-purpose flour
- 1 teaspoon Chinese 5-spice powder (a combination of cinnamon, cloves, fennel, star anise, and peppercorns)
- 1 tablespoon ginger, freshly minced
- 3 pounds apples, sliced in ¼-inch thick wedges
- ½ cup white raisins
- ¼ cup bourbon or calvados
- 2 tablespoons lemon juice
- 1 teaspoon vanilla extract

Directions:

Cut the lard into ½ inch cubes, chilled in freezer for at least 45 minutes.

In a food processor, combine flour, almonds, salt, and brown sugar; pulse to mix. Add frozen lard and pulse 6 to 8 times, until mixture resembles coarse meal, with pea-size pieces of fat. Add water 1 tablespoon at a time, pulsing until mixture just begins to clump together. Test to see if it's ready by pinching the dough. If it holds together, it's ready. If it doesn't, add a touch more water and pulse again.

Remove dough from machine and place on a clean surface. Form dough into two round discs. Refrigerate at least 1 hour before continuing.

Remove dough from the refrigerator. Let sit at room temperature for 5–10 minutes. Sprinkle some flour on top of the discs. Roll them out with a rolling pin on a lightly floured surface to a 12-inch circle, about ⅛-inch thick. Place one on a 9-inch pie plate and return the other to the fridge until needed.

Preheat oven to 375°F. Combine all ingredients for the pie-filling mixture. Spoon in apple filling, mounding slightly in center. Roll out second disk of dough, as before. Gently turn over onto the top of the apples in the pie. Pinch top and bottom of dough rounds firmly together. Trim excess dough, leaving a ¾-inch overhang. Fold dough under and crimp to seal. Cut slits in top crust to allow steam to escape. Brush with a little water and sprinkle with some sugar. Bake pie until crust begins to turn golden, about 20 minutes, then reduce heat to 350°F. Cover edges with a little foil. Continue to bake until crust is golden in the center and juices are thickened and bubbling, about 30–45 minutes. Remove and cool on a rack for at least 1 hour.

Serve with a slice of good cheddar cheese, whipped cream, or ice cream.

Spiced Apple Cider Granita

Granita is an Italian shaved ice. I've heard the name comes from "granite," because when the stone is smashed, it shatters into shards just like this flaky dessert.

This dish is essentially a mulled apple cider in dessert form. If you find the end result is too syrupy or not icy enough, mix in a healthy dash of water and refreeze.

Ingredients:

- 3 cups apple cider
- 1 cup packed brown sugar
- ½ teaspoon Chinese 5-spice powder (a combination of cinnamon, cloves, fennel, star anise, and peppercorns)
- ½ teaspoon allspice
- ½ teaspoon cloves
- 2 cinnamon sticks
- 2 ounces spiced rum
- 1 tablespoon vanilla extract

Directions:

Combine first 6 ingredients and bring to a boil. Stir and allow the sugar to dissolve.

Pour the liquid through a strainer to remove the cloves and cinnamon sticks.

Stir in rum and vanilla.

Let the mixture freeze overnight (or for 3–4 hours minimum). During this time, periodically rake the just-formed ice crystals with a fork.

Serve ice shavings over slices of local apples and garnish with a sprig of fresh mint.

Homemade Apple Butter

I always make apple butter from the apples that fall from the trees in my mother's front yard. Those apples are often wormy and knotted and a little gnarly, but they taste awesome!

Ingredients:

- 8 cups apples (chopped)
- ½ cup brown sugar
- juice of 1 lemon
- 5 strips lemon zest
- pinch salt and pepper
- 1 tablespoon cinnamon
- 1 tablespoon ground ginger
- splash of cranberry juice

Directions:

Combine all ingredients in a pot and bring to a boil. Reduce heat and let simmer 30–45 minutes until apples are cooked down.

Once the apple mixture has cooled, puree in blender until smooth.

Store in an airtight container. As my mom always says, make sure to label and date your containers.

Get Your Home Cooking On: From Restaurant Chef to Frugal Home Cook

CLARA MOORE

In my new life—the one where I live in the woods in the Pacific Northwest, my husband is in school, and we are broke as a joke—I find myself cooking more at home than ever before. I have taken to this lifestyle quite quickly, probably on account of my background as a chef from St. Louis. In a restaurant, it's super important to maintain a financially viable and low-stress kitchen.

Here are some tricks I've picked up over the last several months of my domestication:

I buy lots of milk on sale, usually close to its expiration date, and then I turn it into kefir or yogurt. This extends the life of the milk, and you can still use it for pretty much everything you use milk for. I use it in place of any milk in scones, biscuits, and cornbread. I eat it on my morning granola, sometimes with a splash of milk to lighten the tartness. I add it to smoothies.

I buy all our beans dried. Canned beans are not only packed with salt and weird preservatives, but they usually have such a miserable texture. You don't have to soak your dry beans overnight if you don't want to. Just set them to boil and cook them until done. Better yet, get acquainted with a pressure cooker. I like to cook lots of beans at one time and then freeze what I don't use in small bags. That way I can pull out a bag of chickpeas to make hummus, or I have kidney beans on hand when I want red beans and rice.

Make granola instead of buying cereal. Holy smokes, cereal is so expensive! Granola is easy and relatively cheap to make, and much better for you than most breakfast cereals.

Don't buy things in boxes. Make your own crackers—they last for a really long time! Make your own cookies—it takes literally 15 minutes to put the dough together. Make your own granola bars. Make your own mac 'n' cheese. Make your own stock. Whatever you do, definitely don't say to yourself, "It's too expensive, time-consuming, or difficult." If it is nominally more expensive, it's healthier for you and your family. If it takes a little longer, think about how this can become family bonding time. Not to mention everything is hard the first time. The more you do it, the easier it becomes.

Make food you can enjoy all week long. On Sundays I like to make one soup and one salad. This way when someone gets peckish, there is always something to grab in the fridge. It's even hearty enough to serve as the I-don't-feel-like-cooking-tonight dinner.

Freeze. Freeze. FREEZE! The freezer is your best friend when it comes to saving time and money. Making soup, stock, bread, beans, pastries, and sauces in bulk and freezing them gives you something ready-made to heat up for a quick, cheap dinner. You can also buy big pieces of meat, fish, and chicken on sale and freeze them.

You don't need years of culinary training or tons of money to make great meals for yourself and your family. All it takes is a sense of planning and a few great recipes under your belt.

Make Your Own Crackers

Ingredients:

- 3 cups flour
- 2 tablespoons sugar
- 2 tablespoons salt
- 4 tablespoons oil
- 1 cup warm water

Directions:

Preheat oven to 450˚F.

Mix dry ingredients (flour, salt, and sugar) in a large bowl. Pour in oil and warm water. Mix with a fork until the liquid is incorporated. Use your hands to combine the dough until it has a uniform consistency. Then knead for at least 2 minutes.

Separate dough into 4 balls, and let it rest for about 10 minutes. (If it is dry, you might want to place a damp towel over it.) Cut each dough ball into 6 pieces. Roll out each piece on a lightly floured surface until paper thin.

Slide the rolled dough onto a tray and dock the dough (poke it all over) with a fork. Then, cut the dough into the size crackers you want.

Bake the cut dough in the oven for 5 minutes. Rotate the tray and cook for an additional 5 minutes. Continue cooking until the crackers are golden brown. (They may be a little soft when they come out, but they will crisp up nicely as they cool.)

Vegan Chili That Never Ever Disappoints

Ingredients:

- 1 tablespoon olive oil
- 1 medium onion (diced)
- 1 small can tomato paste
- 2 cans garbanzos (rinsed)
- 2 cans black beans (liquid used)
- 1 can whole peeled tomatoes (liquid used)
- 2 cloves garlic (minced)
- 1 tablespoon chili powder
- 1 tablespoon cumin
- ½ tablespoon salt
- 1 teaspoon black pepper

Directions:

Sweat onions with olive oil in large saucepan until tender. Add tomato paste and stir constantly. Add cans of beans (liquid and all), chopped tomatoes, plus one can of water. Stir.

Add garlic and spices. Simmer for 4 minutes.

Granola Two Ways

Honey Butter Granola

Ingredients:

- ½ cup honey
- 4 tablespoons butter
- ½ teaspoon vanilla
- pinch of salt
- 2 cups oats
- ½ cup pecans (raw and chopped)
- ¼ cup sunflower seeds (I used roasted, but you can use raw)

Directions:

Preheat oven to 250°F.

Place honey, butter, vanilla, and salt in a small pot. Heat until butter is melted and everything is combined.

Combine oats, pecans, and sunflower seeds in a separate bowl. Stir in honey-butter mixture.

Once well mixed, spread onto cookie sheets in a thin layer. Stir the granola and rotate the pan every 20 minutes for 1 hour. It will still seem soft, but once it dries, it will harden into perfectly crunchy granola.

Molasses Hazelnut Granola

Ingredients:

- ¼ cup brown sugar
- 2 tablespoons molasses
- 2 tablespoons grapeseed oil
- ½ teaspoon cinnamon
- pinch of salt
- 2 cups oats
- ½ cup hazelnuts (chopped)
- ¼ cup flaxseeds

Directions:

Preheat oven to 300°F.

Combine brown sugar, molasses, oil, cinnamon, and salt in a small pot. Heat until everything is combined.

Combine oats, hazelnuts, and flaxseeds in a separate bowl. Stir in sugar and oil mixture.

Once well mixed, spread onto cookie sheets in a thin layer. Stir the granola and rotate the pan every 20 minutes for an hour. It will still seem soft, but once it dries, it will harden into perfectly crunchy granola.

Simple Scones

The dos and don'ts of baking . . .

Everything in your kitchen runs out of life eventually. Before you get started with this recipe, make sure your baking powder and baking soda are no more than one year old. It makes a big difference, and it's not that much of an investment.

Use unsalted butter. Always. Salt is a preservative, and that means salted butter is more likely to be older. Plus, you want to be able to control the salt content in your cooking.

Don't get overwrought about "room temperature butter." Just let it sit out for 10 minutes. It just has to be slightly pliable.

Don't overwork your dough. Unless you are making bread or pasta, you don't need to knead dough. Stir it until it is wet and all the ingredients seem evenly distributed.

Last but certainly not least, don't get stressed out! Food is a reflection of your mood. If you are stressed about making something, it will most likely turn out tough or undercooked, for instance, because you nervously opened the oven too often. Relax and enjoy the feel/smell/taste of it all.

Ingredients:

- 3 cups flour
- ⅓ cup sugar
- 2 ½ teaspoons baking powder
- ½ teaspoon baking soda
- ¾ cup butter, at room temperature
- 1 cup buttermilk, milk, cream, or yogurt

Directions:

Preheat the oven to 400°F.

Mix dry ingredients in a bowl. Slice butter into small cubes and toss into the flour mix. Cut the butter into the flour mix either with a pastry cutter or by using your hands. If using your hands, squeeze the butter cubes between your thumb and forefinger and drop them back into the flour mixture. Repeat until the mixture is the size of small bits of gravel.

Add liquid and any other add-ins (e.g., nuts, dried fruit, cheese) and stir until combined.

Separate the dough into thirds, and turn each third on a floured surface until it forms a cohesive ball about 4 inches in diameter. Chill for about 30 minutes. (You can keep the dough like this in the freezer for up to 3 months. Just pull it out and let it thaw on the counter for 1–2 hours, cut into fourths, and bake as usual.)

Remove from refrigerator and cut dough into fourths. Bake on a baking sheet for 15–25 minutes, until slightly browned.

Meal Planning Is Not Lame

CLARA MOORE

Does the phrase "meal planning" makes you a little sick to your stomach, either with anxiety or with the sheer lameness of it all? Well, party people, I am here to tell you that this is simply not true. Meal planning is for you!

Instead of subsisting on PBR and frozen pizza and bumming food off of your friends who cook, it's time to do the cool thing: plan your meals and then cook them.

My life is better when I plan what we eat because:

- I can budget our tiny income.

- I can control what goes into our food, instead of opening a box of food made in a factory and hoping that the owner of the corporation that made it has my best health interests in mind.

- Making food from scratch doesn't become a burden.

- I can use ingredients over and over. For instance, I bought a lot of butternut squash on sale and roasted it all. We ate some for dinner with salt and pepper, and then I used the rest to make a big batch of soup, which we then ate all week long. Another time, I bought strawberries on sale, which I used in morning granola. Then I made strawberry cookies and turned the rest into jam. I made all those dishes in under an hour.

Before you get into the planning groove, be honest with yourself. How much time do you actually have to commit to cooking? It will take a while at first, but once you get the hang of your favorite recipes (and maybe bribe your friends into helping) the process will go so much faster.

Then, crunch your budget. How much money do you have to spend on food? Remember, this is supposed to save you money. Go to the store with a calculator and a budget in mind.

Now for meal planning! This part is the fun part:

1. Plan what you want/need to make.

2. Decide when you can make it.

3. Go shopping.

4. Cook!

My week looks a little like this: Shop on Wednesday and Sunday. Do bulk cooking on Sunday and Monday. Cook dinners as many nights as I can.

Fried Chicken (the Whole Bird)

My mom taught me how to make fried chicken. She would use a whole bird, and that meant we learned how to break down a chicken. Here are her step-by-step instructions.

1. Start by rinsing the bird well. Then be sure you have a sharp knife with at least an 8-inch blade.

2. Cut the chicken completely in half, down one side of the breastbone through one side of the backbone. Now work on each half one at a time. Lay the bird skin-side-up on the cutting board.

3. Cut off the leg section. Grab the leg with your free hand and work the blade along the crease of the leg and breast. If you follow carefully, you should be able to slide right through the joint without hitting a lot of bone.

4. Cut the leg section in half. While holding the drumstick, work the blade along the crease of the thigh and drumstick. Again, if you follow carefully you should slide right through the joint without cutting through bone.

5. Cut the wing section off. Hold the wing tip and work the tip of the blade along the shoulder joint, moving it all the way around in a circular motion.

6. Cut the breast in half. For fried chicken, I generally cut the breast in half while it's still on the bone. The whole breast is just too big to fry. This requires cutting through a lot of little bones, so brace yourself and use both hands.

After you've broken down the chicken, it's important to sanitize your workstation. That includes all knives, cutting boards (it is safest to use wood or bamboo), and surfaces the chicken touched. It all needs to be washed with soap and then sanitized with a weak bleach solution.

Ingredients:

- 1 whole chicken, broken down (instructions above)
- 6 eggs
- ½ cup buttermilk
- 3 cups flour
- 1 cup yellow mustard powder
- 2 teaspoons cayenne
- 4 tablespoons salt
- Peanut oil, for frying

Directions:

Mix eggs and buttermilk in one bowl and flour, mustard powder, cayenne, and salt in another. Set up your thick-bottomed pot for frying with about 2 inches of oil. (I use a big cast iron Dutch oven.) Turn the heat on medium.

With one hand, dip the chicken pieces in the wet ingredients. Toss the chicken in the dry bowl, and with the other hand coat the chicken with the dry ingredients. Then back in the wet and once more in the dry. This ensures a beautiful and crunchy crust. Set the breaded pieces aside while the oil warms. I like to have all the pieces breaded before I start frying.

Once the oil is hot (about 350°F or when a test piece of chicken is bubbling quickly), carefully place just enough pieces of chicken to cover the bottom. Be sure to not overcrowd the chicken. Flip the pieces as necessary and fry until golden brown. Remove and place on a plate covered in paper towels. Store them on a tray in a 200°F oven to keep warm.

Adaptability Is the Name of the Game at the Community Kitchen

It's 11:00 AM. Planning tonight's dinner at the Community Kitchen of Monroe County for 250 to 300 people starts in the pantry. Kitchen supervisor Adam Sommer alternates sipping his coffee with rifling through box after box of packaged food. There's plenty of elbow macaroni, but he cooked that earlier this week, so he's looking for something different. "We had a fantastic donation of egg noodles recently. Let's see if there are any more of those left over," he says. In his ideal world, he would have the time and resources to make egg noodles from scratch, but that's just not possible.

The Community Kitchen gets much of its food from the US Department of Agriculture commodity distribution program. They also receive on-the-edge perishable foods from grocery stores, as well as leftovers from cafeterias. Cooks at the kitchen are used to working with whatever they've got in stock.

Once he collects enough bags of eggs noodles, it's into the freezer. He pulls out some pork. In his ideal world, this *is* the pork he would use. This summer, the Community Kitchen received donations of animals shown at the county fair. The freezer is now packed with meat from three cows, three pigs, and three goats. "This is a pig that was nurtured and loved and it's going to make a beautiful dish today," he says. He sets a dozen packages of meat out to thaw. He also grabs a container of baby potatoes. Then, his favorite part of any dish—homemade chicken stock. "I like to call it liquid gold."

Sommer is formulating his recipe. "I'm kind of leaning toward doing my mom's Hungarian goulash recipe," he says.

Here's where the trick of working in a community kitchen comes in—he discovers they're out of paprika. In a back room, Sommer is standing on his toes, peering into boxes of spices stashed on the top shelf. No paprika. But he does find a bottle of harissa, which is a pepper-based spice blend. This particular bottle lists paprika pretty high on the ingredients list, so that's what he'll use. He tells a coworker to add paprika to the Community Kitchen's wish list.

Back in the kitchen, the countdown begins: three hours until dinner service. He searched for some fresh tomatoes to add to his recipe, but they didn't have any in stock. So his goulash will have to work with spaghetti sauce instead.

"It's going to have to work. That's sort of the name of the game," says Sommer.

Turkey Leftovers Get the Pot Pie Treatment

CLARA MOORE

Each year, I venture to the Pacific Northwest for Thanksgiving. Our head count for dinner this year was 17 people.

That Thursday, I woke up at 7:00 AM. I started by prepping potatoes, brussels sprouts, and two big turkeys. The turkeys were cooking beautifully when, at noon, the head count was down to ten—yikes!

Suddenly we had way too much turkey, but it was a good exercise in what to do with all those leftovers: soups, sandwiches, stock, enchiladas, pasta, casserole, the list goes on. The favorite thing I made this year has been leftover turkey pot pie.

Instead of using a piecrust, which can be finicky and time consuming to prepare, I chose a drop biscuit topping.

Ingredients for stew:

- 1 cup cooked turkey (cubed)
- 2 tablespoons olive oil
- 2 carrots
- 4 stalks celery
- 1 small onion
- 2 cloves garlic
- ½ cup frozen peas
- 3 cups turkey stock
- 2 tablespoons flour
- 2 tablespoons warm water
- salt and pepper to taste

Ingredients for Drop Biscuit Topping:

- 2 cups flour
- 2 teaspoons baking powder
- ½ teaspoon baking soda
- 1 teaspoon sugar or molasses
- 1 teaspoon salt
- 1 cup milk (or buttermilk)
- ½ cup melted butter

Directions:

Preheat the oven to 450°F.

Dice all vegetables and garlic. Make a whitewash, which is a mixture of flour and warm water, whisked together in a small bowl to remove all the lumps.

Place onions in large skillet with olive oil. Cook on medium heat until translucent. Add carrots, celery, and garlic. Stir and cook until softened slightly. Add turkey and peas.

Add stock to pan; bring to a boil. Then simmer for 2 minutes. It should be fairly watery, so now is when you add the whitewash. Add it slowly while stirring constantly. In no time, you should have a delicious thick stew. Salt and pepper to taste.

Remove from the heat and place stew in oven-proof containers with high sides. Set aside to cool.

For the drop biscuit topping, mix your dry ingredients in a large bowl. Add milk, butter, and molasses. Mix just until incorporated. The more you mix, the tougher it gets.

Spread the dough on top of the stew. Bake for 15–20 minutes. Before serving, brush with melted butter for a shiny look.

Later-Winter Soup with Turkey and Quinoa

DANIEL ORR

I like to think of this recipe as a big pot of leftovers.

I shredded some smoked turkey left over from the night before and added a few lonely veggies from my root cellar—carrots, collard greens, leeks, turnips, and parsnips.

Kumquats add some color and a zing of citrus. The bitterness pairs well with the smokiness of the turkey.

Ingredients:

- 2 quarts turkey broth
- 2 cups shredded smoked turkey
- 1 cup quinoa
- 1 ¼ cup water
- 8–12 kumquats
- ¾ cup diced carrots
- ¾ cup shredded collard greens
- 1 onion, diced
- garlic
- olive oil

Directions:

To cook the quinoa, add olive oil, garlic, and salt and pepper to a pot. Add water and bring to a simmer. Continue adding water as necessary. Cook until the sprouts burst forth.

In another pot, combine broth, turkey, kumquats, and vegetables. Simmer for 30–40 minutes. Add cooked quinoa toward the end of the cooking process.

✿ Kitchen Basics

LENTILS 101—DANIEL ORR

Lentils are tiny, lens-shaped seeds. Any busy home cook should learn to love lentils, because they cook up in no time. You can come home from work, put on a pot of dried lentils, and have dinner ready 15–30 minutes later.

Before we start cooking, let's get to know three of the most common varieties of lentils:

Red lentils look more orange than red. These are great in soups and curries because they go from al dente to mush in a matter of seconds.

American lentils are an off-beige, green color. I like these lentils paired with ham hocks.

Lentilles du Puy were classically grown in the Le Puy region of France. Look for their distinctive speckled coloring. They have a nice toothsomeness to them, which makes them good in salads.

Some tips before you get going: Start with a saucepan that is approximately the same width as height. We'll be putting a good amount of liquid in this pan and cooking it down. And be patient! The lentils will slowly absorb the water and become toothsome. The last thing you want to do is dump some of that flavorful broth down the drain.

Basic Lentils

Ingredients:

- 1 cup lentils
- 2 tablespoons olive oil
- 3 cloves of garlic, minced
- ½ cup onions or shallots, minced
- 2 dried bay leaves
- 1 branch of thyme
- 5 black peppercorns, crushed
- 2 slices of lemon
- 3 cups water
- salt and pepper to taste

Directions:

Wash the lentils to remove any dust. Remove any off-colored lentils. Drain well.

Heat olive oil in a medium heavy-bottomed saucepan and add the garlic. Cook until toasted and golden. Quickly add onion and lemon slices and stir. Cook until soft.

Add the remaining ingredients and cover with water. Simmer until cooked tender but not mushy, adding water if needed. (Do not add more water than needed or it will dilute the earthy flavor and your aromatic seasonings.) Season to taste with salt and pepper. Spread in a glass baking dish and cool to room temperature.

Refrigerate until needed.

Curried Lentils Bring the Heat and Sweet

Green lentils are economical and healthy, but they can get boring after a while. I'm spicing them up today in an Indian curry.

While you're assembling all your ingredients, put your lentils on to cook. Rinse them first. Then for one cup of dried lentils, add two cups of water. After bringing the water to a boil, reduce the heat to a gentle simmer and cook for 20–30 minutes.

Some additional tips to keep in mind as you cook:

Chop the ginger east to west, instead of north to south. This cuts through the fibers and prevents any long strands from ruining the texture of the dish.

Allow the garlic to remain fairly raw. The pungent flavor will be nice in this recipe.

I always recommend using organic oranges, especially when you're using the zest. If you're using a conventional fruit, be sure to wash it thoroughly!

This recipe results in a thick paste. If you'd like more liquid, add some vegetable stock to the pan when you add the lentils.

Ingredients:

- 2 cups onions, chopped
- several cloves garlic, minced
- 1 tablespoon ginger, minced
- juice of 1 orange
- 1 teaspoon orange zest
- 1 tablespoon tomato paste
- ⅔ cup dried cherries
- 2 teaspoons curry powder
- 1 cup diced tomatoes
- 1 cup parsley, chopped
- leaves from several branches of thyme
- handful of basil, chopped
- 3 cups cooked green lentils
- salt and pepper, to taste
- dash of olive oil

Directions

In a hot pan, add olive oil. Add onions and allow them to brown. Then add garlic, ginger, orange juice, and zest.

Continue adding tomato paste, dried cherries, curry powder, diced tomatoes, and herbs. This will create a paste.

Add lentils. Season to taste.

Garnish with basil or cilantro. Serve over tofu.

Yellow Lentil Bisque

Ingredients:

- 1 pound yellow or red lentils
- ¼ cup extra-virgin olive oil
- 3 cloves garlic
- 8 plum tomatoes, diced or chopped
- 1 carrot, peeled and diced
- 1 Spanish onion, peeled and diced
- 1 bulb fennel
- 2 tablespoons chili powder
- 4 tablespoons curry powder
- 2 quarts water
- salt, pepper, nutmeg, and Tabasco to taste

Directions:

Rinse the lentils in cold water. Sauté the vegetables and spices in olive oil. Add the lentils, cover with water, and bring to a simmer.

When all the vegetables and lentils are cooked and tender, puree the mixture with a stationary or handheld blender and pass through a fine chinois. Adjust thickness with additional water or vegetable stock as needed. Season to taste.

May be made 2–3 days in advance and reheated gently as needed. Serve in warm bowls with crusty bread. Garnish with ¼ cup thick drained yogurt, cilantro, or other toppings.

earth eats

Bison, Pumpkin, Lentil Chili

This is a wonderful winter dish that you can make ahead and eat for several days. It's great on its own but also nice as a sloppy joe or pita pocket sandwich. Try it on grilled sausages or over pasta, or serve it with my buttermilk biscuits.

Ingredients:

- ¼ cup canola oil
- 2 pounds ground bison
- 2 cups washed green lentils
- 2 medium onions, diced
- 2 carrots, finely diced
- 1 red bell pepper, minced
- 1 green bell pepper, minced
- 6 cloves garlic, minced
- 2 cups diced fresh tomatoes
- 2 cups crushed canned tomatoes
- 2 cups brewed coffee
- ¼ cup sorghum

- ½ teaspoon Chinese 5-spice powder (a combination of cinnamon, cloves, fennel, star anise, and peppercorns)
- 2 teaspoons cumin
- 1 tablespoon onion powder
- 1 teaspoon freshly ground pepper
- 2 pinches cinnamon
- ½ teaspoon cayenne pepper
- ½ cup pumpkin puree
- Assorted garnishes in bowls: diced red onions, scallions, pesto-laced sour cream, grated cheddar or goat cheese

Directions:

Brown bison in canola oil with chopped onions, peppers, carrots, and minced garlic in heavy soup pot.

Cook until vegetables are lightly caramelized and tender. Add coffee, spices, and lentils. Bring just to a boil, then reduce to a simmer until lentils are almost tender (20 minutes).

Add diced and crushed tomatoes, pumpkin puree, and sorghum. Cook another hour or so. Top with diced red onions, scallions, pesto-laced sour cream, grated cheddar, or goat cheese.

earth eats

Lentil Tarragon Soup

NATALIE RAE GOOD

It's soup time! The first snow has dusted the city, and I've pulled my big silver soup pot down from the high shelf.

Soups are the perfect platform for culinary experiments. Try something new with your old soup recipes and if it doesn't work out you can always reverse it by adding more water, acid (lemon juice, vinegar, wine), sugar, or spices.

I worked at a well-loved restaurant with delicious food where we intentionally burned the onions in the lentil soup ever so slightly because one accidental burn yielded surprising results. So roll up your sleeves, raid the pantry, and join me in welcoming the most forgiving culinary season of the year—soup season!

Ingredients:

- 4 teaspoons olive oil
- 1 onion, diced
- 3 carrots, peeled and diced
- 3 ribs celery, diced
- 4 cloves garlic, minced
- 2 teaspoons dried tarragon
- 1 teaspoon dried thyme
- 1 teaspoon paprika
- 3 tablespoons tomato paste
- 8 cups mushroom broth
- 2 cups lentils
- 2 bay leaves
- ½ cup dry red wine
- 1 bunch fresh parsley
- salt and pepper to taste

Directions:

Preheat a large soup pot over medium heat. Add oil and sauté the onion, celery, and carrots until softened (about 7 minutes).

Add garlic, tarragon, thyme, and paprika. Stir for 2 minutes.

Add tomato paste, vegetable broth, lentils, half of the parsley, and bay leaves. Cover and bring to a boil.

Once boiling, reduce temperature to low and let simmer (still covered) for 30 minutes or until lentils have softened. Add water as needed.

Remove from heat. Add wine and salt and pepper to taste. Garnish with freshly chopped parsley and serve with a hunk of fresh bread.

Make Your Own Stock

DANIEL ORR

Nothing makes a house smell like a home more than a good stock simmering away in the kitchen.

Whether it's beef, fish, chicken, or veggie, stocks are the base of most soups, sauces, stews, and broths. A great stock will make a dish.

This recipe uses whole vegetables, but I encourage you to toss in food scraps that would normally go into the compost heap—carrot peels, scallion bases, and mushroom stems. Also be sure to save your meat bones for stock preparation.

Ingredients:

- 6 pounds bones (beef, game, chicken, fowl, fish heads) or assorted veggie scraps
- 1 large onion
- 3 large carrots
- ½ cup water or wine (white for fish or chicken or red for beef or game)
- 1 large tomato
- 2 stalks celery, including some leaves
- ½ cup chopped parsnip
- 8 whole black peppercorns
- 4 sprigs fresh parsley
- 1 bay leaf
- 1 tablespoon salt
- 2 teaspoons dried thyme
- 2 cloves garlic
- 12 cups water

Directions:

Preheat oven to 450°F. Rough chop the onion, scrubbed celery, tomato, parsnips, and carrots into chunks. Roast bones and veggies uncovered in a large shallow roasting pan for about 30 minutes or until the bones and veggies are well browned, turning occasionally. Drain off fat.

Place the browned bones and veggies in a large soup pot. Pour ½ cup wine into the roasting pan. Stir to remove caramelized bits. Pour this liquid into soup pot. Add peppercorns, parsley, bay leaf, salt, thyme, and garlic. Add the 10–12 cups water, just enough to cover.

Bring mixture to a boil. Reduce heat. Simmer for 4–5 hours for beef; 2–3 hours for chicken; 1–2 hours for fish or veggies. Strain stock. Discard solids. Taste and adjust seasoning with salt and pepper. Cool to room temperature and refrigerate or freeze.

❧ Bone Broth with the Hub's Domestic Diva

It's Friday at Mother Hubbard's Cupboard in Bloomington, Indiana, and that means Barbara Lehr is preparing a demonstration in the teaching kitchen. Today, she's brought bags and bags of beef bones.

Lehr's bone broth is a permanent fixture in her home. "I have a stock pot going all the time," she says. "Even though that seems like an odd practice, it was the standard practice before the 1930s. Everybody had it. As a matter of fact, I've seen an old-fashioned stove that has three burners and one hole. And that hole, you put a stock pot in, and you have perpetual broth going all the time."

And it's simple. Lehr's recipe, for instance, has only three steps:

1. Roast chicken or beef bones. (This gives more dimension to the flavor.)
2. Cover roasted bones in water.
3. Simmer for 24 hours.

The result can be used in a variety of dishes, including sauces, steamed vegetables, stews, rice pilaf, and soups.

Michael Hollon is a patron at the food pantry. He came to Lehr's demonstration today to find a healthier alternative to the typical stocks you find in cookbooks.

"All the recipes I've found for it always have a bunch of sodium in it, and I can't have sodium," Hollon says. Lehr explains that, like any recipe, you can add as much (or as little) seasoning as you'd like.

After preparing it, the broth can be placed in the refrigerator, where the fat rises to the top. Barbara explains that this fat could be reused. "You can take that off the top of your container and then you can use that fat to make soap

Barbara Lehr (right) teaches customers at Mother Hubbard's Cupboard how to make bone broth.

with. Or you can use it—it's just pure tallow—you can use it to fry potato chips in."

The broth can last about five days in the refrigerator, six months in the freezer, and about a year if it's pressure canned. It smells and tastes great, but it may not look that great after it's refrigerated. The gelatin from the bones makes its consistency a little like jelly when cooled. It's the collagen that gives chilled bone broth that jelly consistency.

"A lot of people will make broth, it'll gel in the refrigerator, they'll freak out and think that it has gone bad when it's actually fantastic," she adds.

After the demonstration, Hollon, got a chance to taste that squash soup made with Lehr's chicken bone broth. "That's actually pretty good," he remarks. "You can taste the chicken."

He's taking home the recipe plus some beef bones to try making bone broth himself.

Those beef bones can be cooked about three times before all of the nutrients are out of them, Lehr says. After that? Give them to your dogs. They'll love 'em!

Rendering Lard the Right Way

DIANA BAUMAN

Rendering lard is simple. You heat pork fat until it melts. It can take practice to get it just right, especially if you want to make the snow-white odorless leaf lard.

There are several different types of pork fat that you can render.

Back fat comes from the animal's shoulder and rump. It's literally the layer of fat directly below the skin, and it's often sold with the skin still attached. Rendered back fat is great for sautéing and frying.

Leaf lard is the fat from around the pig's kidneys. It's the crème de la crème of pork fat. Leaf lard is used to make perfectly flaky piecrusts and traditional Spanish polvorones.

For this method, I'm using a crockpot. Keep an eye on your fat as it renders. If the pot gets too hot or heats for too long, the cracklings will start to burn. The result will be deep yellow lard that smells and tastes vaguely of pig. If you're using the lard to fry, this isn't a big deal, but if you're making pastries, you don't want your cookies and pies to taste like a hog!

Directions:

Cut your leaf lard or back fat into small pieces. To make it easy on yourself, ask your family farmer to have the fat ground (like I did). The process is much quicker and leads to better results.

Add ¼ cup of water to the bottom of a crockpot and add the cut-up pork fat. (The water prevents the fat from burning before the pork fat starts to melt. It will end up evaporating out.) Then set the crockpot on low and let it cook for 90 minutes to 2 hours, but don't stray too far. It's important to keep an eye on the crockpot to make sure the fat doesn't start to burn. There's no magic number to how many hours it will take. After all, each crockpot is different.

As the fat melts, the little bits called cracklings will separate and settle on the bottom of the crockpot. That's how you'll know your fat has been rendered fully!

Ladle the contents of the crockpot into a cheesecloth-lined colander, separating the liquid fat from the cracklings. The fat should have a pale yellow hue and the cracklings should be soft. Then ladle the liquid fat into pint-sized mason jars. Let it cool on the counter and then store in the refrigerator or freezer.

But wait, there's more! Put the cracklings back in the crockpot and cook until they're brown and crispy. You can use these in a variety of ways. I like them sprinkled on top of salads.

Dried Beans—Soak, Cook, Store

I use a stockpot to boil the beans, but you could use a crockpot. Just make sure to set it on low for at least eight hours, or until your beans are tender.

Directions:

In a colander, rinse the dried beans and pick out any gnarly beans that don't look appetizing. Then completely submerge the beans in water and soak overnight.

    The next day, drain and rinse the soaked beans.

    Add your beans to a stockpot and cover with 2 inches of water. I add sliced onions to the pot as well. Bring to a boil on the stovetop and remove any residue that floats on top. Turn the heat to low and simmer for 60–90 minutes or until tender.

    Once the beans have softened, using a slotted spoon add the beans to mason jars, allowing 2 inches of headspace. Allow the jars to cool completely, preferably in the refrigerator, before freezing.

❧ Sprout It Yourself

SARAH KAISER

The first time I made sprouts was by accident. I left soaked garbanzo beans in the fridge too long and they started to grow little green tendrils. I tried one and it was delicious. I was hooked.

You can sprout almost anything that grows into a plant. My seeds of choice are lentils and quinoa. Lentils make bigger sprouts and I find they have more flavor. If your recipe features sprouts prominently, lentil sprouts would be good. Quinoa sprouts are smaller and probably best utilized as a garnish. But if you're looking for speedy sprouts, go for quinoa.

Here's a quick DIY guide to sprouting your own beans, seeds, and nuts:

1. Soak. Generally, seeds are soaked overnight for around 8–14 hours. However, quinoa only needs 2–4 hours to soak.

2. Drain and rinse. After soaking, the seeds have absorbed water and can be left under a moist towel to rest.

3. Sit. After about a day, you should start to see small sprouts. The quinoa only needed 12 hours to sprout.

4. Rinse and repeat steps 2–3. To get bigger sprouts, rinse your sprouts once a day until they are the desired size.

5. Refrigerate. This halts the sprouting process and keeps sprouts fresh for a few days to a week.

Black Bean Scramble with Quinoa and Lentil Sprouts

SARAH KAISER

Raw sprouts can be tossed into salads, incorporated into sandwiches, or sprinkled on a hot soup. This easy black bean scramble recipe is a favorite in our house.

Ingredients:

- 3 eggs
- ¼ cup milk
- 1 tablespoon olive oil
- ¼ chopped onion
- cumin, salt, pepper, and hot sauce to taste
- 1 can black beans, drained
- 1 cup sprouts
- ⅛ cup grated cheddar

Directions:

Whisk eggs, milk, and spices in small bowl. In a hot pan, sauté onions in olive oil until translucent. Pour egg mixture into pan. Scramble eggs until just done, about 1–2 minutes. Add black beans and heat through. Add sprouts. Mix until heated. Turn off heat and top with cheese.

Sun-Dried Tomato Basil Hummus vegan

As a recent college graduate, I'm always looking for ways to make a cheap yet delicious meal. And as a vegetarian, I find beans and legumes delicious, filling, and full of variation. Take chickpeas; they can be transformed into hummus, falafel, or chickpea curry.

My favorite recipe for chickpeas is hummus combined with sun-dried tomatoes and basil. I recommend buying your tomatoes preserved in olive oil. You'll use some of that oil in the recipe, and it will help infuse your hummus with some extra sweetness.

I think the reason this homemade hummus suits me is the decreased amount of lemon juice. Most store-bought hummus recipes taste very sour to me. If you like that lemony kick, feel free to adjust this recipe to your taste—more juice and fewer chickpeas.

Ingredients:

- 1 7-ounce jar sun-dried tomatoes in olive oil
- fresh basil
- 4 cloves garlic
- salt to taste

- 6 tablespoons tahini
- ½ cup lemon juice
- 4 cups cooked chickpeas (about 2 cans)
- Water or olive oil as needed to get the right consistency. I used some of the cooking water from the chickpeas.

Directions:

Blend all ingredients in food processor or blender. I used a small, handheld blender. It's a bit messy, but it does the trick.

Falafel in a Jiffy vegan

RAMA COUSIK

Ingredients:

- 1 can chickpeas, drained
- 3–4 sprigs of chopped cilantro
- 1 teaspoon crushed red pepper flakes
- ½ teaspoon salt
- 2 cups oil for frying

Directions:

Combine chickpeas, cilantro, salt, and chili flakes in a food processor. (You can also add garlic, lime juice, and ginger if you want a zestier result.) Blend the mix coarsely in a food processor.

Shape the chickpea mixture into balls and gently press them flat. Heat oil in a pan. Deep fry chickpea balls until golden brown.

 ## Gardens Still Going Strong in Fall

DIANNE VENETTA

COVER CROPS

The growing season is winding down and the days are growing shorter, the winds colder. Just when you thought your work was over, your garden still needs your attention.

Row covers will act as blankets to keep your beds warm and weed free during the winter months. Come spring, when you're chomping at the bit to get those vegetables in the ground, it will be much easier to plant your new batch of seeds.

But there's another kind of cover your winter beds will appreciate: crop covers. We're talking rye and legumes, brassicas and flowers. They all have a purpose.

Say you're an organic gardener (of course you are!) and you want to enrich your soil with organic matter. You live in a climate where you can grow year round. Why not plant a crop of beans? They're an excellent choice, not only because they like it warm but also because their wide leaves will shade the ground for extra weed prevention. Their roots will put nitrogen into your soil. Not to mention they're a delicious source of protein for your diet.

Let's say you live up north where beans won't survive the long harsh winter. Rye is cold tolerant and thick enough to provide great weed prevention. It will infuse your garden with a dose of nitrogen. Come spring, simply till it back into the soil after it flowers for maximum soil improvement.

Some cover crops can do more than improve soil and prevent weeds. Mustard plants have been shown to suppress fungal disease in soil by emitting natural toxins.

Brassicas can also release chemical compounds that may be toxic to soil-borne pathogens and pests like nematodes.

Speaking of nematodes, planting marigolds can prevent them from reproducing. That's a good thing, because these microscopic beasts can kill your veggies from the roots up. They are very hard to fend off when you can't see them.

If that isn't enough reason to plant cover crops, consider the benefits against soil erosion. A dense planting of any cover crop will slow down the speed at which rain makes contact with the soil surface, thereby lessening the amount of soil that runs off your garden.

Think of cover crops as a down payment on fertility come spring.

CROP ROTATION

Think of crop rotation as the planned order for planting specific crops on a field or bed. It helps prevent disease and improves the soil by replenishing nutrients.

First thing to keep in mind is that some plants clean the soil of nutrients while others replenish it. Corn uses a lot of nitrogen,

so planting it after a crop of nitrogen-fixing beans will do wonders for your growth. Cabbage and broccoli are heavy feeders, so rotating them with light feeders such as carrots and onions will help keep the soil balanced.

Second thing to remember is that you don't want to plant the same family of plants in the same spot season after season. The pests will be ready and waiting to gobble them up! Some insects and disease-causing organisms are host-specific and will attack plants that are from the same family.

An example of healthy crop rotation for a garden would be beans—leaves—roots—fruits:

- Beans and peas (beans)
- Cabbage, broccoli, and spinach (leaves)
- Carrots, onions, and beets (roots)
- Squash, pumpkin, and tomatoes (fruits)

You can also think of them in terms of light feeders versus heavy feeders:

- Beans and peas (light)
- Cabbage and broccoli (heavy)
- Carrots, onions, and beets (light)
- Squash, pumpkin, and tomatoes (heavy)

The crop rotation not only prevents disease and insect problems; it can also improve soil porosity. Rotating crops with different root systems will help the soil structure by aerating it and adding nutrients at different depths. You can think of these groups by their root characteristics:

- Beans (deep roots)
- Leaves (shallow roots)
- Root vegetables (deep roots)
- Fruits (shallow roots)

You energetic gardening types can get really specialized and alternate based on tall crop section growers like tomatoes, corn, beans, and cucumbers. Or you can go with a low crop section including cabbage, carrots, onions, and peppers. You can also differentiate between nightshades (tomatoes, eggplant, and potatoes) and grasses (corn).

🌿 Next-Level Gardening: Seed Saving

"Every morsel of food that we eat starts with a seed." That's the guiding principle that author and naturalist Janisse Ray follows when she works in her garden. She's the author of *The Seed Underground: A Growing Revolution to Save Food.*

She started growing her own food in Georgia as a way to eat more healthfully. She started saving seeds as a way to save the world. "Seeds are being patented at a rapid rate," she says, and not just GMO and hybrid seeds, but also heritage and heirloom varieties. That worries her because she sees it as corporations gaining control over the food supply. "Our seed supply is our food supply," she says.

She would prefer it if seeds were the property of everyone and no one. "I think seeds belong to the great commons of life, like air, water, fire, and the ocean," she says. "I don't believe they can or should be owned."

THE MAGIC OF POLLINATION

Ray is especially concerned with preserving heirloom varieties of seeds, which means that maintaining a seed's purity is of the utmost importance. Seeds are produced as a result of pollination, so she is acutely aware of how her plants interact with pollinators.

She highlights three of the ways plants are pollinated: self-pollinated, insect-pollinated, and hand-pollinated.

Self-pollinating plants, like tomatoes and beans, do the hard work themselves. When the flower opens up, the pollen is dragged across the stigma—no outside critters or pollen are involved. "Anybody can save bean and tomato seeds and be assured of their purity," she says.

Seeds that are insect-pollinated, like squashes, need a showy bloom with a fragrance to attract beneficial bugs. For instance, as a honeybee collects pollen from the flower's male reproductive part (anther) for use back in the hive, some stray grains will stick to the bee's body. When it travels to the next flower, some of the pollen will be transferred onto that flower's female reproductive part (stigma).

Seed saving gets more complicated, Ray says, when you're dealing with cross-pollination—for instance, when a banana squash pollinates a butternut squash. That compromises the purity of the plants' seeds. In order to prevent a plant from being cross-pollinated by insects, Ray hand-pollinates her plants. This involves some serious gardening:

1. In the evening, find a female bloom and a few male blooms that are set to open the next morning.

2. Tape them shut.

3. The next morning, open the blossoms and rub the pollen from the male flowers onto the stigma of the female flowers.

4. Tape them back shut.

If this seems more hands-on than you'd like to be in your garden, she says you can ensure purity by isolating your plants.

earth eats

🌱 Seed Saving 101

DIANNE VENETTA

Seed saving is all about purity. This is an important concept to keep in mind, because if you're not careful you can create some hybrids of your own.

Step one: Keep your seeds separate, organized by harvest and variety, and learn the recommended "shelf life" for each. Trust me, planting old seeds doesn't work. Not only will they not germinate, but they take up valuable planting space before you discover the error.

Step two: Dry the seeds before storing. There is no greater disappointment than having saved moldy seeds. This happened to my beans one year. I thought they could go straight from pod to packet, but oh no. They needed to be dried. Once dried, pack your seeds away in an airtight storage jar. Peppers are similar to beans in that you remove the seeds and set them out to dry before storing. With the squash family (and okra) you'll want to remove the film coating before storing. Simply wipe them clean and set out to dry.

Not all seeds are treated the same when it comes to storing. Tomatoes require a bit more effort.

Once you remove the seeds, you need to put them in a glass and fill it with water (at least an inch or two above the seeds).

Allow them to sit undisturbed for a few days. When a white mold begins to form over the seeds, scoop it out and any seeds that go with it. The seeds left on the bottom of your glass are the ones you want. (The floaters are duds.)

Drain water from the glass through a fine sieve so you don't lose any of your precious gems. Rinse them with cold water. Place seeds on a paper plate (paper towel over regular plate will also work) and allow them to dry completely. This process may take a few days to complete. Then slip them into your seed saving packet and you're good to go.

Carrots, onions, broccoli, and lettuce are even more complicated. To be honest, they're out of my competency range, but if you're the adventurous type, give it a whirl. You'll need to allow the plant to bolt, or produce flowers, whereby it will produce seeds—tiny seeds, yes, but seeds nonetheless. If you can collect them from the flower before they blow away, you're golden. If not, you'll be back at your local garden shop.

🌱 Walnuts

Walnuts are difficult to prepare, with their hard green hulls and black goo surrounding the nutmeat. Commercial walnut sellers have pricey equipment that hulls the nuts, but forager Tracy Branam does it the old-fashioned way: he runs over the walnuts with his truck. After the nuts are hulled and washed, Branam says, they are dried in the sun for a couple weeks. Then they are bagged and cured for another month.

Customers can watch Branam crack the walnuts at his table at the farmers' market. "That gives me the advantage of seeing whether it's a good meat or not," he says.

Black Walnut and Maple Butter

DANIEL ORR

Before you get started with this recipe, toast the walnuts. This concentrates the essential oils, intensifying the flavor and making the nuts crispier.

The important thing to know about toasting nuts is that they go from brown to black in seconds flat. I suggest setting a timer every few minutes to force you to check on them regularly. If you do burn some nuts, discard the burnt ones and save the rest. Nuts are really expensive, so you don't want burn them too many times.

This recipe features grade B maple syrup from Burton's Maplewood Farm, which has a more robust flavor than grade A syrup. It also includes lemon juice and zest. The acidity will cut a little bit of the sweetness of the maple syrup.

Make a full pound of flavored butter and store it in the refrigerator or freezer to enjoy throughout the winter months.

Ingredients:

- ½ cup toasted black walnuts
- ½ pound butter, at room temperature
- ¼ cup maple syrup or honey
- 1 teaspoon lemon zest
- juice of ½ lemon
- pinch of salt

Directions:

Leave butter out the night before to make sure it's nice and soft.

Toast the walnuts. Combine ingredients and season to taste.

Roll in plastic wrap or parchment paper. Refrigerate or freeze until needed.

Hoosier Autumn Succotash

A succotash is a stew of corn and beans. With that base, you can add whatever ingredients you like. My version is a shout-out to Indiana in the fall, with squash, peppers, mushrooms, and herbs fresh from my garden.

It's a carnival of colors on the plate thanks in part to the last green zucchini and yellow summer squash in my crisper. Discard the inner seeds and dice the outer meat and skin of the veggies into this dish.

Speaking of the dice, you'll notice I include some fairly specific chopping instructions in the recipe. You want all the ingredients to be the same size—about the size of a kernel of corn—so that everything cooks at the same pace.

I like to serve this succotash as a bed for my bacon-wrapped filet mignon, but it would be great with fish or even on its own.

If you want to add this to your Thanksgiving menu, save yourself a headache on the big day and make it a couple of days early. When it's finished cooking, transfer it to a glass dish and cool it down immediately. It will reheat beautifully when you're ready to serve.

Ingredients:

- ½ cup unsalted butter
- 1 medium onion, cut into ¼-inch dice
- 2 cloves garlic, finely chopped
- 1 small butternut or acorn squash, cut into ¼-inch dice
- 1 red pepper, cut into ¼-inch dice
- 1 yellow summer squash, cut into ¼-inch dice
- 1 zucchini, cut into ¼-inch dice
- 1 cup frozen lima beans
- 1 cup fresh or frozen corn kernels
- 1 cup mushrooms, diced
- ¼ cup heavy cream
- salt and pepper to taste
- 2 tablespoons fresh sage, coarsely chopped
- 2 tablespoons fresh tarragon
- 2 tablespoons fresh oregano

Directions:

In a skillet over medium heat, melt butter. Add onion and cook until translucent.

Add garlic, butternut or acorn squash, peppers, zucchini, summer squash, lima beans, and corn.

Add mushrooms and heavy cream. Cook over medium heat until it coats the vegetables and thickens slightly.

Stir in herbs. Season with salt and pepper.

Potato Leek Soup with Chanterelles

I can't tell you the number of times I've seen young cooks throw away perfectly good parts of a leek. You pay as much for the green part as you do for the white part, so you might as well use the whole thing!

You want this soup to have a light green hue to it, so only discard the toughest outer leaves of the leeks. Before you get started, be sure to clean the leeks thoroughly, as dirt and sand can get caught in between the many layers. (Slice off the roots and cut the leek lengthwise. Use warm water to rinse out each layer.)

I'm garnishing this recipe with sautéed chanterelle mushrooms. I'm using rehydrated mushrooms I saved from last year's foraging adventures.

Ingredients:

- 18 leeks, rinsed, rough chop (mostly the white part)
- ½ head celery, rough chop
- 3 onions, rough chop
- 2 cloves garlic, whole
- ¼ cup olive oil
- 2 cups dry white wine
- 1 teaspoon lightly toasted and crushed fennel seeds
- 15 potatoes, large, Idaho, cut into medium pieces
- 2 gallons chicken stock, hot
- sachet thyme, bay leaf, and 1 teaspoon white peppercorns
- cayenne pepper to taste
- 2 ounces chanterelles, sautéed
- 2 ounces leeks, julienned
- 1 teaspoon chopped chives

Directions:

Sweat the leeks, onions, celery, and garlic in olive oil over low heat until translucent.

Add the wine and reduce by half.

Add the fennel seeds, potatoes, chicken stock, and sachet.

Simmer over medium heat for 45 minutes or until the potatoes are cooked through.

Remove the sachet and puree soup with a large immersion blender.

Strain through a large-hole china cap and then a chinois. Adjust the seasoning and chill.

Heat to order and finish with cream and chives. Garnish plates with leeks and chanterelles.

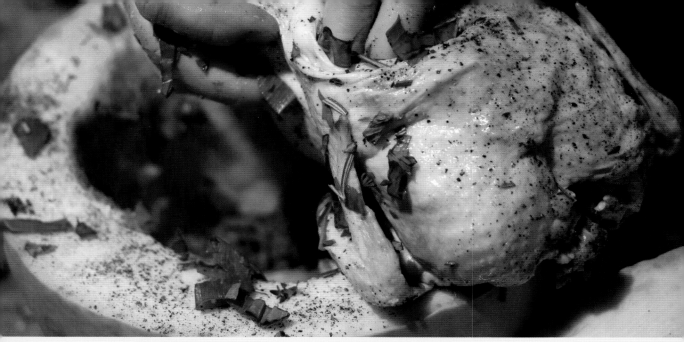

🌿 Beyond the Jack-O'-Lantern

Chicken Baked in a Pumpkin Pot

Ingredients:

- 1 medium pumpkin
- 1 2½–pound chicken
- 2 cups fresh herbs to taste (rosemary, thyme, basil, scallions, sage, fennel)
- 1 cup white wine
- 1 teaspoon smoked paprika
- 1 teaspoon garlic powder
- 1 teaspoon pumpkin pie spice
- olive oil

Directions:

Preheat oven to 350°F. Cut a lid in the top of the pumpkin and remove the seeds and pith. Season chicken and pumpkin with salt and pepper. Throw herbs inside pumpkin and stuff chicken cavity with herbs. For extra flavor, use two fingers to lift the skin on the chicken breasts and thighs. Stuff herbs inside chicken so that they lie directly against the meat. Place seasoned chicken inside pumpkin.

Add wine, paprika, garlic powder, and pumpkin pie spice to chicken and pumpkin. Drizzle with olive oil and replace lid. Secure the lid by sticking the pumpkin with wooden skewers. Add ½ inch of water to a roasting pan so the bottom of the pumpkin won't burn. Place pumpkin in roasting pan and cook in oven for 2 hours or until juices from the chicken run clear. Serve chicken with wedge of pumpkin, and drizzle with juice from the pumpkin.

Vegan Coconut Pumpkin Soup

SARAH KAISER

I wanted to make a creamy pumpkin soup, but most recipes call for heavy cream. In a stroke of inspiration, I decided to substitute some regular coconut milk in our fridge for the cream. It worked like a charm!

Ingredients:

- 1 red onion, finely chopped
- 1 tablespoon vegetable oil
- 2 teaspoons vegetable bullion
- 2–3 cups pumpkin puree
- 1 cup coconut milk
- 1 tablespoon sugar

Directions:

Sauté the vegetable oil and chopped onion on medium high until the onions are soft and translucent. Add 2 cups water or 2 cups vegetable broth. Add the pumpkin puree and coconut milk. Stir to combine. (I used my new food processor to puree the pumpkin, but you could use canned if you wanted.) Heat this mixture to a boil, then lower heat and simmer for 5 minutes.

We enjoyed this soup with some fresh cilantro and sugar 'n' spice pumpkin seeds.

Candied Pumpkin Seeds

BOB ADKINS

I grew up eating pumpkin seeds, but they never did turn out as tasty as I hoped they would.

Then I learned about pepitas. These are not your typical jack-o'-lantern pumpkin seeds. Pepitas are flat, green seeds that come from pumpkins grown specifically for the seeds.

You'll notice that this recipe does not use olive oil or butter in the pan. Just like mushrooms, these seeds won't stick to your pan and will develop a great flavor without any fat.

Ingredients:

- 2 cups pepitas
- ½ cup sugar (enough to cover the top of the seed in the pan)
- a hefty pinch of crushed red chili flakes
- pinch kosher salt and pepper

Directions:

Heat up a heavy-bottomed pan to very hot. Add dry seeds directly to pan. They will pop and brown. Keep moving them, just like popcorn.

Add the sugar, chili flakes and salt and pepper to the seeds in the pan. Once browned, pour seeds onto cookie sheet. While they are still hot, sprinkle sugar over top.

Let them cool and break them up into chunks like peanut brittle. Yum!

Sautéed Pumpkin Slices

BOB ADKINS

The French baking pumpkin we're using in our recipe today is muted green in color, almost white. Like all pumpkins that are good for cooking, this pumpkin is very heavy for its size.

Ingredients:

- 1 2-pound pumpkin
- 1 teaspoon Chinese 5-spice powder (a combination of cinnamon, cloves, fennel, star anise, and peppercorns)
- 2 teaspoons raw sugar
- sea salt
- 5 tablespoons good olive oil
- 2 lemons
- toasted pumpkin seeds

Directions:

Peel and seed pumpkin. Cut into ⅓-inch slices. Toss in olive oil. Toss spices, sugar, and salt in another bowl and pour over pumpkin slices.

Sauté in a nonstick pan until caramelized. Turn and color other side lightly. Remove from pan and season with lemon juice. Sprinkle with toasted pumpkin seeds.

Pumpkin Date Bread Pudding

STEPHANIE WEAVER

Ingredients:

- 15 ounces pumpkin puree (1 ¾ cups)
- ½ cup date paste
- ½ cup agave syrup or honey
- ½ cup sorghum flour
- 2 tablespoons flax meal
- ¼ teaspoon cinnamon
- ¼ teaspoon cloves
- ¼ teaspoon allspice
- ¼ teaspoon ginger
- ¼ teaspoon nutmeg
- ½ cup raisins

Directions:

Soak 4–6 pitted dates in filtered water; 30 minutes for fresh dates, 1–2 hours for dried dates. Drain, reserving the water. Put in a blender with enough of the soaking water to blend into a paste. You can use this to sweeten baked goods and smoothies. The soaking water is a good base for smoothies as well.

Preheat the oven to 350°F. Oil a pie dish or baking dish and set aside. (If using piecrust, no need to oil the dish.)

Put 1 cup filtered water, sorghum flour, spices, and flax meal in the blender. Blend and let sit five minutes. Mix all the ingredients together in a large bowl, blending well. Add the raisins last. Pour into baking dish or piecrust.

Bake for 55–60 minutes or until set.

Pumpkin Flaxseed Doughnuts

NATALIE RAE GOOD

This fall has started out beautifully—wind rustling through fallen leaves (and trash) on these busy Brooklyn streets.

A few sweet and brave friends of mine are leaving the city, and I held a little gathering in their honor in the park last weekend. I made a few caramel apples and a towering pile of pumpkin doughnuts. I've always loved doughnuts, and these pumpkin flaxseed rings are perfectly spicy and sweet.

What better way to ring in the season?

Ingredients:

- 2 tablespoons ground flaxseed
- 6 tablespoons hot water
- ½ cup soy or almond milk
- ½ teaspoon apple cider vinegar
- 4 cups flour
- 4 teaspoons baking powder
- ½ teaspoon baking soda
- 1 teaspoon salt
- 2 teaspoons cinnamon
- ½ teaspoon ginger
- 1 pinch cloves and nutmeg
- 1 cup canned pumpkin
- 1 cup sugar
- 4 tablespoons canola oil
- 2 teaspoons vanilla

Directions:

In a small bowl, mix together the flaxseed and hot water. In another small bowl, mix together the soy or almond milk and vinegar. Set these aside.

In a large bowl, mix the dry ingredients (flour, baking powder, baking soda, salt, and spices).

In another bowl (so many bowls!), whisk together the pumpkin, sugar, oil, and vanilla. Mix in the almond milk and flaxseed mixtures.

Stir the wet ingredients into the dry. Once ingredients are combined, transfer the bowl to the fridge for one hour.

Roll the dough onto a floured countertop. You want the dough to be about ½-inch thick.

Using a round cutter or a widemouthed mason jar lid (like I do), cut the dough into circles. Use a bottle cap to punch the centers out.

In a large, high-walled pot, heat 5 inches of canola oil to 370°F. Use a candy thermometer to monitor the oil's temperature, making sure to keep the oil between 360 and 375°F. Prepare a cooling rack by placing a rack over a baking tray. Carefully drop the doughnuts into the oil and watch them rise to the surface. Flip once, then transfer to the rack to cool. Coat with cinnamon sugar and serve warm!

Gingery Pumpkin Frozen Custard

SARAH KAISER

When I first decided to make pumpkin ice cream for *Earth Eats*, I was planning on doing something simple and vegan—with coconut milk, sugar, and tons of fresh pumpkin.

While that would have undoubtedly resulted in a delicious ice cream, my ambition got the better of me (as it often does), and I decided to go for a custard-style ice cream instead, made with egg yolks and whole milk. Decidedly not vegan! I love how the milk and eggs thicken into a heavy, creamy consistency as you cook them together. And though you can get a similar texture using coconut milk, it really just isn't the same as custard.

I have to give you some warning—this recipe is a bit of a pain to make. You stand there at the stove, stirring and watching, and the minutes can drag on. You'll also need some sort of ice cream maker or machine. Preparing the custard won't be the hardest thing you've ever done, but you will have to be ready for all the steps. So be sure to read through the directions, prepare, then start cooking. You won't be disappointed.

Ingredients:

- 1 ½ cups whole milk
- ¼ cup turbinado sugar
- 1 teaspoon ground ginger (we used dry, but fresh is better)
- ½ teaspoon ground cinnamon
- ½ teaspoon freshly ground nutmeg
- ¼ teaspoon salt
- 3 medium egg yolks
- ⅛ cup turbinado sugar
- ½ teaspoon vanilla extract
- 1 cup roasted, then pureed pumpkin

Directions:

Mix together the whole milk (not skim or 2 percent), ¼ cup sugar, ground ginger, cinnamon, nutmeg, and salt in a saucepan. Continue mixing over low heat until ingredients are thoroughly combined and the milk is warm and starting to bubble around the edges.

While the milk is heating, separate the egg yolks from the whites. Set aside the whites and whisk the yolks. Add half of the warm milk mixture into the egg yolks, stirring constantly. You don't want the yolks to cook, so it's important that the milk not be too hot for this step.

Add the yolk and milk mixture back into the saucepan, stirring constantly. Keep the heat low and continue cooking until this mixture gets a thick, custardlike consistency. You'll notice when it starts to thicken. Pour this mixture into a small metal bowl surrounded by ice. (Fill a large bowl with ice and cold water. Set the smaller metal bowl on top.) After the mixture is placed on ice, immediately stir in the remaining ⅛ cup sugar. Continue stirring until mixture cools. Once the custard has chilled completely in the ice bath (should take about 10–20 minutes), stir in the vanilla extract and pumpkin puree. Chill the entire mixture in the fridge for a few hours, until it is very cold. Then process it through your ice cream maker. Freeze according to its instructions.

Pumpkin Zucchini Bread

One of my favorite childhood memories was going to the farm to visit my mother's side of the family. Her parents own an apple orchard in Maryland, and we would visit during holidays and special occasions.

My grandmother had her own garden and grew beautiful flowers and some fruits and vegetables—including zucchini. I remember during the summer having a thick slice of her homemade (and homegrown) zucchini bread. Her loaves always came out perfect, deep brown in color with gorgeous cracks along the top. They were always moist with a sweet flavor.

Unfortunately, I wasn't all that curious about food as a child, so I never learned her secret. Here is my attempt at zucchini bread, but with a special guest ingredient.

Ingredients:

- 2 eggs (Turn this recipe vegan by substituting ½ cup applesauce)
- 1 ½ cups sugar
- 1 cup pumpkin puree (or half a can of pumpkin)
- ½ cup vegetable oil
- 1 cup oatmeal
- 2 cups flour
- 1 teaspoon baking soda
- ½ teaspoon baking powder
- ½ teaspoon salt
- ½ teaspoon each of ground cinnamon, nutmeg, and cloves
- 1 cup shredded zucchini

Directions:

Preheat oven to 350°F.

Combine sugar, eggs, pumpkin, and oil in a large bowl.

In another bowl, mix together oatmeal, flour, baking soda, baking powder, salt, and spices until well combined.

Add the flour mixture to the egg mixture, and stir with a spatula until just combined. Fold in the shredded zucchini.

Pour the batter into a greased and floured loaf pan. Bake 45–60 minutes, or until the bread is done.

The loaf broke when I tried to remove it from the pan. I'm not an expert baker like my grandma—I'm still learning! Perhaps the key is to wait for the bread to cool a bit before removing it from the pan.

Even in pieces, the bread was delicious—not too sweet. We served it with a bit of maple syrup drizzled on top.

Acorn Squash Tempura

DANIEL ORR

I picked up some local acorn squash for this recipe because you can eat it skin and all. If you purchase it from a grocery store, you will want to peel off the waxy coating.

When mixing the batter, make sure the ingredients are cold. This will help the batter stick to the veggies. Do a test run in your fryer. If the batter doesn't adhere well, add more flour.

Ingredients:

- vegetable oil, for frying
- 2 acorn squash (local, unwaxed)
- ½ teaspoon salt
- ¾ cup unbleached flour
- ½ cup cornstarch
- 2 tablespoons sugar
- 1 large egg, beaten
- 1 cup ice-cold beer

Directions:

Wash and cut squash into thin half-moon shapes. Combine remaining ingredients for batter; mix just to combine.

Heat oil to 350°F. Do a test batch by frying one or two pieces until lightly browned and crunchy. The batter should be light and crisp. If too thin add some more flour, little by little. If too thick add a touch more beer or water. Toss the squash in the batter and fry until crispy, about 2–3 minutes. Drain on paper towel and season with salt while hot from the fryer. Serve straight away with assorted dipping sauces.

Roasted Spaghetti Squash Boat

Ingredients:

- 1 medium spaghetti squash
- ½ cup parmesan cheese
- 3 cloves chopped garlic
- 1 teaspoon lemon zest
- 2 teaspoons crushed red pepper flakes
- truffle oil
- pinch salt and pepper

Directions:

Cut spaghetti squash in half and remove pith and seeds. Rub squash with olive oil. Place the cut side down in ½ inch of water. Roast it in a 375°F oven for 40–45 minutes. It will start to steam.

Use a fork to rake out the squash. Mix the squash with parmesan cheese, garlic, lemon zest, and crushed red pepper flakes.

Stuff the squash mixture back into the shell. Garnish with parsley and parmesan and drizzle with truffle oil.

Cushaw Squash Cutlets

RAMA COUSIK

This recipe is one of my favorites for cold days. These squash cutlets tickle the palate and elevate my mood. I usually only use potatoes in this recipe, but this time I added some heirloom cushaw squash, growing in abundance in my backyard. The results were delicious. Everyone took more than two helpings, and they all wanted to know my recipe.

Ingredients:

- 1 medium-sized cushaw squash (substitute butternut squash if you prefer)
- 2–3 medium-sized potatoes
- ½ cup cilantro
- 1 teaspoon cumin seeds
- 1 teaspoon red chili powder
- 1 teaspoon salt
- pinch of asafetida (substitute garlic powder or onion powder for asafetida)
- 1 cup rice flour

Directions:

Wash and cut squash and potato into large pieces. Cook until soft and drain water. (Reserve the water for use as vegetable stock in another recipe.)

Add everything else except the rice flour. Mash the vegetables using a wire whisk. Add rice flour and mix well.

Shape the dough into rounds and cook on a nonstick pan. You can spray a little olive oil if you want to.

Turn the rounds over and cook until they are golden brown on both sides.

Smoky Butternut Squash Soup

STEPHANIE WEAVER

Butternut squash is a comfort food from way back, when my mom used to buy frozen blocks of it and then serve it with salt and pepper in a pool of melted margarine.

I still sometimes buy the frozen blocks, but I'd much rather buy the actual squash, throw it in a roasting pan, and play with the cooked chunks.

This soup comes together very quickly if your squash is already roasted. The crispy sage leaves and toasted pepitas add crunch and just the right herb note to the smoky soup.

Ingredients:

- 16 ounces butternut squash roasted
- 3 ounces potatoes
- 2 cups vegetable stock
- 1 teaspoon smoked paprika
- ¼ teaspoon dried cumin
- ¼ teaspoon liquid smoke
- ⅛ teaspoon chipotle powder
- 8 fresh sage leaves
- ½ cup raw unsalted pumpkin seeds (pepitas)

Directions:

Preheat the oven to 400°F.

Roast the butternut squash: cut off each end, slice lengthwise. Scoop out the seeds with a grapefruit spoon. Spray or brush cut sides with oil. Place cut side down on a rimmed baking sheet. Bake for 45 minutes or until soft and tender.

Scoop out the flesh from the skin.

Wash the potato and cut up into small cubes. Put in a microwave-safe container with filtered water and 1 teaspoon salt. Cook until fork tender. Drain. (You can also roast the whole potato in the same pan as the squash.)

Combine all the ingredients except the sage and the pepitas in a blender and blend until smooth.

Toast the pepitas in a dry skillet. Remove from skillet.

Lightly spray the skillet and add the sage leaves. Lightly fry on each side until crispy.

Top the soup with crispy sage leaves and the toasted pepitas right before serving.

Gnocchi with Butternut Squash and Gorgonzola

DANIEL ORR

I'm convinced that you could cook anything in brown butter and sage and it would turn out delicious, but this is especially true for gnocchi.

Gnocchi are small potato dumplings with a gentle sour flavor. They can be finicky to prepare, so be careful to not overcook them. When they float to the top of your salted water, they should be soft, tender, and ready to enjoy. For this dish, cool them down after their dip in the boiling water and set them aside as you prepare the other components—but keep that pot of warm water handy!

I also grabbed a butternut squash from a local farmer to add some Indiana flavor to this dish. Just as you cooked the gnocchi ahead of time, roast the squash before you start preparing this dish.

If you're cooking a squash from your garden or grown by a farmer you trust, you can actually leave the skin on. If you pick up a squash from the grocery store, however, chances are it will be waxed. To remove the wax, plunge it into warm water and scrub scrub scrub!

One more tip before you're off and running with this recipe: Never add cheese to pasta still on the heat. Be sure to turn off the burner or remove the pan from the stove altogether and then stir in the parmesan. Otherwise the fat and the milk solids will separate and it will get greasy. Not tasty!

This was a dish our crew simply could not stop snacking on—the plate was practically licked clean!

Ingredients:

- olive oil
- handful of shallots, chopped
- handful of sage, chopped
- nugget of butter (be generous!)
- gnocchi
- 1 butternut squash
- 2 tablespoons water
- ¼ cup Parmesan cheese
- handful toasted walnuts
- sprinkle lemon juice
- crumbled Gorgonzola cheese (garnish)
- sage leaves, fried (garnish)
- salt and pepper to taste

Directions:

Slice butternut squash in half and season with olive oil, salt, pepper, and spices of your choice. Add two tablespoons of water to a roasting pan and place squash cut side down. Roast in a 400°F oven for 20–25 minutes or until soft and caramelized.

To cook the gnocchi, poach it in salted water for 2–4 minutes. Cooked gnocchi will float to the top. Remove them and set aside.

In a large pan, add olive oil and the nugget of butter. Throw in a handful of chopped shallots and a handful of chopped sage.

Cut the roasted butternut squash into cubes. Add them to the pan to heat them through. Add cooked gnocchi to the pan, too.

Add 2 tablespoons of water to the pan and turn off the heat. Stir in parmesan cheese. Season with salt and pepper to taste.

Finish the dish with toasted walnuts, a sprinkle of lemon juice, and as many crumbles of Gorgonzola cheese as you like.

For a special garnish, fry up some sage leaves. (Cook whole sage leaves in olive oil until crispy. Remove from pan and soak up excess oil with a paper towel. Then sprinkle with kosher salt.)

winter

❄ One Farmer, Five Dogs, and the Eighty Sheep They Tend

Denice Rackley uses a cane to get around her farm. She has a brace on her right knee, but she says it's a pre-sheep injury. It's like she's moving in slow motion guiding a couple of baby lambs to join the herd.

Her farm down near the Ohio River is 100 acres. The cropland she rents out, the woodland she leaves alone, and the pastureland is for the sheep. She has about 80 ewes right now that are lambing. Most of them have numbers spray painted on their backs, with matching numbers on their lambs so she can keep them straight.

Inside the barn, the sheep are loud. But Rackley's dogs are quiet. A handful of border collies lay in their cages, looking up at us as we walk by. She opens one of the crates. "This is Meg. She's five years old. She was born and raised and trained here. So I'll use Meg to bring the new mom and lamb up to put behind the barn with the others," she says.

Meg is shaking with anticipation. Rackley gives her commands—lie down, wait. The sheep are focused on the dog. And now it's quieter than it's been all morning. Rackley says border collies are naturally quiet when they work, which is good because barking dogs make sheep nervous. Rackley closes the gate. She gives Meg the okay to start her approach, and the sheep scatter.

"Come by" means to run clockwise around the animals. "Away" is counterclockwise.

"Lie down. That'a girl," she says. Meg drops to her belly. She's isolated the ewe and its new lamb. Rackley commands Meg to lead the animals through the gate to a holding pen. Meg then trots off to drink from a trough of water.

Rackley grabs the lamb and wraps a band around its tail. It'll fall off in 2–3 weeks. Then, it's a dash of purple spray paint. This ewe and her lamb get the number 43.

Rackley has been working with dogs almost as long as she's been a rancher. She's from Cincinnati but moved to South Dakota in 1998 to work on a ranch. A neighbor there told her how helpful dogs can be when working with livestock, so she got a puppy and she trained it. Or rather, the dog trained Rackley. That was Luke. Together, they tended a flock of 50 ewes.

Eight years ago, Rackley moved back to her mother's Midwest farm to raise sheep and train dogs. Here, by the junction of Indiana, Kentucky, and Ohio, she feels isolated. "I really liked it out west, just because of the lifestyle, the people. They're very dependent on neighbors, and there's more of a community-type setting there. Here, you pretty much have to do it all yourself." She says her dogs take the place of several people, in farmwork and, it seems, in companionship.

Rackley breeds border collies, and while she sells most of them, she keeps a select few to train to work with sheep. Her youngest is Zeva. She's about a year and a half old. Zeva and Luke shared time on the farm just briefly.

"When dogs get to 10–12–13 years old, they start slowing down. You have that bond with another dog while you're kind of letting go of the older one," she says.

Zeva jumps up on Rackley's lap and gives her a good lick on the cheek. Then, the dog turns her attention back to the sheep.

❄ Cold Hardy Greens Thrive in the Hoop House

As Stephanie Solomon was preparing the soil inside Mother Hubbard's Cupboard's hoop house in the fall, she had visions of cold hardy greens growing throughout the winter.

Fast forward to a chilly and overcast late-December day. The garden is bursting at the seams with kale, bok choy, salad greens, and collard greens.

"Gardens are exciting that way, watching them change," says Solomon. "It's a good life lesson."

Hoop houses are essentially greenhouses without electricity. They are constructed of a sturdy frame with a special plastic covering.

"It's a great opportunity to figure out methods of growing without needing to be on the grid."

A hoop house absorbs heat and light from the sun while protecting the crops from wind, frost, and extreme cold. It can extend the growing season on both ends by allowing you to plant your seeds sooner in the spring and to continue growing food into the winter.

Solomon says one of the first steps was figuring out how to generate heat inside the hoop house. She placed a couple of 55-gallon barrels filled with water next to the entrances. The water absorbs heat during the day and then emits it at night.

To give the plants even more protection from harsh Indiana winters, she built a low tunnel. Think of it like a mini–hoop house within the big hoop house. When temperatures get below 35 degrees, she pulls a cloth blanket over the top of the low tunnel. This cover protects the plants from frost while still letting light in. When the temperature dips below 28 degrees, she adds a layer of plastic.

In spite of some hard frosts, Solomon is happy to report that everything has survived. The kale in particular is positively thriving. That might change if the temperatures continue to get colder, encouraging the plants go dormant. But for now, she's excited to harvest a couple grocery bags of greens every week.

"That feels like such an exciting thing when all of our other gardens are put to bed for the season," she says.

❈ Cold Weather Greens from the Hoop House

SARAH KAISER

This morning I put on my winter boots, walked out the back door into single-digit weather, and trudged through the snow to our neighbor's hoop house. It's a passive solar greenhouse made of PVC piping and a plastic cover. No electricity necessary for the hoop house. I ducked under the plastic covering and entered a small, warm oasis of growth. Despite the snow and ice, the plants are looking great!

In exchange for help with weeding, I was invited to pick some of the delicious fresh salad greens. There's a great combination of flavors and colors in the spicy salad mix, with deep purple mustardy leaves, spinach, arugula, and lots of other things I couldn't identify. Who knows, I might have enjoyed a few weeds alongside the real salad parts.

The hoop house is a great way to extend the growing season, and I plan on making lots of salads over the winter—at least as long as my fingers don't freeze off while harvesting!

Creamy Tahini Dressing

Ingredients:
- ½ cup tahini
- ½ cup olive oil
- ½ cup water
- ¼ cup soy sauce (or tamari)
- 2 tablespoons red wine vinegar
- 2 tablespoons lemon juice
- 4 cloves garlic
- 1 teaspoon ground ginger

Directions:
Mince the garlic. Combine all ingredients, and whisk until blended. Toss dressing with salad greens and serve immediately.

Swiss Chard Gratin

DANIEL ORR

Most of us probably know the gratin preparation best from potatoes au gratin. But no spuds will be harmed in the preparation of this dish. Instead, we've got some gorgeous rainbow Swiss chard.

I created this recipe when I was cooking in Europe. The funny thing is that Europeans eat the stems and discard the leaves. When I moved back to the States, I noticed that Americans eat the leaves and discard the stems. In the spirit of international diplomacy, I changed this recipe to include both the stems and the leaves.

First order of business is to blanch and shock the Swiss chard. You will cook it in boiling salted water and then plunge it in an ice water bath. Be sure to wring out as much excess water as you can before adding the chard to the other ingredients.

Now for the good stuff . . .

This recipe includes a béchamel sauce. It's ¼ cup flour and ¼ cup butter, cooked down to a roux. Add three cups milk and cook for 10–15 minutes.

While this recipe will never be vegan, you could make it vegetarian by substituting capers or chopped olives for the bacon. And in case you have kohlrabi leaves in your fridge, those would work wonderfully in this recipe as well.

Ingredients:

- 12 bunches Swiss chard leaves and stems, cleaned, cut into 2-inch pieces, cooked
- 1 cup chopped bacon
- 2 ½ tablespoons roughly chopped fresh thyme
- 1 tablespoon lemon zest, cut into brunoise
- 2 teaspoons minced garlic
- 2 teaspoons Chinese 5-spice powder (a combination of cinnamon, cloves, fennel, star anise, and peppercorns)
- 1 teaspoon freshly ground pepper
- 3 cups béchamel sauce
- 8 eggs, beaten
- 1 ½ cups grated parmesan cheese
- 2 cups buttered breadcrumbs
- 3 buttered gratin dishes

Directions:

Blanch and shock chopped Swiss chard. Be sure to wring out all excess water.

Combine chard, bacon, thyme, zest, garlic, and spices. Carefully toss to combine. In a separate bowl, whisk together béchamel, eggs, and cheese. Fold into chard mix. Taste and adjust seasoning. Pour into gratin dishes. Coat with bread crumbs, then sprinkle parmesan cheese on top. Bake at 250–275°F for 1 hour.

Collard Greens with Ginger and Sesame

Break out your largest pan for this recipe. I recommend a 12- to 14-inch diameter pan. It may seem excessively large when you're just cooking for your family, but the large surface area will give your food more heat exposure, so you'll cook quicker. As a result, keep an eye on your garlic. When it has just browned (and it will get to this point quickly!), immediately toss in the greens to slow the cooking process. Any cold ingredient, like onions, will have the same effect.

Ingredients:

- ¼ cup olive oil
- 1 tablespoon sesame oil
- 5 cloves garlic
- 2 tablespoons minced fresh ginger
- ½ teaspoon crushed red pepper flakes
- 2 bunches collard greens, cut chiffonade (very thin ribbons)
- 3 tablespoons oyster sauce (found in the Asian section of your supermarket)
- 2 tablespoons sesame seeds (white, black, or mixed)
- 2 oranges, peeled and cut into slices (garnish)
- 1 teaspoon orange zest
- dash of fresh-squeezed orange juice (garnish)
- salt and pepper to taste
- shredded coconut (garnish)

Directions:

In a large sauté pan, heat the olive and sesame oils over high heat. Add the garlic and cook just until it begins to color.

Quickly add the ginger, chili flakes, and collard greens and toss together.

Add ¼ cup of water and quickly steam the greens. (Do not overcook the greens! They should be bright green and toothsome.)

Remove to a bowl to avoid overcooking and add the oyster sauce, sesame seeds, and orange zest.

Toss to combine and season with salt and freshly ground pepper. Garnish with orange segments, shredded coconut, and a dash of fresh orange juice. Serve hot or at room temperature.

Brazilian-Style Collard Greens

Ingredients:

- 2 bunches collard greens
- 2 tablespoons extra-virgin olive oil
- 1 tablespoon butter
- 1 large shallot, minced (about ⅓ cup)
- 2 cloves garlic, minced
- freshly grated lemon zest
- freshly minced ginger
- sea salt, to taste
- ground pepper, to taste

Directions:

Cut tough end stems off collard greens. Rinse leaves and gather them together into 2 piles. Take each pile and roll it tightly. Cut them into thin strips crosswise. You should have about 8 cups.

Heat oil and butter in a large, heavy skillet over medium heat. Sauté shallot with garlic, stirring often, until lightly browned, about 3 minutes.

Add greens and salt and pepper. Cook, stirring often, for about 5 minutes or until greens are tender but bright green.

Add lemon zest and ginger and stir to incorporate. Taste and adjust seasoning. Collards should be crunchy but tender. If they aren't tender enough add a touch of water.

Polenta with Brussels Sprouts

We're going to turn everyone into a brussels sprouts lover.

This recipe starts off with blanching the brussels sprouts. Keep them a bit crunchy because we are going to cook them more later on. I like them just like this. They're almost like a crudités vegetable. You could eat them cold and dip them into a blue cheese dip.

But this dish is really about the polenta. When cooking the polenta discs in the pan, don't fiddle with them too much. We want to develop a nice crust on both sides, and just like cooking mushrooms, this means putting them in the pan and leaving them alone. You'll know they need to be flipped to the other side when they can move freely in the pan.

Ingredients:

- 2 dozen brussels sprouts
- 1 dozen slices of polenta
- cooking oil
- handful grated parmesan cheese
- 1 teaspoon garlic, minced
- several slices of Taleggio cheese
- salt and pepper to taste
- handful chopped herbs (garnish)
- olive oil (garnish)
- red pepper coulis (garnish)

Directions:

Blanch the brussels sprouts. (Cook in boiling water until al dente, then plunge them into cold water.)

Heat cooking oil in a sauté pan and brown polenta discs on both sides. Sprinkle the polenta with grated parmesan cheese. Don't rush this, and don't fiddle with the food too much! Flip when they move freely in the pan. Set polenta aside.

In the same pan, add oil and garlic. Warm brussels sprouts in hot water, then add them to the pan. Season with salt and pepper, but not too much because parmesan cheese is naturally salty.

Garnish with red pepper coulis, chopped herbs, and olive oil. Finish the dish with slices of Taleggio on top of the polenta.

Fresh Brussels Sprouts Salad

Brussels sprouts are one food that everyone seems to have an opinion about: they either love 'em or hate 'em. Personally, I love brussels sprouts. Even if you've had bad experiences with brussels sprouts in the past, give this raw salad a try. I think it'll change your mind.

Ingredients:

- 1 ½ pounds brussels sprouts, freshest you can find
- 3 tablespoons extra-virgin olive oil
- 2–3 tablespoons fresh lemon juice
- 1 teaspoon fresh thyme leaves
- ⅓ cup fresh scallions or chives, minced
- 1 teaspoon Dijon mustard
- 1 teaspoon minced garlic
- 1 ⅓ cups toasted sunflower seeds
- ¼ cup parmesan cheese
- pinch of red pepper flakes
- salt and pepper to taste

Directions:

Shred the brussels sprouts thinly using your sharpest knife or a kitchen mandoline. Five minutes before serving, place the shredded sprouts in a large mixing bowl and toss with the remaining ingredients, being careful not to break up the sprouts too much. Season to taste with salt and pepper.

Roasted Curried Cauliflower

STEPHANIE WEAVER

First, let me say that I used to hate cauliflower.

I hated it raw. I hated it boiled. I hated it steamed. The only way I would tolerate it was smothered in cheddar cheese sauce. When our friends Will and Carolyn had us over for dinner and served roasted cauliflower, I wanted to be a good guest, so I took a small serving and hoped it wouldn't be too terrible.

It was a revelation. Gone was that bitter, sulfurous taste. It was replaced with lovely chewiness and a crispy exterior.

Ingredients:

- 1 head cauliflower
- 2 tablespoons olive oil
- 1 tablespoon fresh lemon juice
- 1 tablespoon mild curry powder
- ½ teaspoon salt
- ½ teaspoon smoked paprika
- ¼ teaspoon chipotle powder or cayenne

Directions:

Preheat oven to 450°F.

Wash the cauliflower and shake it dry. Remove the leaves and cut out the core. Cut the cauliflower in long slices, about ½-inch thick.

In a large bowl, whisk together oil, lemon juice, curry powder, and salt.

Add cauliflower slices (and optional other vegetables) and toss to coat. Spread vegetables in a single layer in a large baking pan that you have sprayed with oil spray.

Bake until cauliflower is tender, chewy, and brown, 25 to 30 minutes. Stir after 15 minutes, flipping the slices over with tongs.

If you want to create more of a main-dish meal, add 6 red potatoes, scrubbed and then precooked 3–4 minutes (boiled or microwaved). Cut them into medium chunks after precooking. Cut up a peeled yellow, white, or red onion into chunks. Double the oil/seasoning blend and toss all the veggies with the cauliflower. I bake the potatoes in a separate pan, as they often need a little more time, even when precooked.

This is also an excellent and surprising way to prepare sliced plantains. Flip them after 10 minutes of baking, and check after 20 minutes. They will burn more easily.

If you have leftovers, you can throw them in a blender with vegetable stock and puree them into a lovely soup.

Tuscan-Style Roasted Broccoli

DANIEL ORR

Broccoli can often be shoved to the side of a dinner plate, especially if it's competing with a foil-wrapped baked potato and a big hunk of meat. This dish is served with enough extra goodies that it can stand strong as a main course. It's also a quick dish to prepare.

Ingredients:

- 1 head broccoli
- ¼ cup olive oil
- 1 tablespoon chopped garlic
- 10–12 basil leaves, torn
- 2–3 sprigs rosemary
- ¼ teaspoon lemon zest
- ¼ teaspoon crushed red pepper

- salt and pepper to taste
- anchovies
- Gorgonzola cheese
- black olives
- toasted pine nuts
- tomatoes
- juice of ½ lemon

Directions:

Cut broccoli florets into thirds and blanch them. Spread the basil leaves, rosemary, and chopped garlic in a pan. Add blanched broccoli. Sprinkle with olive oil. Cook in broiler for 2–3 minutes, until caramelized. Arrange broccoli, basil, and rosemary on a platter. Top with anchovies, Gorgonzola cheese, black olives, toasted pine nuts, and tomatoes. Dress with a squeeze of lemon juice and a drizzle of olive oil.

❋ All Are Welcome at Joshua Ploeg's Pop-up Café

Eric Ayotte has moved all his chairs, the couch, and the TV out of the way. "We are in our living room that we've now kind of changed and formed into a little café," he says. "Trying to give as much of an authentic café feel as we possibly can here at our house."

It's about one hour before guests should start filing in. At this point, most dinner party hosts would be frantic with last-minute preparations, but the hosts are both relaxed. Charlie Jones says this is one of the easiest dinner parties she's ever thrown. "We get to host people, make people feel welcome, but we don't have to do any of the cooking," she says. "We've got a wonderful chef here to cook all the food."

The chef is a soft-spoken guy who's mopping his sweaty brow and breathing a sigh of relief after a long day of cooking. Joshua Ploeg has scattered the six courses of his vegan feast all over the house. "There's ample space here, but if I'm plating, too, then I have to put things in cubby holes," he tells me, as we admire the brownie shortbread resting on top of the dryer in the utility room.

Ask Ploeg where he's from and he's not really sure how to answer. He's been traveling the country for much of the past decade, and that suits him just fine. He started off as a musician, traveling from basement show to basement show with several different punk bands. Occasionally he would do food demonstrations or prepare snacks for the guests. He received enough positive feedback that he compiled his own cookbook.

He then tapped into his existing contacts in the DIY music scene to jump-start his idea of a traveling pop-up cafe. "The tour model is absolutely from playing in punk bands, and I just decided that it was a great idea to use that model to cook," he says. "It actually works better for cooking than it does for playing music . . . Your band's not going to play seven shows in Minneapolis but I can cook seven dinners without much trouble there."

The details of the menu come to Ploeg as he shops for ingredients. "I write notes in line as we're checking out and everything's going by on the conveyor belt, which is fun because usually the checker is looking at me funny," he says. "Then I explain the whole secret café idea, the traveling paid dinner party, and they're amazed."

Ploeg is calling this his Mediterranean-Meets-Californian Vegan Hoosier Feast:

- Lima bean minestrone soup
- Gluten-free pasta with roasted pepper, tomato, paprika, and cinnamon broth
- Pineapple Caesar salad
- Roasted vegetable terrine with crispy potatoes, rutabagas, spinach, and eggplant
- Black-eyed pea coleslaw with purple cabbage and cider vinaigrette
- Brownie shortbread with fruit compote

This isn't a money-making venture for Ploeg. Guests are encouraged to contribute what they can to help pay for groceries. He takes a little bit to cover his personal expenses, but he doesn't need much to get by.

Once the dinner party is over, Eric and Charlie will move the couch back into place in the living room, and that's where Joshua will crash for the night.

❊ Pizza Party

BAKING THE PERFECT HOMEMADE PIZZA: USING A PIZZA STONE

Plenty of amateur pizza chefs swear by pizza stones. If you've never used one before, it's not just a gimmick. Pizza stones ensure your crust will be baked all the way through without burning the edges and leaving soggy dough in the middle.

But why do they work better than metal cookie sheets? Chemist and science writer Leigh Krietsch Boerner says that it has to do with water distribution. Remember studying capillary action in high school? How when you put the end of a piece of paper into water, the water travels right up the paper? Boerner says that a pizza stone basically does the same thing.

"It has pores the water will travel into," she says. "If you have an area that has a lot of water and an area that is dry, the areas like to even out—nature really loves to make things even out—so the water will travel from the crust into your stone."

That's why there isn't a gooey, undercooked spot in the center of your pizza crust—the stone enables water to escape even from the parts that don't have good contact with the hot air in the oven.

Since pizza stones are just a type of ceramic, the cheap ones will work just as well as the expensive ones. Once you have a pizza stone in your possession, the pros recommend you cure it. First, wash the stone with soap and water to make sure you're starting with a completely clean stone. Then, rub a small amount of vegetable oil evenly all over the stone. Put it in your oven, turn the oven to 450°F, and let it bake for 30 minutes. Then turn off the heat and allow the stone cool down in the oven. Don't open the oven to check on it. Let it do its thing, or you run the risk of your pizza stone cracking!

Baking the Perfect Homemade Pizza

DANIEL ORR

Ingredients:

- 1 cup warm water
- 1 tablespoon sugar
- ¼ ounce dry yeast
- 1 cup cake flour
- 1 ¼ cups all-purpose flour
- 1 cup whole-wheat flour
- 1 tablespoon sea salt
- 2 tablespoons extra-virgin olive oil

Directions:

Combine first three ingredients and proof 5 minutes until foamy. Mix dry ingredients with dough hook. Then add wet ingredients and olive oil. Knead on low for 10 minutes. Place in an oiled bowl and cover. Leave at room temperature for 2 hours. Divide and refrigerate until needed. Proof 1 additional hour before rolling, topping, and baking.

Roll or stretch your dough out on the back of a cooking sheet. Brush a little olive oil onto the dough to prevent moisture seeping into the crust, then add your choice of toppings. Sprinkle coarsely ground grains or cornmeal on a baking stone preheated in a 450–500°F oven. Slide the pie off the baking sheet and onto the stone with a jiggling motion. Bake one pizza at a time until the crust is browned on the edges and crisp throughout (10–15 minutes).

Finish with a drizzle of olive oil or other flavored oil and a sprinkle of freshly ground black pepper, sea salt, and very roughly chopped Italian parsley.

Wild Bianca

Ingredients:

- 2 tablespoons extra-virgin olive oil
- ¼ cup pesto
- ½ cup assorted mushrooms (such as shiitake, oyster, cremini, or foraged mushrooms)
- ¼ cup ricotta
- ½ teaspoon red pepper flakes
- 1 tablespoon parmesan cheese, grated
- truffle oil
- salt and pepper (as needed)

The Veganista vegan

Ingredients:

- 3 tablespoons white bean hummus, loosened with a touch of water
- 1 garlic clove, minced
- 1 red onion ring, grilled
- 1 zucchini slice, grilled
- 3 eggplant slices, grilled
- 6 kalamata olives
- ½ roasted red bell pepper, sliced
- ½ plum tomato, wedged
- extra-virgin olive oil as needed
- fresh rosemary and thyme as needed, chopped
- salt and pepper

Vegan Pizza Party

vegan

NATALIE RAE GOOD

New York is slice city. On any given corner you can get two wide thin-crust slices and a can of soda for just a few George Washingtons. But for those of the vegan persuasion, it can be a bit harder (though not impossible) to grab a slice on the go. Regardless, the city's love for pizza has rubbed off on me, and I am forever in love with heaping vegetable toppings and sweet, thick tomato sauce atop a crunchy crust. Here's an easy recipe for dough that will yield 3–5 pizzas depending on size and thickness. Invite some friends over and be creative with your toppings.

Vegan Pizza Dough

Ingredients:

- 2 teaspoons active dry yeast
- 2 teaspoons sugar
- 2 cups warm water
- 5 cups all-purpose flour
- 2 tablespoons flaxseed meal
- 2 teaspoons salt

Directions:

In a large bowl, whisk together the yeast, warm water, and sugar. Let proof in a warm place for 5 minutes. Once yeast is frothy, add the salt, flaxseed meal, and flour one cup at a time. Knead until the dough is smooth. Let the dough rise in a large oiled bowl for two hours. Don't rush it! Punch down dough and divide into 3–5 balls. Let rest for another 20 minutes. Prepare your toppings.

Nondairy Cashew Ricotta Cheese

Ingredients:

- 1 cup raw cashews
- 3 cloves garlic
- 3 tablespoons olive oil
- 2 tablespoons nutritional yeast
- 2 lemons, juiced (one of these should also be zested)
- 1 pound firm tofu, pressed and broken into pieces
- 1 ½ teaspoons salt

Directions:

In a food processor, blend the cashews, garlic, olive oil, nutritional yeast, lemon juice, and lemon zest until a thick paste forms.

Add the tofu and salt and blend until smooth.

Butternut Squash and Sage Pizza

STEPHANIE WEAVER

Ingredients:

- ¼ butternut squash, cut and roasted until tender
- 1 small red onion
- 1 handful fresh sage leaves
- smoky white sauce (recipe below)
- 1 pizza crust

Directions:

Put the cashews for the pizza sauce in water to soak (see recipe below).

While they are soaking, peel the onion, cut in half, and cut into the thinnest slices you can. Heat 1 tablespoon olive oil in a cast-iron skillet or sauté pan over medium heat. Add the onion, stirring until coated with oil. Turn down the heat a little and cook about 30 minutes, stirring occasionally until tender, golden, and caramelized.

Preheat oven to 375°F. Place a pizza stone in the center of the oven. (You can use a baking sheet if you don't have a pizza stone.) Cut a piece of parchment paper a little larger than the pizza. Thinly slice the roasted squash pieces. Thinly slice the sage leaves into ribbons. Make the smoky pizza sauce. Spread the sauce on the pizza crust and top with squash, caramelized onions, and sage ribbons.

Put the pizza on the parchment and set it on top of the pizza stone or baking sheet. Bake for about 15 minutes, rotating once, until golden and melty.

Smoky White Pizza Sauce

Ingredients:

- 1 cup raw cashews, soaked
- 2 cloves garlic
- 2 tablespoons nutritional yeast
- 2 tablespoons fresh lemon juice
- 1 ½ tablespoons liquid aminos or gluten-free soy sauce
- 1 tablespoon extra-virgin olive oil, or oil from sun-dried tomatoes
- 1 teaspoon smoked paprika
- ¼ teaspoon liquid smoke
- 2 tablespoons filtered water

Directions:

Put the soaked cashews along with the peeled garlic and all the other ingredients into your blender. If you have a high-speed blender with a tamper, use the tamper. If not, you'll have to stop fairly often and scrape down the sides to get everything to blend. Add just enough water, if needed, to get it to blend to a thick, smooth, creamy sauce.

Spread it on the pizza crust, adding your prepared toppings. Bake about 15 minutes until the cashew cream sauce starts to darken.

Zucchini Pizza Crust

DIANA BAUMAN

The zucchini harvest this year has been tremendous. I've been using them in any way that I can—chopping them up and throwing them into anything and everything I'm cooking. Honestly, I was just about done with zucchini until I heard about zucchini crust pizza. My first attempt was good, but the crust was too soft and quiche-like for my taste. It had to be eaten with a fork. What I wanted was a crust that could withstand a lot of toppings and that I could pick up with my hands, so I revamped the cooking process. The result was pizza the way I like it.

Ingredients:

- 8 cups shredded zucchini
- 1 cup shredded cheddar cheese
- ⅔ cup flour (or almond flour)
- 2 cloves garlic, pressed or minced
- 2 teaspoons dried oregano
- 1 teaspoon dried basil
- 2 eggs, beaten
- ½ teaspoon salt

Directions:

Preheat oven to 550°F with a pizza stone inside. In a large bowl, toss the zucchini with 1 teaspoon coarse salt and set aside for 15 minutes. Squeeze the excess moisture out of the squash by wrapping it up in a clean tea towel or cheesecloth and wringing it out. Place the shredded zucchini back into the bowl and add cheddar cheese, flour, garlic, oregano, basil, eggs, and salt. With your hands, mix everything together.

Place the zucchini mixture onto a piece of parchment paper at least 15 inches in diameter, set on something solid that will make it easy to transfer into the oven. Using your fingers, spread the zucchini crust mixture to form a circle about 14 inches in diameter and ½-inch thick. Pinch the edges up so that it forms a nice crust. Transfer the crust on the parchment paper onto the heated pizza stone in the oven. Bake for 8 minutes or until the crust starts to brown. Then, transfer the pizza on the parchment paper out of the oven, onto the solid surface you used before. Top with sauce and topping. Transfer the pizza on the parchment paper back onto the heated pizza stone in the oven and bake for an additional 4 minutes.

Homemade Pizza Sauce

Ingredients:

- 4 large tomatoes, quartered
- 2 tablespoons olive oil
- 2 cloves garlic, pressed or minced
- 1 tablespoon fresh oregano
- 1 tablespoon fresh thyme
- 1 teaspoon salt

Directions:

In a large heavy-bottomed sauce pan, add the tomatoes, olive oil, garlic, oregano, thyme, and salt. Bring to a boil, breaking up the tomato. Lower heat and then simmer for 15–20 minutes. Once simmered, puree all of the ingredients in a blender.

❋ Choose Your Chickens Well

JANA WILSON

January is the time of the year when chicken catalogs arrive in the mailbox. If you're looking to expand your skills beyond gardening, you can take this opportunity to join the bird-raising community.

Just as you need to know whether your plants are annuals or perennials, or for sunny or shady areas, you need to know what purpose you have in mind for your chickens. Remember that chickens have been bred for possibly hundreds of years to get particular characteristics.

How do you choose?

The answer is a combination of what you want to use them for and what you like to look at. If you don't think your chickens are beautiful, then you won't be as happy with them.

EGG LAYERS

These chickens will be smaller and lighter. They will have a higher production of somewhat larger eggs than other types. You can choose between white or brown egg layers.

Did you know that you can tell the color of the eggs a hen will lay by her earlobes? White earlobes mean white eggs and red earlobes mean brown eggs. There are a few exceptions to this, such as Arucanas and Ameraucanas, which both lay green or blue eggs and have red earlobes. These pullets (a female chicken under one year) will generally start laying at around

5 or 6 months and continue on for possibly up to 10 years, though you won't get the quantity of eggs you'll get when they are young.

Popular egg-laying breeds include the Leghorn, Barred or Plymouth Rock, and the Rhode Island Red. Many of the Mediterranean class birds—my beloved Sicilian Buttercups are in this category—are prolific layers.

MEAT BIRDS

Chickens bred specifically for meat production will grow very quickly, as they are meant to be butchered at a relatively young age—usually in 5 to 14 weeks. These birds will not be great egg layers, as most of their energy goes into body weight, not egg production.

Birds that are considered strictly meat birds are not usually a traditional breed but more often a combination of different breeds that results in a large, fast-growing, and tender roast chicken.

The best known of these is called the Cornish X (pronounced "cross") Rock, though another new variety of bird called the Freedom Ranger is becoming more popular. If you are looking for a heritage breed for meat birds, some people have tried the traditional Cornish breed with great success.

DUAL-PURPOSE

Somewhere in the middle are the dual-purpose chickens, those that can be used for both egg laying and meat. They won't lay as many eggs as a Leghorn, but their meatier bodies make them useful as possible Sunday dinner as well.

New Hampshires, Plymouth Rocks, and Wyandottes are all examples of dual-purpose chickens. Also consider two older American breeds, the Dominique and the Delaware.

WINTERIZING YOUR CHICKENS

As winter sets in, like most chicken owners, I've begun taking action to winterize my coop to make life easier for the birds and for me. There are a few simple things you need to know, and after that just relax and enjoy the sight of your colorful birds on the white, snowy ground.

Dampness, not cold, is the enemy most of the time in your coop. This means you still have to have fresh air circulate in your coop even after you seal up all those cracks where the winter wind can creep in. A small wire-covered opening will do the trick while keeping predators out at night.

The birds have all those downy layers of feathers to trap heat in, but trapping the ammonia fumes from the droppings can hurt their lungs or even cause them to get sick.

Depending on the breed of chicken, their combs and wattles can become frostbitten, which can be quite painful. Birds with large combs (usually breeds originating from a warmer place, such as Leghorns) are more susceptible to frostbitten combs and wattles. Birds with smaller combs and wattles usually sail through most weather just fine.

Again, humidity plays a role in frostbite, so keep things dry. Some folks try spreading Vaseline or another oil on the comb to prevent frostbite, but that has never worked for me.

Don't forget to keep an eye on their feet and toes, which also can become frostbitten. (Happily, this doesn't happen too often.)

TO HEAT OR NOT TO HEAT

I remember the very first winter I had chickens. I had to cancel a dinner party one freezing cold Sunday evening after going out in the afternoon and noticing that two of the hens with long, thin red combs were flinging blood from the frozen tips of their combs. I panicked and ran immediately to the hardware store for a heat lamp.

Some say never heat the coop. Others heat at the slightest edge of cold. I fall somewhere in the middle, tending toward only heating if it gets *really* cold. The cutoff point for me is 15 degrees above zero.

If you use a heating device such as a heat lamp or ceramic bulb light, be sure to tie it securely to prevent it falling and causing a fire. Also, place it somewhere above your birds so they cannot snuggle into the light bulb. I've had birds with singed feathers more than once!

Also consider adding 6 inches of bedding to your coop—a method called deep litter. The key is turning the litter to keep it dry while allowing the litter on the bottom to break down. Decomposition gives off heat, which keeps birds a little warmer. I've read that if you throw a little corn on the litter in the evenings, the birds will scratch through it and take care of the turning themselves.

EAT, DRINK, AND BE MERRY

Chickens also need plenty of clean, fresh water at all times in the winter (as well as in the summer). I use plug-in heated dog dishes, which saves a lot of time instead of cracking the ice and adding warm water to the buckets twice a day in the coldest weather.

While the chickens may be fine in freezing temperatures, eggs can freeze, so be sure to gather them more than once a day.

Make sure your chickens have plenty of food to maintain their body weight in the cold. Extra feed, some cakes of suet filled with nuts or fruit, or even plain cracked corn can give your birds a boost. You can throw a handful of corn in the coop in the evening to give the birds a carb-filled snack before hitting the roost.

Taking a few simple steps to prevent trouble and making a point of checking on the birds daily can help them make it through the winter in fine form.

ALL COOPED UP

Now is the time to clean and disinfect your coops. Get your gloves, face mask (to avoid inhaling dust), and a good scraper.

Scrape the roosts, the floor under the litter, the walls, and wherever else there are dried droppings. You can use soap and water or bleach, but make sure it's a sunny day so you can keep the coop open afterward and let it dry.

Sprinkle the floors with an insecticide of some kind, natural or otherwise depending on your methods. I usually coat my roosts with mineral oil to smother any mites or lice hiding in the wood.

It's a good idea to look for unwanted cracks or openings in the coop that could potentially let water in. Yes, you need ventilation, but you don't want rain or snow to get in, as an overly damp coop makes for an unhappy and unhealthy flock.

Let the cold weather begin!

Beef Tongue Pot Roast

CLARA MOORE

I order my grass-fed beef one-half of a cow at a time. Familiar cuts are easy to devour. I make seared tenderloin with crawfish butter sauce, Italian meatball soup, T-bone steaks with local cremini mushrooms and thyme, and lime-marinated flank steak served over rice and beans.

But then I venture into unfamiliar territory—beef tongue.

When I prepare to cook something for the first time, I consult the experts, in this order: *The Joy of Cooking*, the Internet, and my cookbook collection for more ideas. I like to get a cross-section of recipes before I move forward.

In each of these resources, I found the same basic information; the tongue is tough and the skin is almost inedible, but it's incredibly versatile as long as you cook it to tender.

Knowing that people would have a hard time wrapping their minds around tongue, I started with a recipe that most folks would be comfortable with—pot roast.

Ingredients:

- 1 beef tongue
- 10 black peppercorns
- 1 bay leaf
- 2 garlic cloves
- 2 medium yellow onions, chopped
- 3 tablespoons olive oil
- 6 carrots, peeled and cut into 1-inch-long pieces
- 1 head celery, trimmed and chopped
- 8 cups beef stock
- ¼ cup flour
- ¼ cup tepid water
- salt and pepper to taste

Directions:

Place whole tongue in a stockpot. Cover with water and add peppercorns, bay leaf, and whole garlic cloves. Simmer for at least 2 hours, until a knife easily slides in.

Remove tongue from pot and put into ice water. This will make it easy to peel. Remove the skin and cut the tongue into bite size pieces.

In a new stockpot, add olive oil and onions, and cook on medium heat until soft. Add carrots and celery. Cook for 2 minutes.

Add tongue and stock. Simmer until tongue is nice and tender, probably about 30 minutes.

Place water and flour into a small bowl and mix until combined. Add slowly to simmering broth while constantly stirring. Cook for 5 more minutes to remove the taste of flour.

Season with salt and pepper and serve over mashed potatoes.

Garlicky Grilled Beef Heart

Recipes for beef heart were much harder to find, even in my old cookbooks. I ended up being inspired by one that called for marinating and grilling the heart. After a few additions and subtractions, I came up with a garlicky and delicious recipe.

An important lesson I learned from my maiden voyage with beef heart is that you must remove all the veins, as they are way too chewy to eat. Also, overcooked heart is hard to swallow, so it's best to serve it medium rare.

Ingredients:

- 1 beef heart
- ⅓ cup olive oil
- 10 cloves garlic
- 1 tablespoon salt
- 1 teaspoon fresh cracked pepper
- 1 tablespoon fresh rosemary
- splash of apple cider vinegar

Directions:

Wash the beef heart and remove the veins. Slice thinly.

Combine oil, garlic, salt, pepper, vinegar, and rosemary in a food processor. Process into a paste.

Place slices of heart in a bowl and combine with garlic paste. Let marinate for up to 2 hours.

On a hot grill, add marinated beef heart slices. (You can also do this in a hot sauté pan in your kitchen.) Cook for 1–2 minutes on each side, until the pieces are medium rare.

I like to serve this with roasted potatoes and a crisp jicama salad.

Liver and Onions Tacos

BOB ADKINS

I want to change your mind about liver. We're going to cook it right—very simply.

I'm using local lamb livers from our friends at Fiedler Farms. Since I know Jim Fiedler and have seen how he raises his animals, I won't need to cook the livers all the way through. I stop at medium so the livers are still nice and pink in the middle and very moist.

My first step starts the night before when I soak the livers in milk. This leaches out that organ flavor that so many people dislike from the liver.

Ingredients:

- 2 ounces local liver, sliced
- ¼ onion sliced thin
- dry dredge of equal parts cornstarch and cornmeal, with a pinch of salt and pepper
- 1 heaping tablespoon minced garlic
- 1 jalapeño, sliced
- 4–6 warmed tortilla shells
- avocado slices
- fresh pico de gallo
- sliced cabbage
- sour cream

Directions:

Soak liver and onions in milk overnight.

Preheat the oven to 250°F. Wrap flour tortillas in foil and warm them in the oven while you cook the liver and onions.

In a pan, spoon 2 tablespoons of the dry dredge over the liver to cover it. Cook on the stovetop over high heat. Keep it constantly moving. The liver should be cooked to just under medium—as long as you are using local meat from a farmer you trust! Right before the liver is finished cooking, add a heaping tablespoon of minced garlic and jalapeño slices to the hot pan. Cook together to infuse that taste with the liver and onions.

Serve with avocado, sour cream, fresh pico de gallo, and sliced cabbage.

Chicken Liver Crostini

DANIEL ORR

The age-old preservation processes of curing the prime cuts of meat, brining and smoking hams, and making sausages have always been celebratory times in every culture. But what about the remaining parts of the animal? They're known as the offal—the organ meats, the parts that weren't meat or bone.

For many folks, offal just sounds awful. But in Europe, Asia, Latin America, Africa, Australia, and the Middle East, offal is not only accepted—it's prized.

Ingredients:

- 3 tablespoons olive oil
- 1 large sprig rosemary, leaves removed from stem
- 1 teaspoon chopped rosemary
- 3 cloves garlic very thinly sliced (so they may be fried for garlic "chips")
- ½ cup finely minced red onion
- 3 cloves garlic, minced
- ½ teaspoon coarse kosher salt
- ¼ teaspoon freshly ground black pepper
- ½ teaspoon Chinese 5-spice powder (a combination of cinnamon, cloves, fennel, star anise, and peppercorns)
- 8 ounces (about 1 cup) chicken livers, cut into small pieces
- ¼ cup Madeira (or any dry port or sherry)
- ¼ cup roughly chopped parsley
- 12 baguette slices, toasted

Directions:

Line a plate with paper towels for draining rosemary and garlic chips and set aside.

Heat oil in medium skillet over medium-high heat. Add rosemary leaves; sauté until crisp, about 30 seconds. Using slotted spoon, transfer sautéed rosemary to paper towels.

Quickly add garlic slices and cook until just golden and crisp. Do not overcook or they may become bitter. Add to plate with rosemary.

Quickly add red onion to same skillet; sauté until golden, about 3 minutes. Sprinkle in the salt, pepper, and spice powder. Add the minced garlic, liver, and 1 teaspoon chopped rosemary. Cook until liver starts to color then turn. Continue cooking and turning until all sides are lightly browned, about 3 minutes.

Deglaze with Madeira, and cook until wine has evaporated, about 2 minutes. Add chopped parsley and toss. Taste and season as needed.

Spoon onto toasted baguette slices and sprinkle with crispy garlic and rosemary to garnish.

Corned Beef Tongue for Saint Patrick's Day

Throughout history, people have corned beef as a way to preserve it, but in North America, we most associate it with Irish American food traditions—and specifically with St. Patrick's Day. It's usually made with brisket or beef round, but Seth Elgar, executive chef and general manager at No Coast Reserve, is using a fresh, local cow tongue. He will transform it into a corned beef tongue and cabbage terrine for a Saint Patrick's Day special.

Is he worried his guests will be turned off by tongue? Not at all. The corning process infuses plenty of flavor into the meat. "These very strong flavors will help overcome some of the associations people have with a muscle cut like tongue," he says.

Elgar says he has his restaurant's carbon footprint in mind when he uses organ meats in his dishes. "I believe from a sustainability standpoint you have to be willing to use the whole animal and we try to set that example," he says.

Note: This recipe requires some planning, as the tongue will soak for 4–5 days before it's cooked.

Ingredients:

- ¾ cup kosher salt
- ¼ cup sugar
- 2 teaspoons pink salt
- 10 cloves garlic, sliced very thin
- 4 tablespoons pickling spice
- 2 quarts water
- 4 carrots, diced
- 1 head celery, diced
- 2 onions, diced
- 7 cloves of garlic, diced
- 2 bay leaves
- beef tongue
- 2 quarts water

Directions:

Soak the tongue in salt water for 2 hours at room temperature. While it soaks, make the brine. Combine kosher salt, sugar, pink salt, 3 diced garlic cloves, and pickling spice into 1 quart of water. Bring it to a boil, then turn off the burner. Set a 20-minute timer to allow for hot infusion of spices. Pour the brine into a 6-quart container. Add the remaining quart of water. Cool to room temperature, then add the tongue. Cover with a gallon plastic bag filled halfway up with cold water. This will keep it from floating up and out of the brine. Refrigerate for 4–5 days, rotating it in the brine each day to ensure an even cure.

Remove the tongue from the brine and place it in a 4–5-quart pot with a lid. Add carrots, celery, onions, and garlic to the pot. Add enough water to cover vegetables and tongue by 2 inches. Add bay leaves. Bring to a boil, then reduce to a simmer and cook until a paring knife can be inserted into the tongue with no resistance (approximately 4 hours, checking on it every 45 minutes or so). Once the tongue is cooked through, cool it to room temperature by placing the pot in an ice bath in your kitchen sink. (Cooling the meat in its own liquid helps keep it moist.) Once cooled to room temperature, peel the tongue and enjoy!

Traditional Corned Beef

DANIEL ORR

Ingredients:

- raw brisket
- fennel seeds
- coriander seeds
- cumin seeds
- allspice (crushed)
- mustard
- crushed red pepper flakes
- Spanish paprika
- ½ cup pink salt
- bay leaves
- white wine
- white wine vinegar
- Dijon mustard
- thyme leaves (with stems)

Directions:

Mix dry and wet ingredients, to taste, into a brine.

Pour the mixture over a raw cut of brisket. Massage it in a bit, and then refrigerate for about 4–5 days or even up to 2 weeks. Turn the meat on occasion so that it gets evenly spiced. The longer you leave the spice mixture on the beef, the more flavor you'll get.

On the day you plan to enjoy the corned beef, remove the beef from the brine and put it in a pot of cold water. Bring to a boil and cook until tender (about 2 ½ hours).

Add a variety of vegetables to the same broth and cook until tender so they absorb the flavor of the corned beef.

Serve on a big rustic platter with some freshly grated horseradish, some really pungent mustard, and crusty Irish soda bread.

❊ Root Vegetables

BEETS

Big, beautiful, bright red beets. Daniel Orr always plants a row or two in his garden.

"Plant more beet seeds than you're going to need, and then you can thin them as they grow," he says. He was born and raised in southern Indiana and has tended a garden his whole life. "Then you can use those nice tender beet greens in dishes."

Root vegetables love sandy soil. Orr adds some sand to the middle of the row to help his beets, carrots, and turnips grow. "Otherwise, you'll get these gnarled roots that aren't attractive and that can be discouraging," he adds.

The Roast

When it comes to cooking root veggies, the difficulty is allowing enough time for them to cook—45–60 minutes in the oven. But it's worth it, as roasted beets taste sweeter than other preparations.

Place your whole beets (skins intact) on a pan covered in a bed of salt. You'll roast them in a 350°F degree oven until you can insert and easily remove a knife from the beets. Place them directly into a covered plastic container; the steam will make them easier to peel.

The Salad

Chef Orr likes to combine 3 medium-sized beets, 1 crunchy Bosc pear, and a fennel bulb. Dice all the ingredients to the same size. He adds several thin slices of red onion and as much feta cheese as you would like.

The dressing can be as simple as olive oil, lemon juice, and a dash of rice wine vinegar. Adjust the seasoning to your taste, and be careful to not oversalt, as feta is naturally salty.

Pickled Golden Beets

DANIEL ORR

People always complain to me that they don't like beets because they taste like dirt. I think golden beets are a little less that way. I especially love them pickled.

First things first, be sure to steam or boil the beets for at least 45 minutes. Use a sharp knife to test if they're cooked through. If you feel any resistance as the knife pierces the beets, keep cooking. You want the blade to move easily in and out of the veggies.

When all's said and done, here's a storage tip. My grandma taught me to seal the jar lid nice and tight and then turn the jar on its top. This helps it seal as it cools. Once you put it in the fridge (right side up), the flavors will have permeated every single bit of these beets.

Ingredients:

- 4 large golden beet roots
- 1 ½ tablespoons sugar
- 1 teaspoon ginger, minced
- ½ cup vinegar
- ¼ cup water
- 1 cinnamon stick
- ½ hot pepper (you choose)

Directions:

Boil the beets in a large pan of water until tender. Depending on how large the beets are, this could take 45 minutes to 1 hour.

Cool the beets, then peel off the skins. Slice them into wedges. Stuff them into a mason jar.

Heat the sugar, ginger, vinegar, and water until just boiling. Add the cinnamon stick and hot pepper.

Pour the brine over the sliced beets and allow to sit until cooled. Screw the lid onto the jar.

These will stay good in the refrigerator for three weeks. The longer you wait to pop them open, the more pickled they'll taste!

Fennel, Beet, and Blood Orange Salad with Citrus Vinaigrette

DIANA BAUMAN

In my family, we eat a salad nearly every day. This time I decided to come up with something a little bit different using seasonal ingredients.

The more I learn about fennel, the more excited I am to grow it this year in my garden.

It's a delightful herb with a wonderful aroma of anise. The bulb is often eaten raw in salads or chopped and cooked like a root vegetable. The greens can be used as aromatic garnishes to top all kinds of dishes.

It has found a nice place for itself in this salad alongside cooked beets, blood oranges, and red onions.

To top it off, I made citrus vinaigrette with freshly squeezed orange juice, infused with red onions and fennel.

Ingredients:

- 1 large red beet, boiled and sliced
- 1 blood orange, peeled and segmented
- ¾ cup freshly squeezed orange juice
- ½ cup extra virgin olive oil
- 2 tablespoons white wine vinegar
- 1 tablespoon raw honey
- ½ teaspoon salt
- 1 tablespoon minced red onion
- 1 tablespoon fresh fennel leaves
- red onion, thinly sliced, to garnish
- fennel leaves and shaved fennel from bulb to garnish

Directions:

For the vinaigrette, mix orange juice, olive oil, vinegar, honey, salt, onion, and fennel in a dressing or mason jar. Allow flavors to meld in the refrigerator for at least 1 hour before using.

On a plate arrange 4–5 slices of freshly boiled beets that have cooled.

Top with shaved fennel, sliced red onions, and blood oranges. Drizzle with citrus vinaigrette and garnish with fennel leaves.

Cold Marinated Beet Salad

NATALIE RAE GOOD

Cold marinated salads may bring to mind ideas of a summer barbecue, but who cares? Sometimes, even in the middle of winter, I get a hankering for a cool vegetable dish.

Beets are grown in a wide range of colors and sizes, so choose any combination of tones for this recipe.

Boil each beet variety separately to ensure color retention. Let the salad marinate for at least a few hours before serving.

Ingredients:

- 1 pound golden beets
- 1 pound red or purple beets
- ½ cup apple cider vinegar
- 1 large lemon, juiced
- ½ cup red onion, finely chopped
- scallions or chives, to taste
- salt, pepper, and sugar, to taste

Directions:

Boil the beets whole in salted water until just soft when pierced with a fork. Remove the beets and let cool.

Once cooled, peel and slice into quarters.

Place in a large bowl with the vinegar, lemon juice, and red onion and place in the fridge for at least 2 hours. Mix and add sugar or salt to taste. Top with chives or scallions and serve!

Parsnip Soup with Sweet Potato Leaves

DANIEL ORR

Parsnips look somewhat like white carrots. They have a sweet, floral flavor. I recommend using water as the base for this soup instead of stock so that the flavor of the parsnips is at the forefront.

Like their root vegetable sibling horseradish root, parsnips can last in the garden through the winter or until you get a super hard freeze. The ground serves as their own personal refrigerator.

As for the sweet potato leaves, make sure to pick them before the first frost. They keep in the fridge for a couple weeks. (If you'd rather, you could substitute spinach in this recipe.)

For a special holiday treat, finish the soup with fresh oysters. A quick note if you're planning to cook oysters: cook them until they just start to smile or crinkle around the edges. Don't bring them to a boil.

Ingredients:

- 3 cloves garlic, roughly chopped
- ¼ cup olive oil
- 2 white onions, diced into ¼ inch bits
- 2 shallots, diced
- 6 parsnips, peeled and diced
- 3 cups water
- salt and pepper to taste
- 2 cups heavy cream
- large bunch sweet potato leaves (or spinach), torn into pieces
- squeeze lemon juice

Directions:

Start by browning the garlic in a pan with the olive oil. Add onions and shallots to the pan and increase the heat. Cook the onions and shallots until they are translucent. Add parsnips and cook.

Add water or stock and pinches of salt and pepper. Cover and bring the soup back to a boil, then let it simmer for 15–20 minutes.

Add heavy cream and sweet potato leaves. Cook until the leaves wilt.

Parsnip Cakes

These little bite-sized snacks make great appetizers.

You could substitute any other root vegetables for the parsnips (think rutabagas, celery root, or turnips). The only thing to keep in mind is that some of these veggies have more water in them than others, so you may need to adjust the amount of flour to give the batter the right consistency.

Alternatively, you could add a bit of sugar to the mix and serve these for breakfast with a dollop of maple syrup.

Ingredients:

- 2 pounds parsnips, peeled and roughly chopped
- ¼ cup heavy cream
- 2 large eggs, divided and beaten
- 1 tablespoon flour
- 3 tablespoons unsalted butter
- ½ teaspoon salt
- ¼ teaspoon freshly ground black pepper
- 1 cup panko crumbs
- ¼–½ cup vegetable oil, for pan frying

Directions:

Place the parsnips in a pot, with enough water to cover by 1 inch. Bring to a boil and cook until tender, about 20 minutes.

Drain and transfer to a large bowl. Mash with the cream, an egg, flour, butter, salt, and pepper. Let sit until cool enough to handle.

Form into small cakes, about 3 inches in diameter and 1 inch high.

Place the panko in a small bowl. Heat ¼ cup of oil in a large skillet over medium-high heat.

Brush the cakes on both sides with the remaining beaten egg and dip into the breadcrumbs.

In batches, pan fry the cakes in the hot oil until golden brown on both sides, adding more oil as needed.

Remove from the pan and serve immediately.

Roasted Parsnips and Carrots with Mustard

SARA CONRAD

I could eat roasted root veggies every day of the week, and in the wintertime we eat a lot of them in my family. When the carrots are roasted, they get nice and sweet. We always fight over the slightly burnt ones—my son usually wins!

Ingredients:

- 1 pound carrots
- 1 pound parsnips
- 1 medium golden beet
- ¾ pound small potatoes (skin on)
- ¼ cup olive oil
- 1 tablespoon Dijon mustard
- 1 tablespoon mustard seeds
- dash of balsamic vinegar (optional)
- salt and pepper to taste

Directions:

Heat oven to 425°F.

Skin parsnips and beet. Cut everything into cubes. Put veggies in a large casserole dish.

In a separate bowl, mix olive oil, mustard, mustard seeds, balsamic vinegar, salt, and pepper. Pour over veggies.

Roast 30–40 minutes or until tender.

Curried Carrot Soup

DANIEL ORR

Ingredients:

- 1 onion, peeled and chopped
- 1 fennel bulb, roughly chopped
- 4 garlic cloves
- 2 ounces olive oil
- 1 tablespoon curry
- ½ tablespoon turmeric
- 1 tablespoon kosher salt

- 8 medium carrots, peeled, and roughly chopped
- 3 sprigs thyme
- 2 bay leaves
- 1 orange, juiced, plus 2 teaspoons zest
- 4 tablespoons honey (or agave nectar)
- 1 quart water
- salt and pepper to taste
- 1 cup cream or coconut milk (optional)

Directions:

In a large pot, place onion, fennel, garlic, and spices and sauté in olive oil for 4 minutes. Add the rest of the ingredients and cook until carrots are soft. Puree in blender until smooth. Pass through fine strainer. Add heavy cream to soup and return to a boil. Season to taste, then chill the soup in an ice bath.

Grandma Orr's Polish Rutabaga Mash

Rutabagas are often coated in wax to preserve them, so make sure to slice off that shiny outer layer before cooking. To get rid of some of their bitterness, blanch the rutabagas before cooking. And don't be surprised to see them turn a carrot-like orange when they cook!

Ingredients:

- 1 medium rutabaga (about 1 pound), peeled and cubed
- 4 medium potatoes (about 1 pound), peeled and cubed
- 2 cups chicken stock or broth
- 1 teaspoon salt
- 2 teaspoons sugar
- 4 tablespoons butter
- ½ cup heavy cream
- freshly ground black pepper

Directions:

In a large saucepan, cover rutabaga with water and bring to a boil. Cook halfway, about 15 minutes. Drain.

Place stock, rutabaga, potatoes, salt, and sugar in saucepan. Bring to a boil, lower heat, and cook until vegetables are tender. Drain.

Mash to a smooth consistency, adding butter, heavy cream, and pepper. Adjust seasonings if necessary.

Garnish with fresh herbs and carved apple slices.

Caramelized Turnips and Pears

It's a family affair at my restaurant FARMbloomington. My mom shows up with truckloads of food from our farm on the Ohio River. A lot of times I see what she brings and I base the weekend specials on those ingredients.

It's been a bumper year for our harvest. Lots and lots of beautiful veggies, like turnips. Not your favorite? Well, hang tight. These are prepared with sweet maple syrup and crunchy pears to take the edge of the turnips' slightly bitter flavor.

Baby turnips are wonderful for this preparation—toss them in the pan whole! If you use larger, more mature turnips, be sure to dice them into cubes.

Ingredients:

- 3 average-sized turnips, with skins, washed, cut into ½-inch squares
- 2 Bosc pears, peeled, cut into ½-inch squares
- ⅓ cup organic apple cider (or apple juice)
- pinch of sea salt
- ¼ teaspoon freshly ground pepper
- ¼ cup maple syrup
- dash of Chinese 5-spice powder (a combination of cinnamon, cloves, fennel, star anise, and peppercorns)
- 2 tablespoons butter
- 1 tablespoon lemon juice

Directions:

In a small, heavy-bottomed pan with a lid, bring the turnips, cider, and pears to a boil on a high flame. Turn to low, cover, and simmer for 8–10 minutes until just tender. Do not overcook.

Remove the lid and add the salt, pepper, syrup, and spices. Increase the heat and cook, stirring, until liquid reduces and begins to caramelize. Be careful not to burn.

Add butter and lemon juice and remove from heat. Stir to coat. Taste and adjust seasoning.

West Indian Slammin' Yam Salad

I worked on Anguilla for two years, so I'm fond of Caribbean flavors. I also learned to love cooking with yams.

We're using full-fat coconut milk for this recipe because you can't get the same luxurious mouth feel from the low-fat version. I'm also including some Spanish sherry vinegar called Xeres. It's got a nice smoky flavor. If you don't have the sherry vinegar, you could use cider vinegar instead.

Ingredients:

- 2 pounds steamed yams, peeled, cut into cubes, and chilled
- 1 cup coconut milk
- ¼ cup honey
- 1 tablespoon curry powder
- 1 red onion, thinly sliced
- ¼ cup cilantro, roughly chopped
- ¼ cup mint, roughly chopped
- ¼ cup scallions, chopped
- ¼ cup Spanish sherry vinegar (or apple cider vinegar)
- 2 limes, juiced
- ½ cup toasted coconut
- salt and pepper to taste

Directions:

Cook and reduce coconut milk, honey, and curry powder until the mixture is the consistency of heavy cream. Cool to room temperature.

Combine all remaining ingredients, except the vinegar and lime, in a large bowl and season with salt and pepper. Add the coconut milk mixture, lime, and vinegar and toss to combine.

Adjust the seasoning and serve topped with coconut flakes.

Sweet Potato Fries

SARA CONRAD

Sweet potatoes can range from pale yellow to vivid orange and purple. (Consider using a mix of these for a beautiful presentation.) My son loves these fries. Sometimes he will eat an entire sweet potato when I prepare them this way.

Oven "fried" sweet potatoes can be a bit tricky because sweet potatoes have high moisture content. If you want really crunchy fries, dust the potatoes with potato starch or use Okinawan sweet potatoes.

Ingredients:

- 2 pounds assorted sweet potatoes cut into ¼-inch strips
- 1 tablespoon canola oil
- ½ teaspoon salt
- ½ teaspoon ground black pepper
- 2 tablespoons potato starch (for those crispy fries)

Directions:

Preheat oven to 450°F.

Toss sweet potatoes in oil, salt, pepper, and starch. Arrange potatoes in a single layer on baking sheet.

Bake 10 minutes. Turn potatoes with spatula. Bake another 12 minutes, or until golden brown.

239

winter

Jerusalem Artichoke Soup

DANIEL ORR

The Jerusalem artichoke (also called a sunchoke) is neither from Jerusalem, nor does it look much like an artichoke. It's actually a type of sunflower that grows in the eastern United States and is cultivated for its tuber, which is used as a root vegetable.

Ingredients:

- 2 ounces olive oil
- 2 onions
- 6 cloves garlic
- 2 pounds sunchokes
- 2 potatoes
- 1 apple, peeled and cored
- 5 sprigs thyme
- 1 bay leaf
- 3 quarts water
- 1 cup cream
- ¼ teaspoon nutmeg
- salt and pepper to taste

Directions:

In a large pot on medium high, add the olive oil, onions, and garlic. Cook gently for about 3–4 minutes. Add herbs, sunchokes, potatoes, apple, and water; simmer until veggies are very tender. Add the cream and bring to a boil, then remove from the heat. Puree in blender until smooth. Pass through fine strainer. Season to taste then chill the soup in an ice bath.

Honey-Roasted Sunchokes

STEPHANIE WEAVER

Ingredients:

- ½ tablespoon honey or brown rice syrup
- 2 tablespoons fresh lemon juice
- 1 tablespoon extra-virgin olive oil
- 1 pound sunchokes (also called Jerusalem Artichokes), cut into ½-inch-thick slices
- 3 large shallots, peeled and cut into wedges
- kosher salt
- freshly ground black pepper

Directions:

Preheat oven to 425°F. Warm the honey until it's runny, then whisk in the lemon juice, olive oil, salt, and pepper. Scrub the sunchokes and slice into thirds lengthwise. Peel the shallots, cut off the root ends, and cut into quarters. Put the sunchokes and shallots in an ovenproof baking dish and pour over the marinade. Toss until everything is evenly coated.

Bake until vegetables are tender and caramelized (about 35 minutes), stirring every 10 minutes.

Roasted Celery Root Soup

I'm trying to be more adventurous with my soup ingredients this year, and I realized that I had never roasted celery root.

Celery root, also called celeriac, is the root of a specific type of celery that's grown for its large root. It's another starchy root vegetable, although not as starchy as potatoes. It blends up into a creamy, thick soup.

I roasted elephant garlic (much milder than regular garlic) and fennel bulbs with the celery root, and blended it all together with coconut milk and homemade chicken stock. Vegetarians and vegans can simply sub in vegetable stock. I reserved some of the fennel fronds for the garnish.

Ingredients:

- 3 celery roots, skin removed and cut into chunks
- 2 fennel bulbs, trimmed and quartered lengthwise
- 6 cloves garlic
- 2 tablespoons extra-virgin olive oil
- 1 can coconut milk
- 5 cups chicken stock or vegetable stock
- 1 teaspoon freshly ground pepper

Directions:

Preheat the oven to 425°F.

Toss the trimmed chunks of celery root, fennel bulbs, and unpeeled garlic cloves in 1 tablespoon extra-virgin olive oil. Sprinkle with pepper. Roast for 20 minutes, then stir. Stir again after 15 minutes. After another 10 minutes of roasting, check the celery root for fork tenderness. If it's not extremely tender, use tongs to remove the fennel pieces and garlic cloves and set aside. Drizzle the celery root with the last tablespoon of olive oil, stirring to coat. Roast 10 more minutes, then let cool.

Warm the coconut milk. Then, working in batches in a food processor, puree ¼ of the roasted vegetables, ¼ of the coconut milk, and 1 cup of stock until smooth. Repeat until everything is pureed, adding as much stock as needed to make a smooth, creamy soup.

Stir together in a large saucepan with the pepper and warm through until it reaches serving temperature.

Celery Root Remoulade

DANIEL ORR

Ingredients:

- ½ cup mayonnaise
- ¼ cup sour cream or crème fraîche
- 2 tablespoons Dijon mustard
- 1 tablespoon fresh lemon juice
- 2 tablespoons chopped parsley
- 1 pound celery root, quartered, peeled, and coarsely grated just before mixing
- ½ tart green apple, peeled, cored, julienned
- salt and freshly ground pepper (to taste)

Directions:

Slice off the tough brown skin of the celery root. Using a mandoline, julienne the celery root and apple (matchstick cut).

Combine the mayonnaise, sour cream, mustard, lemon juice, and parsley in a medium-sized bowl.

Fold in the celery root and apple and season with salt and pepper.

Cover and refrigerate until chilled, at least 1 hour.

CHEESE

Welsh Rarebit

DANIEL ORR

Don't be fooled by the name. This traditional English appetizer is made of seasoned cheese and toast—no rabbit meat in sight!

When I cook with beer, I often suggest using a light, cheap brew, but not with this recipe. I've popped open a dark ale; a porter would also be nice for this. Add some butter, dried mustard, and a healthy serving of cheese and you've got a rich football-watching snack.

The traditional way to serve this fancy Cheez Whiz is poured on top of a thick slice of toast. Put it under the broiler and eat it like an open-face grilled cheese sandwich. I also like serving it fondue style with some biscotti. Be like the English and include a dish of pickles on the side.

You might consider inviting some friends over to enjoy the Welsh rarebit, because this recipe can serve 10–12 people. If you have any left over, put it in your omelet the next morning.

Ingredients:

- 3 ¼ cups grated cheddar cheese (set ¼ cup of this aside)
- 1 ounce butter
- ½ cup dark ale (Pabst Blue Ribbon won't cut it. Use a darker beer you would enjoy drinking on its own.)
- 1 teaspoon freshly ground pepper
- 2 teaspoons mustard powder
- ground black pepper and salt
- 8 slices of baguette, cut on a long bias

Directions:

Combine 3 cups of cheese, butter, and ale in a heavy-bottomed saucepan. Over medium heat, allow the cheese to melt.

Season with mustard and salt and pepper to taste. Set cheese sauce aside.

Butter the baguette slices; sprinkle with salt and pepper if you like. Toast the slices of baguette.

Then, place the baguette slices in a baking dish. Pour cheese sauce over top and sprinkle with extra grated cheese. Broil in a toaster oven until the cheese has a nice brown crust

Baked Brie Cooked over an Open Fire

I like brie that is packed in wooden containers. That way I can use those containers when I bake the cheese. The wood might catch fire, but that will give the cheese a nice smoky aroma.

Don't worry if you don't have an open fire over which to cook this. You can stick it in an oven and then cut into it once it becomes warm and melts.

Ingredients:

- 1 round of brie, packed in a wooden container
- dried cherries
- hazelnuts
- apricots
- walnuts
- pine nuts
- salt and pepper
- honey

Directions:

Cut brie in half to expose the creamy interior. Place back in the wooden box. Sprinkle with salt and pepper.

Place dried cherries and apricots in the middle. Push hazelnuts down into cheese and arrange walnuts and pine nuts around the outside. Finish by glazing the cheese, fruit, and nuts with a drizzle of honey.

Position it over an open fire. Eat the cheese once it starts to warm and melt.

Goat Cheese Ball with Pecans, Cherries, and Bacon

Ingredients:

- 1 pound soft goat cheese
- dried cherries (or cranberries)
- pecans, roughly chopped
- pepper bacon, cut into little pieces
- 1 teaspoon pepper
- 1 teaspoon salt
- rosemary leaves
- thyme leaves

Directions:

To the goat cheese, add cherries, pecans, and bacon. Add salt and pepper.

Mix the cheese and add-ins by hand. (It should end up looking like a very large softball.)

Decorate the outside with rosemary and thyme leaves.

Flourless Chocolate Torte

BOB ADKINS

Ingredients:

- 4 eggs
- 1 cup sugar
- pinch salt
- 2 cups chocolate morsels
- 1 cup heavy cream
- 1 stick butter, cubed
- 1 teaspoon orange zest

Directions:

Preheat oven to 350°F. Spray 8-by-8-inch pan with nonstick spray and dust with cornstarch. Cut parchment paper to fit inside pan with some overhang. Spray parchment and dust with cornstarch.

In a large mixing bowl, combine eggs, sugar, and salt. Whisk to combine. Set aside.

In a large saucepan, scald heavy cream and slowly whisk in chocolate morsels over low heat. Remove from heat and whisk in orange zest and butter, a little at a time.

Use hot cream and chocolate to temper the egg/sugar mix. (Add cream little by little, whisking constantly, to slowly heat up the eggs. Be careful with this step or you'll get scrambled eggs!)

Pour mixture into the lined pan. Bake at 350°F for 1 to 1 ½ hours, until edges begin to set. The middle of the cake will still be loose. Cool at room temperature for 2 hours and refrigerate overnight.

Don't Forget the Ganache

For this, you'll need an additional cup of heavy cream, 2–3 cups of bittersweet chocolate chips, and a teaspoon of orange zest.

After your cake has chilled overnight, invert it onto a parchment-lined sheet tray. It should fall out easily.

Then, just as with the cake, scald your cream. Turn the heat to low and whisk the chocolate chips into the cream. Add your zest while the mixture is still warm.

Allow the ganache to cool a bit, and then slowly pour it over the inverted cake, using a spatula to spread it evenly.

Chill the finished dessert at room temperature for an hour. If you have leftover cake (heaven forbid), store it in the refrigerator overnight.

Flan

SETH ELGAR

This recipe for custard is simple—eggs, half-and-half, sugar, fresh vanilla bean, and a pinch of sea salt. It's the caramel sauce that transforms the custard into the best flan you've ever had.

Ingredients:

- 1 cup sugar
- 2 tablespoons water
- ¼ teaspoon sea salt
- ½ fresh bean vanilla, split and scraped, or 2 teaspoons of real vanilla extract

- ¼ teaspoon sea salt
- 1 cup half-and-half
- 1 cup whole milk
- 1 cup sugar
- 4 large eggs

Directions:

Preheat the oven to 325°F. Place 1 cup of sugar, water, and salt in a small saucepan over medium heat. Bring to a simmer and cook until a medium brown caramel is achieved. (DO NOT stir caramel, as foreign material will harden your caramel.) Pour the caramel into ramekins and let it harden.

Put your vanilla bean and scraped interior (or extract), salt, and milk in another pot and bring up to a simmer. Turn off heat and allow to steep for 30 minutes at room temperature. Remove the vanilla bean chunks (if used) and add the half-and-half to the pot. Bring the mixture back up to a simmer.

Whisk the sugar and the eggs together until homogenous and pale. Place a damp towel under your egg mixing bowl. While whisking rapidly, slowly pour the hot dairy mix into the eggs. Whisk until smooth.

Pour custard mix into ramekins, on top of hardened caramel, and place the flan(s) into a baking pan. Using a pitcher, or measuring cup with a pour spout, pour hot water into the pan until it comes halfway up the custard cups. Transfer the baking pan to the oven, making sure not to splash water into the custard. Cover in parchment foil to trap the steam.

Bake for 30 minutes, gently rotate the pan 180 degrees, and then cook for another 15 minutes. (This may take an additional 5 or more minutes.) You'll know the custards are done when they jiggle uniformly (as in, the centers aren't looser than the exterior ring). Remove custards from the water bath, cool to room temperature, and refrigerate until service.

Elgar pulls a finished cup of flan from the refrigerator at No Coast Reserve. Looking at the plain light yellow custard, it's easy to forget the surprise that's waiting at the bottom.

He uses a paring knife to separate the custard from the edges. He turns it upside down on the plate, giving it a good *tap tap tap*. The custard releases and is quickly followed by a rush of oozing dark amber caramel.

Now we have flan!

Caribbean-Inspired Hot Chocolate

DANIEL ORR

Ingredients:

- 1 pound bittersweet chocolate, melted (top quality)
- 8 cups milk
- 4 cups cream
- 2 vanilla beans, split
- ½ orange zest, peeled with a vegetable peeler
- 3 cinnamon sticks
- 1 teaspoon Chinese 5-spice powder (a combination of cinnamon, cloves, fennel, star anise, and peppercorns)
- 1 cup brown sugar
- ½ teaspoon salt
- 1 cup rum (optional)
- whipped cream or steamed milk

Directions:

Heat milk and cream with the zest, cinnamon, spices, and sugar just to the boiling point. Allow to sit 10–15 minutes to infuse. Strain. *Slowly* add to chocolate and finish with immersion blender. Steam with espresso machine milk steamer. Add a shot of rum to a hot coffee cup and top with the hot chocolate and a bit of milk foam or whipped cream from the espresso machine.

Eggnog, a Holiday Favorite

Back in the day in England, they would milk the cow directly into the punch bowl—talk about local! This eggnog recipe incorporates heavy cream, milk, and half-and-half purchased from area farmers. We're also using a local spirit for the booze: W. H. Harrison Bourbon, made in Brazil, Indiana. I would always use the freshest, local eggs for eggnog. If you have any suspicion that the eggs might be old, don't consume them raw. Cheers!

Ingredients:

- 4 egg yolks
- ½ cup sugar
- 1 tablespoons grated lemon zest
- ¼ teaspoon nutmeg
- ¼ teaspoon cinnamon
- 1 ½ cups heavy cream, whipped
- 4 egg whites, whipped
- 3 ounces bourbon
- 1 cup milk or half-and-half

Directions:

Combine egg yolks, sugar, and lemon zest and beat for 1 minute or so.

With a handheld spatula, fold in nutmeg and cinnamon, whipped heavy cream, and whipped egg whites.

Finish by stirring in bourbon and milk or half-and-half. Garnish with a sprinkle of nutmeg.

Cranberry Apple Shake-up

This interactive cocktail will get conversations started as revelers do the shaking themselves. I love using mason jars as glasses not just because they come with their own screw-on lids, but because they give an especially homey feeling to my get-togethers.

You can create any kind of shake-up cocktail using this basic premise—fill a mason jar with fresh ingredients and local spirits. Make sure the lids close tightly on the jars so when your guests start to shake, the cocktails don't decorate their holiday best.

This recipe tastes like a cranberry apple martini.

Ingredients:

- 1 ½ tablespoons chopped cranberries
- 1 large peel of orange rind
- several leaves fresh basil, crunched up to release essential oils
- 1 ½ ounce applejack liquor
- ½ ounce Clément Créole Shrubb rum (or Grand Marnier or triple sec)
- ½ ounce lemon or lime juice
- 1 peel of lime rind
- 1 ½ ounces apple cider
- ice cubes
- club soda
- mason jar and lid

Directions:

Combine first 8 ingredients in a mason jar. Store jars in the fridge until your guests arrive.

Right before serving, fill jars ¾ full with ice cubes. Screw the lid on and tell your guests to give the jar a good shake.

Add a splash of club soda for fizz. Enjoy!

Warm Wine with Mulling Spices and Honey

Your house will smell *amazing* by the time this potion is ready to drink.

Something to remember is that the alcohol cooks off as the wine mulls, so you might want to add a splash of vodka to this before serving. To really spice up your night, serve this up in a caramel-rimmed glass.

Ingredients:

- 3 750-milliliter bottles of your favorite local red wine
- 2 cups brown sugar, or to taste depending on sweetness of wine
- 1 cup honey
- 3 branches thyme
- 3 fresh bay leaves
- 12 cloves
- 14 cardamom pods, lightly crushed
- 2 tablespoons freshly ground pepper
- 3 pieces star anise
- 3 3-inch cinnamon sticks
- 2 oranges, sliced in half moons
- caramel-rimmed glasses (dip glass rims into a little honey, then into cinnamon sugar to create a caramel ring)
- splash of vodka as needed

Directions:

Pour the wine, sugar, and honey in a noncorrosive (stainless) pot and bring to a simmer.

Place the remaining ingredients, except the orange, in a cheesecloth, tie, and place in the warm wine. Allow to infuse for 10–15 minutes over heat and then add the oranges. Taste and adjust sweetness and spices; keep in a thermos.

Let mull for 45 minutes to an hour. Serve in caramel-rimmed glasses with a splash of vodka as the final touch to add a little kick.

❋ First Meal

Abigail Carroll's breakfast of choice is a little unorthodox. On the day I chatted with her, she had ground grass-fed beef with tomato puree and sautéed Swiss chard, "which is very colonial of me, I must admit."

And she should know. She wrote the book *Three Squares: The Invention of the American Meal*. She says breakfast holds a unique place in the discourse about the American meal structure.

"What I love about breakfast and find quite fascinating about it is the way people talk about it in moralistic terms—you should and you shouldn't eat it in certain ways or have certain things for it or eat it at certain times, or just the fact that you should eat it. There's that whole debate over whether you even should eat breakfast. You don't see that around the other meals as you do around breakfast," she says.

In the 1600s and 1700s, breakfast foods as we know them today didn't exist. "People were eating like I had for my breakfast, they were eating leftovers for breakfast. Or they might have cornmeal mush, bread and cheese or butter, a slice of pie."

Fast forward to the mid-1800s, Americans were suffering from a collective bout of indigestion. Food reformers started to promote a new idea of breakfast—eating less and eating lighter. "And they were all about health food, and their number-one health food was what they called graham flour, which was flour that still had the bran in it," she says.

Sylvester Graham invented the flour. John Harvey Kellogg helped bring cold breakfast cereals onto American tables. Between those two inventors was Henry Crowell, founder of Quaker Oats. In addition to being the first packaged breakfast food, Quaker Oats had a reputation for purity, thanks in part to the logo featuring the Quaker man. Purity was important to consumers at the turn of the twentieth century, as they believed packaging meant the food reached them virtually untouched.

There are a number of reasons why breakfast evolved from heavy and meat-centered to light and grain-centered, but our work culture was the most influential factor. "If they were going to eat a farmers' breakfast and then head to work and sit at a desk, they were not necessarily going to be very productive and efficient. So the lighter breakfast is an example of a new emphasis on efficiency," she says.

Woodstone Oven Eggs with Local Sausage and Parmesan

DANIEL ORR

Ingredients:

- 1 pound local Italian-style sausage
- 1 tablespoon garlic, chopped
- 1 teaspoon chili flakes
- 1 tablespoon each rosemary and thyme, chopped
- 3 tomatoes, roughly chopped
- ½ yellow pepper, roughly chopped
- ½ red pepper, roughly chopped
- 1 can artichoke bottoms, diced
- 1 cup tomato juice
- 4 red-skin potatoes, quartered and cooked just tender
- 4 Yukon Gold potatoes, quartered and cooked just tender
- kosher salt and black pepper
- 12 farm-fresh eggs
- ½ cup cheese of choice, grated (a mixture of parmesan and gruyère is nice)

Directions:

Brown the sausage. Drain off extra fat. Add the garlic, herbs, and chili flakes. Add the peppers, artichokes, tomatoes, and tomato juice and simmer for 15 minutes or until the sausage mixture reaches the desired consistency.

Add potatoes and heat through. Season to taste.

Divide ragout into baking dish(es) in equal amounts. Top with grated cheese and place potatoes cut in half around the edges.

Top each serving with two fresh eggs and finish in oven until egg whites are firm yet the yolks are slightly runny.

Garnish with roughly chopped Italian parsley.

Breakfast Gravy Meets Winter Veggies

CLARA MOORE

Working seasonally can be a drag sometimes.

Over the summer I couldn't stand the sight of yet another tomato. By fall, the apples were piled on the prep table. Now, it's the season of root vegetables. Life sure is tough when you have the misery of cooking with extremely fresh, local vegetables. Woe is me!

I've been searching for new ways to cook the usual suspects (think parsnips, beets, and potatoes). A few weeks ago, I threw some root veggies in my biscuits and gravy, and it turned out great.

Ingredients:

- 3 cups of winter vegetables, diced (e.g., carrots, potatoes, parsnips, beets)
- olive oil
- 3 tablespoons butter
- 6 tablespoons flour
- 5 cups cold milk
- salt and pepper to taste

Directions:

Preheat oven to 350°F.

Peel and dice all the veggies. Toss in olive oil and arrange on a pan. Bake for 45 minutes, or until veggies are soft enough to pierce with a fork.

Melt butter in a saucepan. Add flour to melted butter and stir with whisk until well incorporated. This might get lumpy. Don't worry, just keep whisking! Cook on medium heat for about 5 minutes. Stir occasionally or constantly, whichever makes you more comfortable. Just try not to let it brown.

Add the cold milk slowly, whisking the entire time. (This might also get lumpy, but again don't worry. Just keep whisking!) Cook on medium heat until it begins to thicken.

Add roasted vegetables. Cook it until you achieve the desired consistency. (The longer you cook it, the thicker it will get.) Add salt and pepper to taste.

Pour over Daniel Orr's Grandma's Buttermilk Biscuits (see page 44), and enjoy!

Vegetable Breakfast Scramble

STEPHANIE WEAVER

Ingredients:

- 1 carrot
- 1 small sweet potato
- 2 green onions or ½ sweet onion
- ½ package cremini mushrooms
- ½ package tofu
- ½ cup black beans (half of one 15-ounce can)
- ¼ head red cabbage
- 1 broccoli stalk
- 3 cloves garlic
- 2–4 tablespoons low-sodium soy sauce, tamari, or Bragg's liquid aminos
- 2 tablespoons sesame seeds
- 2–3 teaspoons toasted sesame oil
- 1–2 teaspoons hot chili oil

Directions:

Rinse and drain the beans. Wash all the vegetables, leaving the skins on.

Slice the mushrooms. Cut the carrot into thin diagonal slices. Thinly slice the cabbage. Cut the sweet potato into small dice (about ¼-inch cubes). Peel and mince the garlic cloves. Thinly slice the green onions or mince the sweet onion. Cut the broccoli into small chunks.

Heat about 2 tablespoons olive or grapeseed oil in a large skillet or nonstick sauté pan. When the oil is shimmering, add the onions, carrots, mushrooms, and the sweet potato.

Cook, stirring every couple of minutes, for about 10 minutes. Break up the tofu with your fingers and add to the pot.

Add the tamari, sesame oil, and sesame seeds. Add the garlic, broccoli, beans, and cabbage and continue to cook for another 5 minutes.

Taste and adjust seasonings.

Banana Hemp Pancakes

DANIEL ORR

These pancakes will actually include three different hemp ingredients—the seeds, hemp powder, and some hemp oil.

Before we get to the recipe, let's make sure we're all on the same page. Yes, hemp is edible, and no, it does not have the physical and psychological effects of its cousin marijuana. At the printing of this book, only 13 states allow farmers to grow hemp. Since Indiana is one of those states, we were able to score these local hemp products.

The powder has a mild, almost neutral flavor. The seeds will add a nice crunch. We're using the oil in the pan for cooking the pancakes, and that too, is clear and neutral.

The liquid ingredients for this recipe are bananas and eggs. Your pancakes will end up being more tender than regular pancakes because there's no dairy and not too much flour in this recipe.

As you're mixing the batter, embrace the army-green color. It will turn a deep brown as it cooks. But don't worry, kids. Slice into your pancakes and you'll see the green again!

Ingredients:

- 1 teaspoon Chinese 5-spice powder (a combination of cinnamon, cloves, fennel, star anise, and peppercorns)
- 1 banana
- 2 medium eggs
- ¼ cup hemp powder
- ¼ cup all-purpose flour
- 1 teaspoon baking powder
- pinch of sea salt
- 1 tablespoon hemp seed oil (for cooking)
- hemp seeds
- fruit and syrup of your choice

Directions:

In a large bowl, mash the banana until completely broken down, but not liquefied. Set aside.

In a separate bowl, whisk the eggs until well combined. Fold in mashed bananas, sea salt, hemp powder, and all-purpose flour. Mix until combined.

Heat a nonstick pan. Add hemp oil to a hot pan and add pancake batter. Cook until lightly browned. Sprinkle hemp seeds on the pancakes and then flip.

Serve with your favorite toppings, like yogurt, fruit, butter, maple syrup, or honey.

Chia Seed Breakfast Pudding

Remember Ch-Ch-Ch Chia Pets?

The novelty items might be a thing of the past, but the chia seeds themselves are enjoying new life as one of the latest "it" foods for the health conscious.

This dish requires some planning because you have to soak the chia seeds in milk for 24 hours. (I prefer making it vegan with soy, almond, or coconut milk.) The soaked seeds look similar to rice pudding. Add some fresh fruit on top and it will look more like breakfast.

Ingredients:

- ⅔ cup chia seeds
- 2 ¼ cups milk (soy, almond, coconut milk)
- several slices of kumquats
- a handful of blueberries and blackberries
- agave syrup (to taste)
- juice from ½ lemon
- pinch of salt
- sprig of mint (garnish)

Directions:

Soak the chia seeds in milk of your choice overnight or for 24 hours. The next morning, add agave syrup, lemon juice, and salt to chia seeds. Top with fruit and mint.

❋ A Farmer and a Chef Walk into a Bar . . .

When farmer Dave Fischer decided to sell his beef, pork, and chicken directly to area restaurants, he knew he needed to cultivate consistent customers.

The first step was to meet the people in charge. He started in Bloomington, Indiana.

"Usually I'd drag one of my kids along, and we would go knocking door to door at the different restaurants," he remembers. One of the doors he knocked on was Nick's English Hut. Managing partner/owner and chef Gregg "Rags" Rago answered. "It's kind of interesting how Dave and I met," Rags remembers. "Dave came by as a cold call, just walking from restaurant to restaurant wanting to know if I wanted to buy his beef."

Now, they collaborate on the Nick's burger, a special blend of meat developed by Fischer and Sander Processing. Nick's also offers Fischer steaks and pork loin on its menu. The chili features Fischer beef and pork. Ground turkey from Fischer is in the turkey burgers. All this can total up to 500 pounds of meat per week, depending on the time of year. "It's kind of what all of us really want to do when you have an independent, smaller restaurant, where you can trust the person who is raising your beef and processing your beef," says Rags.

Chefs like Rags call or text Fischer on Mondays to place their orders. Fischer then sends that information to Sander Processing, which receives the animals and prepares the various rib eyes and sausages. Fischer delivers the orders to the restaurants on Wednesdays. That meat could then make it onto customers' plates by Friday.

The challenge Fischer faces is selling all parts of the animal. "I've got so much rib eye, so much filet, so much strip steak, so much sirloin each week, and I've got to figure out which restaurants those are going to," which is what makes his relationship with Rags and Nick's English Hut so special. "I'll call him up and say 'I'm just swimming in sirloin, can you put a sirloin on your menu?' They've been super to do that," says Fischer.

Week in and week out, Nick's changes its specials based on what extra cuts Rags can purchase from Fischer. Since Nick's tries to keep its food under $20 a plate, the customers may be the ones who benefit the most from this arrangement.

Beef Stew with Winter Vegetables

DANIEL ORR

Ingredients:

- ¼ cup extra-virgin olive oil for frying, plus more to drizzle
- 3 tablespoons butter
- 2 cups all-purpose flour
- 2–3 pounds beef chuck shoulder roast, cut into 2-inch pieces (this cut is also called chuck roast boneless)
- sea salt and freshly ground pepper
- 1 bottle good quality dry red wine
- 8 fresh thyme sprigs
- 6 garlic cloves, smashed
- 1 orange, zest removed in 3 1-inch strips

- 2 bay leaves
- 2 ½ cups beef stock
- 9 small new potatoes, scrubbed clean and cut in half
- ½ pound carrots, peeled and sliced
- 2 cups assorted root vegetables such as celery root, turnips, parsnips
- 2 onions, roughly chopped
- 1 pound white mushrooms, cut in half
- fresh flat-leaf parsley, chopped (garnish)
- sour cream (garnish)
- crusty bread

Directions:

Preheat a large heavy-bottomed saucepan or Dutch oven over medium-high heat with the oil and butter.

While the pan is heating, arrange the flour on a large dish. Season the cubed beef with some salt and freshly ground black pepper and then toss in the flour to coat. Shake off the excess flour and add the beef chunks in a single layer to the hot pan, being careful not to overcrowd the pan. You might have to work in batches.

Thoroughly brown all of the cubes on all sides. Once all the meat has been browned, remove it to a plate and reserve.

Add the wine to the pan and bring up to a simmer while you scrape the bottom of the pan with a wooden spoon, being sure to loosen up all those tasty bits.

Once the wine has gotten hot, add the browned meat, thyme, smashed garlic, orange zest strip, freshly ground black pepper and salt to taste, bay leaves, and beef stock.

Bring the mixture up to a boil and then reduce the heat to a simmer and cook uncovered until the liquids start to thicken, about 15 to 20 minutes.

Cover and cook on low heat for 2 ½ hours.

After 2 hours add halved potatoes, sliced carrots, root vegetables, onions, and mushrooms, along with a touch of honey or molasses to balance out the acid from the red wine.

Turn the heat up slightly and simmer, uncovered, for 30 minutes more, until the vegetables and meat are tender.

Season with salt and pepper and remove the thyme sprigs.

To serve, place the stew in a soup bowl and garnish with parsley, drizzle with olive oil, and add a dollop of sour cream. Serve with a slice of crusty bread.

No-Meat Chili with an Indian Flair

RAMA COUSIK

Veggie chili is a staple food in my family, particularly in winter. It is a blessing to have veggie chili when you have a cold, as it is packed with healthy ingredients that tickle your taste buds and help clear your upper respiratory system.

I soak beans overnight and cook them in a pressure cooker. Alternatively, you can use one can of cooked beans.

If you like more liquid in your chili, add another cup of water with the beans. Add a dash of oregano or a few mint leaves for variety. I like to add a cup of mashed pumpkin or cooked sweet potato instead of flour for that special, sweet taste.

Ingredients:

- 1 tablespoon oil
- 1 teaspoon cumin seeds
- ¼ teaspoon fennel seeds
- pinch asafetida (substitute garlic powder or onion powder for asafetida)
- 1 small onion chopped
- 2 cloves garlic crushed
- ¼ teaspoon turmeric powder
- ¼ teaspoon ginger powder
- ½ cup chopped red, yellow, or green pepper

- 2 medium-sized tomatoes chopped
- 4 sprigs cilantro
- ¼ teaspoon black pepper
- 2 cups cooked beans (e.g., red, garbanzo, black, black-eyed, pinto)
- 1 tablespoon rice flour or whole wheat flour mixed with ½ cup water
- 2 cups water
- 1 teaspoon salt
- ¼ teaspoon juice of lemon

Directions:

In a large pot, heat ½ tablespoon of oil. Add cumin seeds, fennel, and a pinch of asafetida.

Now add chopped onion and garlic and cook until onion is slightly brown. Add chopped pepper, turmeric, ginger powder, and a pinch of salt.

Add tomatoes, chopped cilantro, and black pepper and cook for 2 minutes.

Add cooked beans, water, and salt. Stir well and let it boil for 10 minutes on medium heat. Then reduce heat.

Mix flour and ½ cup of water into a smooth paste. Add this paste to the chili and cook for another 1–2 minutes.

Turn off the heat and mix in the lemon juice.

Lima Bean Ragout

DANIEL ORR

Cooking beans from dry may take longer, but it's worth it in the end. The thing with cooking beans from dry is that you can inject a lot of flavor into the beans.

I start off with some olive oil and garlic in a pan and then—this is one of my secrets— once the garlic starts to brown, I add rosemary for a nice rustic flavor. You can use this trick when you're trying to spruce up some canned tomato sauce. It will taste like you've been cooking it for hours.

You certainly can presoak beans if you prefer. They will cook much faster. To do this, add one part beans to three parts water. Soak them for six hours before you start this recipe.

Whatever you do, make sure to pick through the beans and remove nonbean materials before you start cooking. And don't forget to rinse the beans to wash off any . . . insect material.

Ingredients:

- ½ pound washed lima beans
- 1–2 tablespoons minced garlic
- olive oil
- 1 sprig rosemary
- 1 15-ounce can chopped tomatoes
- ½ chopped onion (red or white)
- ½ cup chopped carrots (or other root vegetables of your choice)
- 2 bay leaves
- 2 ½–3 cups water

Directions:

In a large pot with olive oil, toast the garlic. Add leaves from the rosemary sprig once garlic has browned.

Add beans, chopped tomatoes, chopped onion, carrots, bay leaves, and water. (Err on the side of adding too little water at first. You can always add more later, but you can't take it out!)

Bring to a boil, then simmer until beans become soft.

Serve as a soup or a sauce over fish.

Mulligatawny Fights the Winter Blues

RAMA COUSIK

Mulligatawny is a Tamil word that means pepper water. I remember drinking it as a child, particularly during the winter season and especially when I had a cold. My fussy high school senior will vouch for it. He even asks me to make it for him every time he's sick.

The traditional recipe I grew up with included split mung beans, black lentil flour, and curry leaf. The addition of mushrooms is my special touch.

Ingredients:

- 2 cups mushrooms, sliced and washed
- 1 teaspoon oil
- 4 garlic cloves, crushed
- ½ teaspoon ginger powder
- 1 teaspoon cumin powder
- ½ teaspoon fresh ground pepper
- 4–5 cups water
- 1 teaspoon salt
- 1 teaspoon honey or brown sugar
- 1 teaspoon lemon juice
- ½ teaspoon dried basil leaves

Directions:

Heat oil. Add crushed garlic, ginger powder, and cumin powder, and roast for a few seconds.

Add sliced mushrooms and salt. Sauté till the mushrooms are a little tender.

Add water and freshly ground pepper and rest of the salt. Let it boil for 10 minutes. Add honey or brown sugar and mix well. Add 1 teaspoon lemon juice and a sprinkle of basil.

You can have this soup as is or with a dash of cream or butter. Alternatively, place a cup of cooked rice in a serving bowl, pour two ladles of Mulligatawny over it, and enjoy it as a complete meal.

Vegetarian Curry

Chef Bob Adkins doesn't shy away from including less popular ingredients in his dishes (see page 223). He encourages his guests to step outside their comfort zone; maybe they'll surprise themselves.

He stepped out of *his* comfort zone with his first attempt at a real Indian curry on the menu. First order of business: he learned to make his own curry paste. He has handfuls of fresh herbs on hand—mint, cilantro, fennel—along with heaping portions of ginger and garlic. Be sure not to skip toasting the cumin and curry powders. This brings out more complex flavors that you will love in the finished dish.

Ingredients:

- 1 rib celery
- 1 red bell pepper
- 1 jalapeno
- ½ large onion
- 1 carrot
- 1 bulb fennel
- 1 leek, cleaned
- homemade curry paste
- 1 3-ounce can tomato paste
- 1 can diced tomatoes, drained
- 2 large red potatoes, diced
- 1 can coconut milk
- 2 tablespoons vegetable base
- 4 cups water
- salt to taste

Directions:

Slice all the vegetables to the same size and thickness. In a large pot, sauté the curry paste in a little oil until very fragrant. Add the sliced vegetables and sweat until translucent. Add remaining ingredients and simmer just until potatoes are tender. Remove from heat, adjust seasoning to taste and eat immediately over rice.

Homemade Curry Paste

Ingredients:

- 2 ounces ginger
- 10 cloves garlic
- 2 tablespoons curry powder, toasted
- 1 ½ tablespoons cumin powder, toasted
- 4 large sprigs mint
- ½ bunch cilantro
- 1 stalk fennel, stripped of soft fronds
- 1 ½ tablespoon yellow curry paste
- ¼ cup oil

Directions:

In a hot and dry pan, toast curry and cumin powders until very fragrant. Combine all ingredients in a food processor and blend to a fine paste.

❋ And a Happy New Year!

GOOD EXCUSE FOR A PARTY

When you "go a'wassailing," you could be doing one of two things.

There's the house-visiting wassail, which is the practice of singing carols door to door during the Christmas season.

The other type is the orchard-visiting variety. That's Maria Kennedy's bread and butter. "I went to my first wassail at the Leominster Morris Wassail," she says. She worked with cider makers in England as part of her studies in folklore at Indiana University. "I showed up at this pub in the middle of nowhere in a little village in the north part of the county of Hertfordshire." She was one of 300 people at that wassail. "They led us all out to the orchard, carrying torches and banging drums."

And singing. The noisy procession into the orchard is meant to wake up the cider trees and scare away evil spirits.

"They poured some cider on the roots of the tree to give it back some of the juice it had produced," she says. Some people even beat the trees with sticks. "Let's encourage the fertility of the trees and encourage lots of apples for the next year."

Wassails are traditionally held on the evening of either January 5—Twelfth Night— or January 17, which is the date of Old Twelfth Night, before the introduction of the Gregorian calendar to Britain in 1752.

Kennedy helped revive the wassailing tradition on Broome Farm in Hertfordshire when she was there in 2012.

In addition to the singing and noisemaking and general merriment, "We built twelve little fires around the biggest apple tree. The twelve fires are said to represent either the twelve months of the year or the twelve apostles. Then you build a thirteenth fire, which is the Judas fire." Revelers are supposed to stamp out the Judas fire.

It's hard to know how long people have been wassailing, but the tradition likely originated long before Christianity came to Britain—since AD 600. Kennedy says it was practiced by agricultural laborers.

"It's kind of like a contract almost," she says. "The laborers are saying, 'You're going to give us some cakes and things to eat tonight, and hopefully for the rest of the year, you're going to pay us well and be a good employer. In exchange, we're going to sing to your trees and make sure they bear a lot of fruit.'"

Then it's back to the fields the following week for what's called Plow Monday.

These days, Kennedy says wassailing is a good excuse for a party before the work starts up again.

"You have to think like it's really dark in England in the middle of winter," she says. "It's rainy and it's cold and it's really dark all the time. And then you get together with a group of people and light some torches and go out in the orchard and sing some songs and bang some pots and drink a lot of cider. It's a good thing."

Black-Eyed Pea Salad for Luck in the New Year

DANIEL ORR

The tradition of eating black-eyed peas to bring prosperity dates back to AD 500. The Talmud mentions the eating of black-eyed peas on Rosh Hashanah, the Jewish New Year. Jews brought this tradition to the southern United States in the 1730s, and it started spreading during the American Civil War.

The peas are traditionally served with ham or bacon, collard or mustard greens, and cornbread. While that preparation is absolutely delicious, I wanted to create something a bit healthier. This salad is served over arugula, but feel free to substitute any late-winter greens you have growing in the garden.

Ingredients:

- 3 tablespoons extra-virgin olive oil
- 2 tablespoons lemon juice (plus a teaspoon of the grated zest)
- 1 tablespoon minced garlic
- freshly ground pepper to taste
- 4 cups peeled and diced cucumbers

- 1 14-ounce can black-eyed peas, rinsed
- ⅔ cup diced red bell pepper
- ½ cup crumbled feta cheese
- ¼ cup slivered red onion
- 2 tablespoons chopped black olives
- ¼ cup toasted walnuts
- a big handful of herbs such as mint, cilantro, parsley, and scallions—roughly chopped

Directions:

Whisk oil, lemon juice and zest, garlic, and pepper in a large bowl until combined. Add cucumber, black-eyed peas, bell pepper, feta, onion, and olives. Toss to coat. Just before serving, add the walnuts and herbs. Serve at room temperature or chilled.

Black-Eyed Peas and Cornbread

HELEN COBB

Having grown up in the South, I understand bacon's effect on a big pot of vegetables. It softens and seasons everything it touches with its salty, smoky flavor.

But not all of us want to eat bacon with our vegetables. Yet we still want our turnip greens and black-eyed peas to be as rich and melt-in-your-mouth as those cooked in fat for several hours.

This recipe produces tender, mouth-watering black-eyed peas. You'll enjoy coating your cornbread with this perfect pea gravy.

Ingredients:

- olive oil
- 1 large shallot, diced
- 5 cloves garlic, diced
- 1–2 tablespoons red pepper flakes
- leaves from 1 bunch thyme
- 2 bay leaves
- 1 bag presoaked black-eyed peas (I soaked mine for 2 hours)
- 1 quart water (or more, if the peas absorb too much)
- 2 vegetable bouillon cubes
- 2 large tomatoes, diced
- 1 small carrot, chopped
- 3 tablespoons tomato paste
- salt and pepper

Directions:

Heat a little olive oil in an enameled cast-iron pot on medium-low. Add the shallot to the hot oil, season with salt, and cook until translucent.

Add the garlic, red pepper flakes, thyme, and bay leaves and cook about 1 minute.

Add the peas, water, bullion, tomatoes, carrot, tomato paste, salt and pepper, and a generous drizzle of olive oil. Bring to a boil, reduce heat to just above low, cover with a heavy lid, and simmer for several hours, stirring occasionally.

During the last 30 minutes or so of cooking, check the water level in the peas. If the peas seem too soupy, you may want to remove the lid so more water evaporates. Likewise, you may need to add water if the mixture is too thick. Remember that when the peas cool, they will thicken considerably. They should be like stew.

Jalapeño Onion Cornbread

STEPHANIE WEAVER

Ingredients:

- 1 cup soy milk
- 1 tablespoon apple cider vinegar
- 1 tablespoon ground flaxseeds
- 2 tablespoons water
- ¼ cup agave syrup or honey
- 2 tablespoons olive oil
- 1 cup yellow cornmeal
- 1 cup gluten-free flour mix
- 2 teaspoons baking powder
- ½ teaspoon baking soda
- ½ teaspoon sea salt
- ½ teaspoon xanthan gum
- 1–2 jalapeños, minced
- ½ onion
- ½ cup shredded cheddar cheese

Directions:

Preheat the oven to 400°F. Put a cast iron skillet in the oven to preheat. (Or you can use an 8-inch round or square pan. In that case, line the pan with parchment paper.)

Add the vinegar to the soy milk, stir, and let stand to curdle.

Put the flaxseeds and water in your mixing bowl, and let stand to thicken.

Peel the onion and cut into fine dice. Sauté in about 1 tablespoon olive oil until golden.

Whisk together the cornmeal, flour, baking powder, baking soda, sea salt, and xanthan gum in a medium bowl.

With a wooden spoon or a stand mixer, mix together the curdled soy milk, flaxseed mixture, agave syrup (or honey), and olive oil until blended. Add the flour mixture and mix just until incorporated. Do not overmix. Stir in the jalapeños, onion, and cheese just until mixed.

Remove the skillet from the oven with a hot pad. Put about 1 tablespoon of oil in the skillet and tilt to cover the bottom and sides of the pan evenly.

Pour the batter into the pan and spread evenly. Place in the center of the oven and bake for 15–20 minutes. Remove, cool, and cut into wedges.

About the Authors

Bob Adkins is the head chef at FARMbloomington Restaurant. He is an anthropologist by training and a chef through the school of hard knocks, from dishwasher to daycare cook to culinary schoolteacher and nearly every position in between.

Diana Bauman is a mother of three. She spends her time urban homesteading in Iowa. She can be found online blogging at *My Humble Kitchen*.

Eoban Binder is Director of Digital Media at Indiana Public Media (WFIU/WTIU), and is the principal photographer for *Earth Eats*. Originally from Milwaukee, he graduated from Indiana University in 2008.

Helen Cobb is a writer living in Manhattan with her husband and two young daughters. She was raised on a small farm in rural Georgia. Helen loves sharing the healthy side of Southern cuisine through her blog *Why I Consume Art*.

Sara Conrad studied Tibetan culture at Indiana University. She loves to cook with fresh, organic, vegetarian ingredients, but also has never turned down fake mashed potatoes in a buffet line.

Annie Corrigan is an announcer and producer for WFIU. She has produced *Earth Eats*, a weekly radio program and podcast, since its inception in 2009. Originally from Ohio, she moved to southern Indiana to pursue a degree in music. It's thanks to her work with *Earth Eats* that she's always hungry for good food grown close by.

Rama Cousik grew up in India watching and helping her mom cook. She now lives in Fort Wayne, Indiana. No matter where she lives, the idea of seasonal food is an essential part of her food philosophy.

Seth Elgar is the executive chef and general manager of No Coast Reserve (Bloomington, Indiana). He graduated from the Kendall College School of Culinary Arts in Chicago and Purdue University's program for Hospitality & Tourism Management. He has spent eighteen years in kitchens, from Bloomington to Fishers, Indiana, and Chicago to Beaurecueil, France.

Natalie Rae Good is a Brooklyn-based artist, musician, and food blogger committed to sharing wholesome, vegetable-centered meals. She blogs her recipes, photos, and ideas at *The Veganette* and runs the design and print studio Etc. Letterpress.

Sarah Gordon earned a PhD in folklore from Indiana University. In addition to southern Indiana, she has lived in Montreal, London, Japan, Seattle, and the Canadian Arctic. She is now a freelance writer, adventurous cook, and wannabe gardener.

Sarah Kaiser fell in love with Bloomington's foodie culture when she attended Indiana University. Now a sociology instructor in Buffalo, New York, Sarah has rediscovered the joys of summer. Backyard gardening, outdoor cooking, and vegetarian cuisine are some of her recent interests. Buffalo winters will do that to a person.

Arlyn Llewellyn is the chef at Function Brewing (Bloomington, Indiana), which she owns with her husband, brewer Steven Llewellyn. She focuses on fresh, bright, spicy, and often vegetarian food made with local ingredients.

Clara Moore is a chef from St. Louis. She currently resides in Portland, Maine, with her partner and their child. In addition to cooking and writing, she works with Low Income Access at the local farmers' market.

Daniel Orr is a chef and the owner of FARMbloomington as well as the author of several cookbooks. He draws from a lifelong curiosity about individual ingredients combined with extensive training in the art of finding food's true essence and flavor. The result is simple, yet sophisticated; the best of American food tempered by classic European training.

Sarah Ostaszewski studied anthropology and fine arts at Indiana University. She moved to the Pacific Northwest to explore lush green landscapes and to join the local trail running community. She still dreams of fresh summer tomatoes from her family's garden.

Heather Tallman is a freelance writer and mother to two busy boys. She is the creator of the cooking blog *Basilmomma*. She writes about her culinary hits and misses and all of the life that goes along with it.

Dianne Venetta is an author, entrepreneur, and mother. She writes the blog *BloominThyme* and volunteers as garden coordinator for her children's school garden. She lives in Central Florida with her husband and two children.

Stephanie Weaver is a writer, health coach, migraine advocate, and food blogger based in San Diego. Her work has been featured on the *Huffington Post*, the *New York Times* Well blog, Buzzfeed, *Cooking Light*, *Cosmopolitan*, *Bon Appétit*, and *San Diego* magazine. She has a master's in public health in nutrition education from the University of Illinois.

Jana Wilson lives on 20 acres just outside of Bloomington, where she writes her blog *The Armchair Homesteader*. In addition to chickens, she has ducks and border collies to help her with her various efforts at becoming more self-sufficient.

David Wood is an early music specialist, traditional singer, educator, runner, and aspiring urban farmer and chicken rancher living in the Kansas Flint Hills. David formerly served as WFIU's music director, program content coordinator, and arts bureau chief, where he was involved with *Earth Eats* from its very beginnings.

Index

index

EDITOR   Ashley Runyon

BOOK & COVER DESIGNER   Jennifer L. Witzke

PROJECT MANAGER/EDITOR   Rachel Rosolina

MARKETING AND SALES DIRECTOR   Dave Hulsey

EDITORIAL & PRODUCTION DIRECTOR   Bernadette Zoss